Chicago
BEARS

THE COMPLETE ILLUSTRATED HISTORY

Chicago
BEARS
THE COMPLETE ILLUSTRATED HISTORY

Lew Freedman

Foreword by Dan Jiggetts

Voyageur Press

Page 1: Superstar linebacker Brian Urlacher acknowledges the fans' applause after making a tackle against the Minnesota Vikings in 2004.
Jonathan Daniel/Getty Images

Pages 2–3: Bears fullback Neal Anderson dives for yardage in a 1992 game against the Atlanta Falcons.
Andy Hayt/Getty Images

Right: Walter Payton running against the Green Bay Packers in 1980. Payton is the second most prolific rusher in NFL history.
Focus on Sports/Getty Images

First published in 2008 by Voyageur Press, an imprint of MBI Publishing Company and the Quayside Publishing Group, 400 First Avenue N, Suite 300, Minneapolis, MN 55401 USA

Copyright © 2008 by Compendium Publishing Ltd.

Voyageur Press titles are also available at discounts in bulk quantity for industrial or sales-promotional use. For details write to Special Sales Manager at MBI Publishing Company, 400 First Avenue N, Suite 300, Minneapolis, MN 55401 USA.

Library of Congress Cataloging-in-Publication Data

Freedman, Lew.
   Chicago Bears : the complete illustrated history / Lew Freedman.
      p. cm.
   Includes bibliographical references.
   ISBN 978-0-7603-3231-3 (hb w/ jkt)
   1. Chicago Bears (Football team)—History. I. Title.
   GV956.C5F7315 2008
   796.323'640977311—dc22

2008009843

Printed in China

CONTENTS

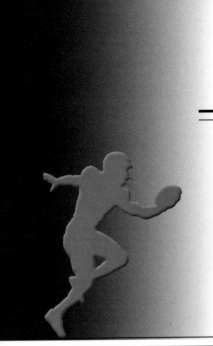

FOREWORD
BY DAN JIGGETTS

Once a Chicago Bear, always a Chicago Bear. Once you've been associated with the club I think that lasts forever.

I was drafted by the Bears in the sixth round in 1976 as a tackle out of Harvard. I grew up on Long Island and thought about pro football, but it was always "Boy, I wonder what that would be like?" By the time I got drafted I was negotiating with Toronto in the Canadian Football League. They had put some money on the table. At the time I did not know a lot about the Chicago Bears. One of my roommates in college was from Chicago. He was constantly telling me all the great things about the city, but I wasn't sure because he had gone to secondary school in England! When I signed my contract I was invited to give a little talk at the Harvard Club. I got my first look at Chicago and I was excited about it.

I loved it. They had me staying at the Hyatt downtown and from O'Hare when you drive down Lake Shore Drive, especially at night, it is an awesome sight. You see the lights and the city is laid out before you. It was fabulous. I was a government major in college and this place was ground central for a lot of what was going on in politics. I had a Harvard degree, but I didn't want to go into pro football with the attitude that it wasn't important. It was important to work hard at playing professional football and try to be as good as I possibly could be. I had some other things in my mind about looking into politics and the business environment, but I felt those things would work themselves out during the course of the off-season.

Right away you could tell how important the Bears were to Chicago. From the first day, when you land at O'Hare and the people look at you and they understand why you're there, you find out that the Bears are No. 1 in this town. There had been struggling years after the 1963 team won the championship and it had been a struggle pretty much right up to 1976. We were .500 in my first season and the fans were acting like that was the playoffs. That's when you got an idea how tough it had been, but also how near and dear this team was to everyone. You understand that the fans in this city love this football team. They may not always love the way it is run, but they love the football team itself.

After I retired I went into sports broadcasting—not a career I envisioned for myself until I had been playing for about five years—and through all of those years and later, the fans were the same. In the Super Bowl era, 1985 and 1986, it was just frenzied. The feeling was just off the charts.

The funny thing was that I played with a lot of those guys and I had a really good idea of the personalities. It was just fascinating. It was a great football team and you knew it was coming. There was a batch of wild and crazy guys who had a lot of fun, but when the whistle blew it was time to play. You talk about walking in and going after somebody, my goodness.

That team endures in the public mind like no other and there's no question it's because of the personalities in addition to winning. Recently, somebody came up to me and they were talking about "The Super Bowl Shuffle" because that was unique at the time. Imagine that, a rap video from a pro sports team in the mid-80s—this was more than twenty years after they dropped the song—it was and is iconic. People tell me that they still remember when they were kids hearing "The Super Bowl Shuffle" and how it opened their eyes to the ways sports and entertainment merged. It was a unique group of people and it definitely was a unique time in Chicago sports. Even with the great success of the Chicago Bulls and Michael Jordan I don't know if it had that spirit, or if that spirit has ever been recaptured by any team in Chicago.

A lot of those guys stayed around Chicago and if they're not around Chicago they are involved somehow or another with the NFL. There's been a lot of success after they finished playing and that is a sign of something. Football is such a short period in your life and then you have the rest of your life to live. Hopefully, you live it in a productive way and you do something that's positive.

With all of the personalities on that Super Bowl team, I don't think there was anyone who was more fun than Walter Payton. He was a great friend and a unique human being. You had to be careful with him because he was such a practical joker. If you got him back it just escalated. It didn't end. That was the beginning of hostilities. Like when he would have a sock-throwing contest with our very staid general manager, the late great Jim Finks. Here's a 60-something man with silver hair and people telling him he should be the next commissioner of the league and he's sneaking around the locker room trying to surprise Walter and hit him with the balled up socks.

As soon as I got to training camp everyone started in on me, "Hey, Harvard. Hey, Harvard." I'm like, "OK, here we go." But the veterans pretty much left us alone because there were a lot of guys who came in just a year earlier. In thinking back on what it meant to be a professional we had a clear example in Walter. His credo was that he was never going to be out-worked. This is how great he was. For all the things he did on the field, in reality when you watched him day in and day out, all those great things, none of it surprised you. I think what would surprise you was if something magical didn't happen. It was all a result of him putting in his work and not looking for shortcuts.

We had a great time playing against Green Bay. The rivalry is intense. That is not a joke. The first time we drove up there we were on a bus and we could see kids about eight or nine years old out on a Saturday afternoon playing football and it's an idyllic setting with the leaves turning colors. So we waved to them from the bus and the kids flipped us off. But you develop a lot of respect for their players. It's fun when you have a rivalry that goes on like this one has.

Chicago fans hunger for a winner. They understand what they had in 1985 was something really special. I think what they're looking for is consistency. They want a team that year in and year out gives everything they've got. I think they want the team to reflect their character in the city, hard-working people. The team and the city have a bond. Chicago has hard-working folks. Even if you're in the white-collar world, you roll your sleeves up. When you go out to eat, you don't eat sushi. You go out to eat real food. It's that kind of place. You know you live hard and you play hard and you work hard. That's what this city is about.

Coming to the Chicago Bears changed my life. I don't know if I would have ended up in Chicago. You look at how things unfold in your life and it's had a huge impact. The wonderful thing has been to be able to stay on once my playing days were over and enjoy the city and become part of the city. It's home for me.

Dan Jiggetts was an offensive lineman for the Chicago Bears from 1976 to 1982.

Dan Jiggetts became a popular Chicago sports broadcaster after retiring from the game.
Scott Boehm/Getty Images

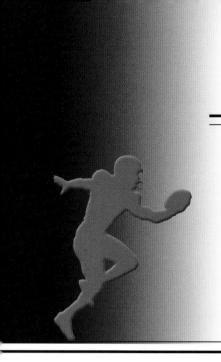

INTRODUCTION

Fans approaching Soldier Field before a Bears game against the Kansas City Chiefs in 2007. *Jonathan Daniel/Getty Images*

It is game day in early autumn along the shore of Lake Michigan in downtown Chicago and the surface of the Great Lake, one of the biggest lakes in the world, glitters in the sunshine. Sailboats cruise the placid waters, skippers glancing at the great structure on shore that is the focal point of activity this day, the hive where all of Chicago's worker bees are gravitating for a taste of honey. Soldier Field looms large on land, a monstrous stadium where the Chicago Bears entertain other National Football League clubs on fall Sunday afternoons.

On the water, looking towards shore, the scene seems soundless, almost as if occupants of the boats are looking earthward from the space shuttle. Those ants scurrying around are people, fans bedecked in dark blue sweatshirts with orange trim, blue baseball caps with a big "C" on the front, waving pennants, all pledging sartorial allegiance to their favorite team. The stadium, particularly since it was remodeled in the early 2000s, resembles nothing less than a spaceship itself, where the fans march in, almost as if they are going on a long journey to another solar system.

From the water, Soldier Field is a beautiful building, its new glass panels gleaming in the sunlight, a distinctive shoreline presence that fits nicely along the Chicago skyline. Up close and personal it is all different. Those exuberant fans who could not be heard from the lake are abuzz with the anticipation of a gladiatorial game where the hometown heroes will grunt and growl and bare their grizzly-bear teeth at the Giants, the Cowboys, the Lions, or the Packers, rivals for decades

The Monsters of the Midway, as the Bears were long ago nicknamed in homage to the World's Fair carnival grounds, have become the signature sports team of a pulsating city that is the crossroads of the American Midwest. Chicago was hog butcher to the world, the hub of water, train and then air transportation, very definitely a city of big shoulders, as Carl Sandburg, its most famous poet, intoned. Now it is alive with modernity, from theater to symphony, from

financial markets to museums and professional sports franchises.

Chicago loves its Cubs and White Sox baseball teams, its Blackhawks hockey team, and its Bulls basketball team, especially when they succeed. But the relationship with its football team runs deeper. These players all have big shoulders, even without wearing shoulder pads. They play a rougher, tougher game that rewards hard work, hard hits, and hard heads. Something in that mix always resonated with the Chicago immigrant communities that had experienced hard times. And in the nearby farm communities, too, where hard toil in the hard soil paid off (sometimes) if you worked dawn till dusk. Football was a game played in the rain, the mud, the wind, the cold and the snow. You just kept on going. Much like life raising a family or raising crops.

It was right and proper that the paternalistic leader of the Chicago Bears was a man who was there at the birth of the National Football League, a man who had a gruff voice and a prickly demeanor, strictly following his own advice and beliefs because he was always correct. The man's name was George Halas, and they called him "Papa." He was the papa Bear, the alpha leader. He grew up in Chicago, a son of Czech immigrants, and he never misjudged his audience.

Halas ruled the franchise with an iron fist for more than 60 years, passionate at all times, addicted to winning, cantankerous to the many, quietly generous to the few who could not help themselves. A similar outlook governed his relations with people and other NFL teams, where he assuredly believed in the common good.

Halas had the foresight to sign Red Grange in the 1920s and spent the next six decades promoting the NFL every way he could. The Bears were often and somewhat regularly the dominant team in the league and that fed his ego. Whatever the byproducts of rules changes, or looking ahead with new policies, Halas still burned to win.

When it all began, Halas' men played in less-glamorous settings and made a few hundred bucks on

A panoramic view of the modern Soldier Field before a game.
Scott Boehm/Getty Images

Tailgating and grilling came back into fashion in the parking lots outside Soldier Field in the 2000s.
Scott Boehm/Getty Images

their paychecks. Mike Ditka, the all-pro tight end and prodigal son, whom Halas anointed coach the year before his death, once famously said of his boss, "He throws nickels around like manhole covers." Ditka was not complimenting Halas' discus throwing, but rather his cheap ways in salary negotiations. Now the stadiums shine in the sunlight and the men who wear the uniform colors he chose get paid millions of dollars.

Not Ditka, not the fans, not the sports media, could discern how much fear Halas lived in that one day he would lose control of his baby. He survived the Depression and close calls financially and that guided his penny pinching and shaped him. In an era when the

NFL is flush and TV and ticket money roll in almost as fast as slot-machine payoffs, Halas might have behaved differently. But it should be noted that his family does still control the Bears.

Game day is a party in Chicago. Streets around Soldier Field are blocked off officially, or they are clogged with traffic, vehicular and pedestrian. The 61,500 fans who jam the stadium for each home game take up a lot of space. In another of his spot-on observations, when Ditka transformed from player to coach in the 1980s, he noted that his team was a blue-collar group, made up of "a bunch of Grabowskis." The Bears were still in touch with the past.

Since then Chicago has morphed into a more sophisticated city. Immigrants are more likely to identify with soccer than football. And livings are more likely to be made in towering skyscrapers than on manure-covered farms. But the link to the rough-and-tumble era remains. Those fans who turn out 60,000-strong do not care much who the Bears are playing, for it is the Bears they have come to see. They hunger for victory, behave with borderline delirium if the team wins consistently, but win or lose the spectators still come.

For the Bears belong to Chicago and Chicago belongs to the Bears.

Bears fans display their passion for their team at an October 2007 game at Soldier Field.
Scott Boehm/Getty Images

ACKNOWLEDGMENTS

The author would like to thank the research team at the Pro Football Hall of Fame in Canton, Ohio, for their assistance in bringing the past to life with the museum files.

In addition, the always helpful Scott Hagel and Jim Christman in the Bears communications department provided valuable assistance.

Thanks also to Chicago Bears players past and present who were interviewed and offered insights and their memories of what it is like to play for one of the most revered franchises in the National Football League.

CHAPTER 1

THE 1920s:
THE FOUNDING FATHER AND THE RISE OF PRO FOOTBALL

The legendary George Halas once reportedly said, "Nothing is work unless you'd rather be doing something else."

There was nothing in Halas' life that he enjoyed more than his association with the Chicago Bears. He was the team founder, a player, coach and owner. His entire life was defined by the Chicago Bears and the Chicago Bears were defined by George Halas. He was

Young George Halas, a player with the Chicago Bears in the early 1920s when he was owner, coach and player simultaneously of one of the original clubs in the fledgling National Football League.
Bettmann/Corbis

present at the creation and his spirit hovers over the franchise a quarter of a century after his death.

Halas was fortunate enough to discover his calling as a young man and forceful and insightful enough to transform his own private passion into a public one. He shaped a sports team into a civic institution and allied the sensibilities of franchise and community into overlapping paths until the goals and aspirations of one meshed with the goals and aspirations of the other.

Halas was the offspring of a family of Czech immigrants. Born in 1895 and raised on the West Side of Chicago, he attended Crane Tech. Father Frank was a tailor and then a grocer. Halas shoveled coal and did other maintenance chores. He became a devoted follower of the Chicago Cubs and his first athletic success was in baseball. There were many gang fist fights and sometimes, outnumbered, Halas ran rather than stood his ground. He said later that was how he developed his speed for sports. At the University of Illinois, Halas earned a degree in civil engineering. The Illini won the Big Ten football title in 1918 and Halas was the Most Valuable Player of the 1919 Rose Bowl. During World War I he was an ensign in the Navy.

Perhaps resentful that his family had to scrap for everything it earned, perhaps on the lookout for slights, perhaps wary of a world that he knew could deliver danger around the corner, whether in the way of bullies or other unforeseen challenges, Halas was quick to anger. His temper erupted regularly. Whether it was arguing with Illinois football coach Bob Zuppke, in consultation with other NFL owners, in public with journalists, or with players, Halas used to bluster to prove he was right. He felt intimidation was half the battle in getting what he wanted. Throughout a long life of 88 years, he never changed.

Halas was a good enough baseball player to excel on the semi-pro level and briefly earn a spot in the New York Yankees' lineup. During the 1919 season, Halas played 12 games in the outfield for the Yankees. However, he hit .091 at the plate. In one of the most dissected trades of all time, New York bought Babe Ruth from the Boston Red Sox and placed him in Halas' right-field spot. Ruth became the most famous home-run hitter of all time. Halas went on to other things.

Halas made one more minor league stop, his infamous temper getting him tossed out of a game in St. Paul, Minnesota, when he screamed at an umpire to listen to him and pulled the man's coat off. His next job was in the bridge design department of the Chicago, Burlington, and Quincy Railroad for $55 a week.

Bored without sports, Halas gravitated to a 14-member semi-pro football outfit that included John "Paddy" Driscoll and Jimmy Conzleman in the lineup and even played the Canton Bulldogs with Jim Thorpe. In March of 1920, Halas was recruited to work for the A. E. Staley starch-making company of Decatur, Illinois, about 175 miles south of Chicago. His job included playing baseball, possibly starting a basketball team and

playing for, coaching and organizing a semi-pro football team that was expected to be among the best in the country. Halas wangled permission to practice on company time.

Decades later, in a written reflection about the company, Eugene Staley wrote about the 1919–22 era when starch and pigskins mixed. He also jotted down some of his thoughts about why Halas was the man to run the team. "His drive, energy, pep, and ambition made him a standout football star and on top of this he was a keen student of the game," Staley wrote. "He also had some experience in pro football as he played Sunday football with the Hammond, Indiana, pro team while holding down his job as bridge engineer. The personal interview clinched the deal for all concerned."

Applying his knowledge of regional talent, Halas recruited All-Americans and other experienced players to make starch, blocks and tackles. Among the first players joining the Staleys was Chuck Dressen, later a famous big-league manager, and Dutch Sternaman, a recent Illinois star, and later Halas' business partner with the Bears. The Decatur Staleys took the field in the fall of 1920 and played a schedule that included games against the Rock Island Independents, the Moline Tractors, and teams from Chicago, Rockford and Hammond, Indiana. The first

A view of Soldier Field in its early days when it opened in the 1920s.
Bettmann/Corbis

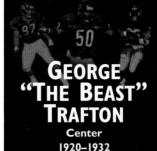

GEORGE "THE BEAST" TRAFTON
Center
1920–1932

Along with George Halas, George Trafton was a Decatur Staley before he became a Bear. Trafton was a local, graduating from Oak Park High—Ernest Hemingway's school—and he was an eight-time all-star and fearsome lineman. Trafton then played for Notre Dame, but coach Knute Rockne threw him off the team for playing semi-pro ball in his spare time.

The 6-foot-2, 230-pound Trafton's nicknames indicate what he was like in the trenches. Besides "The Beast," Trafton was called "The Cyclone." During the first 12 plays of a 1920 game, Trafton sent four Rock Island players to the sidelines with injuries. "Trafton was the only guy who claimed he was the world's greatest at his position and actually was," said Hall of Famer Jimmy Conzleman.

Away from football, Trafton fought an exhibition fight against White Sox player Art Shires in 1929 for $1,000 at a time he was making $100 a game from Halas. Trafton also tried professional wrestling, managed boxers and ran a gym after retiring from jobs as an assistant coach with the Packers and Los Angeles Rams. He had delusions of being a heavyweight contender and won a bout on the undercard of a Jack Dempsey fight, but when he tried to move up a class he was knocked out by Primo Carnera in one round.

Trafton was nominated for the Pro Football Hall of Fame in 1964 and died of a heart attack at age 74 in 1971.

Red Grange (right), who put pro football on the map by touring nationally with the Bears, made big money partnering with promoter C.C. Pyle, and bought himself a fur coat.
Underwood & Underwood/Corbis

game produced a 20–0 victory over Moline in front of 2,000 fans at Staley Field. There were 5,000 fans on the road for the Staleys' second game of the year against the Independents.

Halas banned his players from betting on their games—a wide-open practice at the time—but Staleys' supporters cleaned up when their club bested Rock Island 10–0 the first time. There was a lot of trash talk on both sides (years before derogatory diatribes were acknowledged with the words) and Independent fans singled out the Bears' rugged 6-foot-2, 230-pound tackle George Trafton, who never met a man he didn't mind slugging.

Early in the game, Trafton used his craft to level a Rock Island player, necessitating repair work of 19 stitches in his head and a cast encasing a broken wrist. It was a 0–0 game and before embarking for the trip home, the Staleys changed at their hotel. Halas gave the gate-receipt payoff (variously mentioned by Halas as $3,000 or $7,000) to Trafton and told him to bring it to the train. "I would run for the money, but Trafton would run for his life," Halas said later, explaining his strategy.

Player and money arrived safely for the train ride to Illinois.

The first evidence of a football player being paid dates back to the late 19th century, but the first evidence of a time and place for the establishment of a true league dates to the period immediately after World War I. The age of the millionaire franchise owner lay in the future. Businesses formed teams to aid their fortunes, offering jobs at the company to occupy players between stints on the field. Individual players not employed by companies might earn $100 a game.

By November of 1919, a group of teams in the Midwest seeking to schedule games, decided to form a league organizing their far-flung individual enterprises under one umbrella. The public hadn't accepted the concept yet, but team owners and players recognized that the quality of play was better among the play-for-pay crowd than it was in college. A plan was implemented for a schedule for the 1920 season. A preliminary planning meeting was held in August 1920, with the agreement made that a league would be formed.

A more critical meeting was conducted on September 17, 1920. This meeting—attended by

Half back Red Grange scores a touchdown for the Bears in a 1925 game against the Yellow Jackets in Philadelphia.
Bettmann/Corbis

"Chicago cops had more fear for Trafton than they had for the Capone mob."
—*Red Grange on tough guy teammate George Trafton.*

George Halas, representing the Decatur Staleys—formally created the American Professional Football Association and is regarded as the official establishment of the predecessor of the National Football League. Those joining were assessed a fee of $100, but it is believed the franchise bills were never paid. Jim Thorpe, who eight years earlier had won the Olympic gold medal in the decathlon in Sweden, and played pro football and major league baseball, was elected president of the league.

When Jim Thorpe won the Olympic gold medal in the decathlon at the Summer Olympics in 1912, the presentation included a speech by the king of Sweden proclaiming, "You, sir, are the greatest athlete in the world." It was no exaggeration. However, Thorpe was not the greatest administrator in the world. Think Enron without the corruption. His comfort zone was on the playing field, not behind a desk. It was unclear if Thorpe's election as a figurehead league president to exploit his name paid any dividends, but by 1921 he was out of office and back on the field.

The nation was enjoying prosperity, but pro football was not an established business. The owners and team representatives gathered in the crowded Hupmobile showroom owned by Ralph E. Hay in Canton, Ohio, to draft the original league constitution, were taking a risk with their money. They sensed the time was right to bring more organization to the pro game, but they did not know if the league could succeed.

If there was a sign of this uncertainty, the organizational meeting took place in no fancy rented conference room. If there was a sign of enthusiasm and optimism, it was that the turnout was so great there was not enough room to sit at chairs and tables. Members of the overflow crowd seized seats where they could find them such as resting their rear ends on the running boards of cars for sale. Room to pace was

ORIGINAL 14 TEAMS OF THE AMERICAN PROFESSIONAL FOOTBALL ASSOCIATION

Akron Pros

Buffalo All-Americans

Canton Bulldogs

Chicago Tigers

Columbus Panhandles

Detroit Heralds

Cleveland Indians

Dayton Triangles

Decatur Staleys

Hammond Pros

Muncie Flyers

Racine Cardinals

Rochester Jeffersons

Rock Island Independents

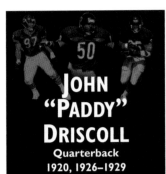

JOHN "PADDY" DRISCOLL

Quarterback
1920, 1926–1929

The personal history of Paddy Driscoll as a professional football player criss-crossed several important moments in Chicago football history. Not only did he star collegiately at North-western in suburban Evanston, where he was born, during World War I Driscoll played at the Great Lakes Naval Training Station, where he teamed up with George Halas. Later, Driscoll was a member of the original Decatur Staleys, switched to the Chicago Cardinals, and then was purchased by the Bears for $3,500 in 1926.

Even by NFL standards of the 1920s, Driscoll was small. He had the physical stature of a high school player at 5-foot-11 and 160 pounds, but he was fast, shifty, creative and could throw long and kick far. In one game with the Cardinals, Driscoll drop-kicked four field goals.

Driscoll shared the Bears' backfield with Red Grange and later returned to the club as an assistant coach. He served in that capacity between 1941 and 1956 and, in two seasons as head coach during a Halas hiatus, Driscoll led Chicago to an NFL championship game. In his autobiography, Halas wrote that he planned to lend out the job for two years to Driscoll, "my friend and colleague for 40 years. I felt I owed him the satisfaction of being head coach before he ended his career."

at a premium, but beer, in buckets, was plentiful. None of these men could have imagined a world of Super Bowls, billion-dollar TV contracts (they were barely imagining radio), and stadiums filled to overflowing every Sunday nationwide. The attendance at their games was more likely to be 1,000 than 5,000 and half the people in the grandstands probably had the same last names as the various players.

Among the first professional teams recognized by the league were: the Dayton Triangles, Canton Bulldogs, Decatur Staleys and Buffalo All-Americans. There had been New York-based all-star teams and famed New York baseball Giants manager John McGraw sponsored some.

The game of football in the 1920s would be recognizable to the fan of the 2000s, but there were differences. The players were not nearly so large, even at the strength positions. The passing game existed, but rules prohibited the quarterback throwing from less than five yards behind the line of scrimmage and most coaches adhered to the philosophy espoused later by famed college coach Woody Hayes. Hayes said that if you throw the ball only three things can happen and two of them are bad—an incompletion or an interception.

Teams of the 1920s relied more on running. Their game plans centered on pushing the ball downfield on long drives, like bulldozers. The quick strike on offense usually meant a runner broke free through a large offensive line hole. Then, of course, teams had small rosters—none of this 53-man stuff that is the current team limit—and most players competed on both sides of the ball. You were a tackle and a defensive tackle. Quarterbacks were usually defensive backs, too. It was common for players to play the entire 60 minutes.

Red Grange (third from left) and his Bears teammates at a practice in the 1920s.
Bettmann/Corbis

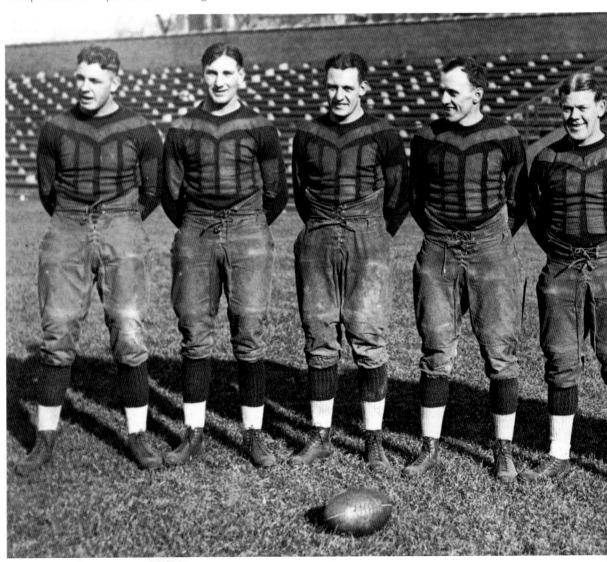

Generally speaking, without elaborate air attacks, scores were lower. There was much less sophistication in training, less emphasis on drinking water to stay hydrated, virtually no focus on diet and nutrition. Equipment was primitive. Shoulder pads were thinner and more likely to break. Helmets were leather and had no face bars. Some players still lined up bareheaded. A 250-pound lineman was unusual and was probably comparable to the 330-pound linemen of today. A 200-pound running back was huge. It was possible to field an entire row of linemen whose weights barely exceeded 200 pounds.

A home-and-home, everyone-plays-everyone schedule was not in the cards for 1920. Teams made their own schedules. Some teams played 11 games. Decatur played 13, finishing with a 10–1–2 record. The Muncie Flyers played just one game against a league opponent. The Akron Pros went undefeated, 8–0–3 and despite the Decatur record were voted champs.

Fritz Pollard, the first black player in league history, was the Akron team leader. A year later Akron also fielded Paul Robeson, the Rutgers All-American who became a famous singer and black political activist.

Slowly, through better cooperation, schedules that made better sense were worked on and worked out.

Halas was in the right place and at the right time when he was summoned by the Staleys—he thought. But Eugene Staley's dream of developing powerhouse sports teams to spread the name of his starch far and wide fizzled. Business problems at headquarters, reflecting a declining market for starch, meant that financial cutbacks were in order. At least one report suggested Staley lost $14,000 on the ventures. In gratitude for Halas building him a football team out of thin air, Staley suggested Halas move the club to Chicago for its second season and offered $5,000 in additional backing provided Halas retain the name of the Staleys for one more season. Halas agreed.

In 1922 the Decatur Staleys, the same franchise which had already been located in Chicago for a year, became the Chicago Bears. Thinking back to his youthful rooting for the Chicago Cubs and their cute, cuddly mascot, Halas named the team the Chicago Bears. The Bear was a grown animal and a bit meaner-

Bears and Giants face off at the Polo Grounds in 1925.
Bettmann/Corbis

Runner Red Grange shows off his other skills as he goes back to pass for the Bears against the New York Giants in 1925.
Bettmann/Corbis

looking than the Cubs' symbol. Halas' affection for the Cubs was genuine, but he also wanted to capitalize on the public's identification with the baseball team. It couldn't hurt if anyone thought his football team was connected to the popular baseball club.

The Bears played their home games at Wrigley Field, then and now the home of the Cubs. However, in the 1920s Wrigley was called Cubs Park. Halas made his deal with Bill Veeck, Sr., president of the team, and father of Bill Veeck, Jr., who became baseball's most storied promoter between the 1940s and 1970s when he owned the Cleveland Indians, St. Louis Browns, and Chicago White Sox twice. Veeck, Sr. warmly embraced a deal with Halas. The ballpark had no tenants in the fall.

Veeck knew that college football was king, but he saw the possibilities in the pro game. During those days many Americans worked a six-day week and could not attend college football games. Veeck saw Halas providing something for the working man to do on his day off. "They'll jump at the chance to see pro games if you play on Sunday afternoon," Veeck told Halas.

When the Bears became the Bears, Halas was not the sole team operator. His co-owner was Dutch Sternaman, like himself a former University of Illinois star, who had scored 98 of the Staleys' 164 points during their first season. The Bears were a success in Chicago in 1922, finishing the season with a profit of $1,476.92.

"He did it all a little bit better than anyone else of his era and there seems to be little doubt that he would have done it just as well in any era."
—*National Football League Encyclopedia on Roy Lyman.*

Halas was a better football player than he was a baseball player and during the 1923 season he made the most memorable play of his career. A 1920s photograph of Halas shows him with a thick head of dark hair, hands on hips, in uniform. His long-sleeved dark shirt resembles a sweater and has what appear to be streaks of leather layering the front. He's got cleats on his feet, tight socks, and baggy pants. He is smiling and that figures because George Halas was in his element, dressed for a practice, perhaps, on a dusty field.

During the 1923 contest against the Oorang Indians, Halas, playing defense, went up against Jim Thorpe. Thorpe was a player-coach playing both ways

on offense and defense. Back on the gridiron, Thorpe was doing what he did better than anyone else around—carry the ball downfield for touchdowns just about any time it was handed to him.

It was rainy and the field was muddy. On this particular play Thorpe tucked the ball under his arm and started a run to the nearby Bears goal-line. Only the ball slipped out of his hands, bounced around on the turf and was scooped up by Halas on his own 2-yard-line. One reason Thorpe excelled at football was his fierceness on the field. He enjoyed leveling other ball-carriers to put doubt in their minds. Halas began running towards the other end zone. It seemed to be in the next community.

It was during this long journey slogging through the mud that Halas recalled Thorpe's desire to crush ball-carriers. He knew Thorpe was mad at himself for fumbling and he knew Thorpe should be able to run him down with his superior speed. But Halas ran fast,

Red Grange at the end of the bench on the right during his first professional football game in 1925 against the Chicago Cardinals.
Underwood & Underwood/Corbis

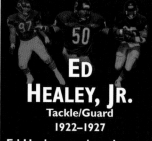

ED HEALEY, JR.
Tackle/Guard
1922–1927

Ed Healey may have been as tough as George Trafton and Roy Lyman, but compared to them he was pint-sized. He stood 6-foot-1, but weighed just 207 pounds. Today's running backs outweigh Healey.

Healey grew up in Massachusetts, attended high school in Springfield, and then college at Dartmouth in New Hampshire. He was an Ivy League guy, but he was no genteel bookworm. When he moved to Chicago Healey's part-time job was boxing. He lied to his parents and eight sisters, saying facial bruises stemmed from defending the honor of the Irish in the wrong neighborhood.

The first pro team on Healey's resumé was the Rock Island Independents in 1920. Healey played against Bears founder George Halas. It was said that Healey once hit Halas so hard he re-arranged his molecules and that when Halas' headache went away he offered Healey a contract. If Healey was on his side, Halas reasoned, he would get bashed by him no more.

In an era of bargain rates, it cost Halas $100 to acquire Healey. Joining a team like the Chicago Bears that played in a big-time facility like Wrigley Field was like going to heaven. Healey did not nominate Rock Island's Douglas Park for a photo spread in *House Beautiful*. Being afflicted with athlete's foot was not the main locker room worry. "There was only one shower, and you never knew what kind of a bug was going to bite you," Healey said.

Chicago Bears lining up with Red Grange in the back field in a warmup before a 1920s game.
Bettmann/Corbis

Left to right, Dutch Sternaman, Red Grange, and George Halas, at practice in November 1925.
Bettmann/Corbis

sprinting for a score with a maximum amount of fakes thrown in. "I could feel Thorpe breathing down my neck all the way," Halas said many times over the years as he re-told the story.

Whether it was because of his late start, the sloppy field, or Halas running faster than he ever had before, Thorpe never caught up. Halas scored a 98-yard touchdown. It was a league record for returning a fumble the farthest, and it stood for 49 years.

The returns were slow in being measured, but the new league, which changed its name to National Football League at Halas' urging, was making inroads with the public. Pro teams could not yet compete with college teams for local allegiances, but they were another entertainment option.

Like any other league in any other sport, the NFL had growing pains, many of them related to money. In the 1920s, it might be more attractive for a player to start his career in an established profession that paid better and guaranteed year-round income. Becoming a professional athlete now is akin to winning the lottery, earning enough salary to be set for life. At that time, particularly if a player was married, there was considerable pressure to settle down.

Players tried football for a couple of years and decided it wasn't worth it financially. Or their wives did. Teams disbanded, teams went under. The Chicago Bears endured successfully. The Racine Cardinals became the Chicago Cardinals (and later the St. Louis Cardinals and Arizona Cardinals), but they survived. Amazingly, by 1933, only the two Chicago teams remained of the charter league members. Only one charter player from 1920, Hall of Fame center George Trafton of the Bears, was still in the league.

The speedy halfback Red Grange certainly appreciated the way Trafton blocked for him and revealed a few hints as to how Trafton was able to persevere. Grange called Trafton, "The toughest, meanest, most ornery critter alive." And he meant that in a nice way. Once, in a game at Rock Island, a Trafton tackle broke a player's leg. Fans hooted and mocked

him. When the game ended, Trafton quickly donned a sweatshirt to try and hide his trademark No. 13 uniform number worn in defiance of superstition. He dove into a taxi cab, but fans caught up and pelted the car with rocks. Trafton jumped out and sprinted down the road ahead of the mob.

In the 1920s, the U.S. economy was riding high, so a new venture had a fighting chance to succeed. The Bears made a $24,000 profit in 1924, but Halas cast his eye southward, to the University of Illinois campus, scene of his own collegiate exploits. Being in the same state, being so close, Halas could not overlook the powerful presence of Red Grange.

When Grange—who wore the very identifiable No. 77 jersey—and the Illini played, the newly constructed Memorial Stadium was jam-packed with 67,000 fans. Cubs Park did not seat anywhere near that many people. The Illini bought programs and popcorn and loved their team.

Halas knew an All-American when he saw one and he featured such linemen like Trafton and Guy Chamberlain out of Nebraska on the Bears. But linemen don't sell tickets. Even in the modern game

coaches can't evaluate linemen's performances on the spur of the moment after games. They all say they need to look at the films. Fans only care about offensive linemen when they miss a block so egregiously that the naked eye can see it from the 40th row. They only care about defensive linemen if they see them flatten a ball-carrier in the open field or sack the quarterback.

What Halas wanted was a headliner. Someone he could use to push tickets. Someone so glamorous that the casual football fan would be lured to watch a game. Someone so famous that diehard fans of college football might even be enticed to see a pro game— and keep on coming back. Of course, there was only one player who fit that description. After Grange rushed for 363 yards to ruin Penn in a game, the train back from Philadelphia was met by 10,000 shouting students. Halas craved seeing Grange switch his blue and orange uniform of the Illini to the blue and orange uniform of the Bears. He was determined to sign Grange.

C. C. Pyle, the P. T. Barnum of the period with an outlook towards sports, and the man who

Jim Thorpe, Olympic gold medalist in decathlon, was named the first president of the National Football League when it formed in 1920.
Bettmann/Corbis

Hunk Anderson (left) who helped fill in as Bears coach during World War II when owner George Halas was serving in the Navy, talking to quarterback Sid Luckman.
Bettmann/Corbis

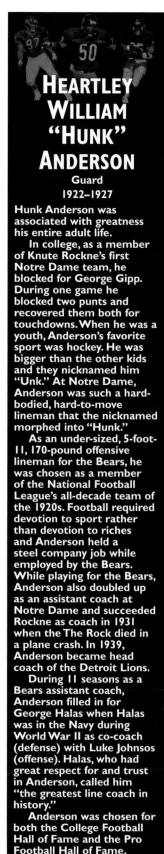

HEARTLEY WILLIAM "HUNK" ANDERSON
Guard
1922–1927

Hunk Anderson was associated with greatness his entire adult life.

In college, as a member of Knute Rockne's first Notre Dame team, he blocked for George Gipp. During one game he blocked two punts and recovered them both for touchdowns. When he was a youth, Anderson's favorite sport was hockey. He was bigger than the other kids and they nicknamed him "Unk." At Notre Dame, Anderson was such a hard-bodied, hard-to-move lineman that the nicknamed morphed into "Hunk."

As an under-sized, 5-foot-11, 170-pound offensive lineman for the Bears, he was chosen as a member of the National Football League's all-decade team of the 1920s. Football required devotion to sport rather than devotion to riches and Anderson held a steel company job while employed by the Bears. While playing for the Bears, Anderson also doubled up as an assistant coach at Notre Dame and succeeded Rockne as coach in 1931 when the The Rock died in a plane crash. In 1939, Anderson became head coach of the Detroit Lions.

During 11 seasons as a Bears assistant coach, Anderson filled in for George Halas when Halas was in the Navy during World War II as co-coach (defense) with Luke Johnsos (offense). Halas, who had great respect for and trust in Anderson, called him "the greatest line coach in history."

Anderson was chosen for both the College Football Hall of Fame and the Pro Football Hall of Fame.

sponsored "The Bunion Derby" as the foot race from coast to coast came to be called, was the conduit between Halas and Grange. Pyle promised Grange he could make $100,000 by taking a football tour with the Bears. Pyle and the Bears put together a national tour and except for Grange getting hurt in the middle and missing a couple of games (something that hammered the gate in Detroit and wounded it during one Chicago stopover) things unfolded spectacularly.

It was difficult to say that permanent converts to pro football were made throughout the country, but there was little doubt Grange made friends everywhere.

When he joined the Bears for good after a hiatus in a rival pro league started by Pyle, Grange's style and elusiveness did bring converts to the pro game.

In the first game of the fabled 1925 tour, the Bears, with Grange in the lineup, faced the Chicago Cardinals and their star Paddy Driscoll. Besides being a renowned quarterback, Driscoll was the squad's punter. On a day when his team could not move the ball well against the Bears, Driscoll was called on to punt 23 times. Grange was sent back to receive the kicks. Catching punts and returning them great distances was one of Grange's strengths because he could build up momentum in the open field.

Red Grange dives for a touchdown and loses his helmet in a game against the Los Angeles Tigers in 1926.
Bettmann/Corbis

"We'd only need two."
—George Halas in 1973 on how the Bears with Ed Healey and Joe Stydahar in their line wouldn't need a 40-man roster to win a title.

Time after time, however, Driscoll steered his kicks away from Grange. Either to the other side of the field or out of bounds. Grange could make plays on only three returns and he did the Cardinals little harm. The fans soon recognized what Driscoll was doing and as

he kept up the strategy the booing became louder and louder.

Exhibition game or not, Driscoll admitted afterwards he had given much thought to his approach. He didn't mind the booing, he just didn't want to get burned by a Grange breakaway. "It was a question of which one of us was going to look bad," he said, "Grange or Driscoll. I decided it wasn't going to be me. Punting to Grange is like grooving a pitch to Babe Ruth."

The fates of the NFL, the Bears, and Grange were heavily intertwined during the 1925 season in particular and for the rest of the 1920s. As flamboyant as Grange was on the field, his manner was understated off of it. He knew his value, but he never flaunted his talents in conversation. He was not aloof from his teammates, made friends among them, and despite establishment of the legend that followed Grange throughout his life, he remained grounded.

"One of a kind," said Abe Gibron, a later Bears coach. "He was one of the most honorable and honest people I've ever met."

If Grange was disbelieving when Pyle first approached him and told him he could become rich playing football, Pyle lived up to every pledge. Not only did Grange strike gold on the playing tour, Pyle brought him six-figure paydays from making movies, making personal appearances, and by setting up product endorsements for everything from sweaters and shoes to ginger ale. Overwhelmed by the attention and the windfall, Grange did go Hollywood briefly, buying a $500 raccoon coat and a pricey car. Newspapers estimated that Pyle helped make Grange $1 million. "He was the biggest thing in the United States," said Charles "Ookie" Miller, who roomed with Grange on Bears road trips. "I had a lot of respect for Red."

One reason for that attitude was Grange's sense of responsibility to the paying customers who made him rich and famous. Sometimes he made decisions that were detrimental to his own health and future, Miller said, playing hurt, even when Halas wanted Grange out of the game. One game Halas told Grange he would play him on defense for a while, but he didn't want his injury to worsen, so he wasn't going to run the ball. "But Red stayed in for three or four plays," Miller said, "and got jammed up again. Halas was raising Cain on the sideline and Red came over and said, 'Look, George, these people paid to see me play and I'm going to do it as long as I possibly can.' That was Red."

It was the sportswriters, not his teammates, who referred to Grange as "The Galloping Ghost," and it was one of the more (continued on page 27)

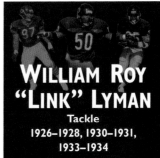

WILLIAM ROY "LINK" LYMAN

Tackle
1926–1928, 1930–1931,
1933–1934

At 6-foot-2, Roy Lyman was not a gigantic presence in height but at 252 pounds, he was in girth. He was an advance model of the modern lineman—big, strong, with quick feet—and he played tackle both ways. Lyman's ability to stunt along the line was the prototype for future linemen. Being athletic as well as large at a time when 200-pound linemen were common, made him virtually unstoppable.

Lyman played collegiately at Nebraska, broke into pro football with the Canton Bulldogs, Cleveland Bulldogs and Frankford Yellow Jackets, and then in 1925 joined Red Grange on his barnstorming tour of the country. When Grange became a Bear, so did Lyman. It was an association that worked out well for Lyman and George Halas. Wherever Lyman went— Nebraska, the Bulldogs, Frankford, the Bears—his teams won championships.

In an illustration that demonstrates how salaries were sub-par in the early days of the NFL, Lyman twice took leaves from the Bears. One fall he played semi-pro ball in Texas and another he spent clearing up ranching problems. Lyman also later had an insurance agency.

Later, with the roots of his pro football years in his thoughts, Lyman lobbied heavily for the Hall of Fame to be situated in Canton, Ohio. Lyman was enshrined in 1964. He died aged 74 in 1972 in an automobile accident.

THE GALLOPING GHOST

He ran like the wind and the wind trailed in his wake. Strong men could not tackle Red Grange and fast men could not catch him. On a football field, he was like the god Mercury, with wings on his feet and magic in his stride. He was both mythological and human and, although he did not invent professional football, he elevated it.

When Red Grange came along, electrifying crowds of 67,000 at the University of Illinois, he was a step ahead of the pack, the man who with a zig or a zag could outdistance pursuers. All eyes were riveted upon him when he carried the ball. With Grange in the lineup, football was less about brute strength than slipperiness and daring. The sport was less about wrestling and more about ballet. And the audience loved it. Sure, football was for stout-hearted men with their bulging muscles, but it turned out fans appreciated touchdowns scored in spectacular style even more.

George Halas, who participated in the formation of the National Football League and operated the Chicago Bears a mere 150 miles north of the Illini excitement, recognized the potential of a name drawing card and the value of adding Grange to his team. Better yet, Harold "Red" Grange, so nicknamed for the color of his flaming hair, was a local boy. Born in 1903 in Pennsylvania, where his father supervised a logging camp, Grange grew up in Wheaton, a suburb of Chicago, where for eight summers through high school and college he held a job carrying ice, making as much as $37.50 a week. These were good wages at the

Red Grange caused a sensation when he moved from college to the Bears in 1925.
New York Times Co./Getty Images

time and the work built up the power in Grange's arms and shoulders on his 5-foot-11, 175-pound frame.

"The Wheaton Iceman," another Grange nickname, was the real deal. He paid his way through school, he was muscular and handsome, carried the ball out of the backfield, returned punts, passed sharply, and was a devastating tackler on defense. The public imbued Grange with an "aw-shucks" personality because that's what people wanted to believe. In the Roaring Twenties, Grange was as popular and well known as heavyweight champ Jack Dempsey, baseball slugger Babe Ruth, golfer Bobby Jones, tennis player "Big Bill" Tilden and swimmer Johnny Weissmuller, later the movies' Tarzan. They shared the headlines and captured the fancy of an American population riding the crest of good times after World War I.

Halas was down-to-earth, but realized the need for more publicity lest his beloved football franchise fail. Grange was a sexy personality. Girls swooned over him and men admired his skills. It didn't hurt that Halas was an Illinois man, too.

Grange made his name and left others to magnify it in newspaper headlines and in bright lights elsewhere. As a sophomore he scored 12 touchdowns and rushed for 1,260 yards as the Illini went undefeated. As a junior he scored 13 touchdowns and rushed for 1,164 yards. Grange's legend was cemented, however, with a single game in 1925 that remains, more than 80 years later, one of the best ever produced by a collegiate football player.

Before playing Michigan, the Wolverines' legendary coach Fielding Yost said, "Mr. Grange will be carefully watched every time he takes the ball." Watch is pretty much what Wolverine tacklers did as Grange accounted for six touchdowns in the 39–14 romp. He ran 95 yards with the opening kick, scored on runs of 67, 56, and 45 yards, and passed for two touchdowns on throws of 12 and 18 yards.

Halas plotted to ensure Grange would move directly from the Illini to the Bears. But as expansive a thinker as Halas was, someone else in the shadows thought bigger. Charles Pyle, a Champaign, Illinois, movie theater owner and promotional wizard, was called "Cash and Carry" Pyle by those who knew his flamboyant style. One day Pyle literally stalked Grange into the movies, cornered him and advanced one of the most famous sporting propositions of all time. "How would you like to make $100,000?" Pyle asked Grange. Goggle-eyed at the thought, Grange signed on for a national football tour with the Chicago Bears to begin Thanksgiving Day, 1925, immediately after exhausting his collegiate eligibility.

Pro football was in its infancy. Fans rooted for colleges because they were students, graduates, or local supporters, and considered the pros ruffians. Transplanting Grange from one setting to the other was genius, but not appreciated by all. "The only thing I could have done worse was kill somebody," Grange said. "I was called everything possible. I would

Top: Actress Marian Davies and Bears star Red Grange.
Underwood & Underwood/Corbis

Above: Red Grange carrying the ball in a 1926 practice.
New York Times Co./Getty Images

have been more popular if I had joined the Capone mob."

The 66-day, 19-game swing throughout the United States, from Chicago to New York to Florida to California, spread the gospel and excitement of pro football using Grange as the centerpiece selling point. Not every game did huge box office, but many did. About 75,000 fans observed the Bears playing the Los Angeles Tigers in the LA Coliseum and about 73,000 saw the Bears play the New York Giants in the Polo Grounds.

Grange got his money from a percentage of the gate receipts, Halas got his publicity, and when the exhibition tour ended, the Bears had a star player who contributed to their early championship clubs and later evolved into a long-time team broadcaster. At the peak of his fame, Grange had a candy bar named after him, and a doll as well. "He brought pro football out of the closet," said later Bears quarterback Sid Luckman.

Grange understood his own worth, but was no blowhard. He could tell a joke on himself and there was never a better one than the story of Grange and Halas visiting the White House to see President Calvin Coolidge. They were introduced as Halas and Grange of the Chicago Bears. "How are you, young gentlemen?" Coolidge asked. "I have always admired animal acts."

The Bears were not yet world renowned.

CHICAGO BEARS–RED GRANGE TOUR OF AMERICA

1925

Date	Opponent	Place	Attendance
Nov. 26	Chicago Cardinals	Cubs Park, Chicago	36,000
Nov. 29	Columbus Tigers	Cubs Park, Chicago	28,000
Dec. 2	Donnelly Stars	Sportsman's Park, St. Louis	8,000
Dec. 5	Frankford Yellow Jackets	Shibe Park, Philadelphia	35,000
Dec. 6	New York Giants	Polo Grounds, N.Y.	73,000
Dec. 8	Washington All-Stars	Griffith Stadium, Wash. D.C.	7,000
Dec. 9	Providence Steam Rollers	Braves Field, Boston	15,000
Dec. 10	Pittsburgh All-Stars	Forbes Field, Pittsburgh	6,000
Dec. 12	Detroit Panthers	Navin Field, Detroit	4,000
Dec. 13	New York Giants	Cubs Park, Chicago	15,000
Dec. 25	Miami All-Stars	Coral Gables, Fla.	5,000

1926

Date	Opponent	Place	Attendance
Jan. 1	Tampa Cardinals	Tampa	8,000
Jan. 2	Jacksonville All-Stars	Jacksonville	6,700
Jan. 10	Southern All-Stars	New Orleans	6,000
Jan. 16	Los Angeles Tigers	Los Angeles Coliseum	75,000
Jan. 17	Cline's Californians	San Diego	not available
Jan. 24	San Francisco Tigers	Kezar Stadium, San Francisco	23,000
Jan. 30	Longshoremen	Portland, Oregon	not available
Jan. 31	Washington All-Stars	Seattle	5,000

19 Games, 66 days on road, 17 cities, 13 wins, 5 losses, 1 tie

> **"I liked George very much, but we didn't always agree and he had a control over me I wasn't happy about. He used to fine the heck out of me."**
> —*Early Bears player Charles "Ookie" Miller on George Halas.*

euphonious and appropriate of nicknames of all time. Football was considered a brutish game (one of Trafton's nicknames was "The Brute") and what Grange did with his slick moves was add a touch of elegance. He was the first true slashing, open-field runner who brought fans out of their seats. When Grange died in 1987, NFL Commissioner Paul Tagliabue took note. "Red Grange was one of the NFL's first superstars who gave pro football credibility and recognition," Tagliabue said.

Superstar? Nobody used that word in the 1920s, but when newspapers wrote stories about Grange's impact on the "fair sex" simply by running down the field, clearly he had transcended support solely from the factory-worker crowd. Grange never acquired the superstar strut or attitude, however. Even while playing for the Bears, he returned to his Wheaton ice-carrying job though the boss asked him to park his $5,000 Lincoln somewhere besides the front of the building so he wouldn't get confused about who was working for whom.

If women took notice of Grange's swivel hips, if football was trying hard to appeal to mainstream sports fans, if pro football was showing collegians there were respectable ways to continue their careers, it was still a man's game. And Halas was a man's coach. He was a dictator who yelled at his players and referees. Winning was the only thing for Halas, much as for any coach. He was not out to make friends, but he wanted to influence outcomes.

In Halas' mind it was important to out-work, out-smart, and out-hustle the other guys. Then on game day, out-muscle, out-think, and out-perform them. Halas came from poverty and in the Chicago Bears he was building something. It was no overnight job, either. It was a years-long project. Halas wanted to put fannies in the seats so his team could thrive and he wanted to put wins on the scoreboard so his fans would cheer.

It was a long process, but Halas also had a long memory. He remembered his friends when times were tough. "Loyalty speaks for itself," he said. "I believe it to be the most important characteristic a man can have." By the end of the 1920s, the National Football League had stabilized, and even during the worst of the Depression years to follow it showed it was not going away.

1920s CHICAGO BEARS YEAR BY YEAR

1920	10–1–2*
1921	9–1–1*
1922	9–3
1923	9–2–1
1924	6–1–4
1925	9–5–3
1926	12–1–3
1927	9–3–2
1928	7–5–1
1929	4–9–2

* First two seasons played as the Decatur Staleys

Red Grange (left) and coach George Halas discuss strategy as Grange is about to turn professional.
Corbis

CHAPTER 2

THE 1930s:
THE BEARS BECOME MONSTERS

Bronko Nagurski's reputation preceded him and George Halas was not asking for directions from a stranger when he first saw him. Halas went to the University of Minnesota campus to see what this behemoth of the gridiron was like, though Halas would likely have signed Nagurski sight unseen anyway.

It has always been difficult to separate myth from reality when discussing Nagurski, but one cold, hard fact stands out when football people marvel at his talents and size. Nagurski's ring size was 19½, the largest ever measured for a player's championship prize.

Right: Bears fullback Bronko Nagurski bursts through the line to score a touchdown in Chicago's 1935 exhibition victory over the Pacific Coast All-Stars. *Bettmann/Corbis*

Far right: Red Grange displays his throwing form. *Bettmann/Corbis*

The arrival of Nagurski for the 1930 season went a long way towards making sure the Bears had championship rings at all. Just as he had the wisdom and persuasiveness to sign Red Grange, Halas got Nagurski's name on a Bears contract. But a decade after the creation of the National Football League, many things off the field were changing that affected Halas, the Bears, and American society. The Roaring Twenties, with their party-time outlook, were coming to an end, indeed, crashed to an end with the collapse of the stock market that heralded the Great Depression. After the 1929 season Halas retired as a player. And he chose to take his first break from coaching.

Teams came and went in the NFL. Clubs whose owners' ambitions out-reached their pocketbooks departed and often the city where their team was located was left without football. Even those owners who were more grounded found their cash flow impeded by the nation's changing economic conditions. The Wall Street panic had struck. Gradually, inexorably,

"Many people flounder about in life because they do not have a purpose, an objective toward which to work."
—Bears owner George Halas.

the United States was sliding into the Depression, which destroyed fortunes, uprooted despondent families in search of employment, drove many to suicide, and shattered American spirits. From a wildly optimistic country that was living high in the 1920s, the U.S. sank to desperate depths.

Halas was no longer playing end. Halas was no longer coaching. As the 1930s began, he was pre-occupied with three tasks. The first was fielding a competitive team with enough talent for the championship race. The second was serving as a member of league committees that examined the rules of the pro game with an eye towards beefing up scoring and attracting more customers. The third, from Halas' standpoint, was probably the most critical. He had to use his wiles to retain control of his Chicago Bears.

When the Staleys morphed into the Bears, moving from Decatur to Chicago, Halas was in charge, but partnered with Ed "Dutch" Sternaman, another star player. They had an agreement that if one or the other wanted to dissolve the partnership, the other had the right of first refusal to buy his share. By 1931, Sternaman was broke. He did not have money for basic living necessities and was going to have to move out of his home. Sternaman needed the cash infusion and Halas wanted the team. There was little precedent for selling football franchises and it was guesswork what the Bears were worth during the Depression. Eventually, the two men settled on a $38,000 payment from Halas for Sternaman's half.

Halas did not have that much money. He paid $25,000 up front and agreed to make two additional payments within a year. Ralph Brizzolara, one of Halas' best friends, whose family has been involved with the Bears over the generations, lent Halas a chunk of the money. But he needed more. Business partner and friend Jim McMillen, another former Illini football player, who also played for the Bears under Halas' tutelage between 1924 and 1929, was one of the few people around making money in 1931. McMillen had become a professional wrestler and grappled more than 100 times in a year. It was a big raise from Halas' $100 per game. Promoters in the professional wrestling industry paid fees in advance. Who knew that the hokiest thing on the planet would become one of its most reliable financially? McMillen invested in the Bears when Halas

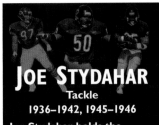

JOE STYDAHAR
Tackle
1936–1942, 1945–1946

Joe Stydahar holds the distinction of being the first player ever drafted by the Bears after the collegiate player draft was instituted. He was a 235-pound tackle at a time when linemen weighed only perhaps about two-thirds of what they do in the modern game. Stydahar was nicknamed "Jumbo Joe."

An all-star left tackle in his first years, Stydahar missed prime years to serve his country in the Navy during World War II, then returned to play two additional seasons for the Bears. He played collegiately at West Virginia, where he grew up, and was selected for the College and Pro Football Halls of Fame. He also coached the Los Angeles Rams and St. Louis Cardinals. Stydahar led the Rams to an NFL title.

In 1963, Stydahar returned to the Bears as an assistant coach, proclaiming at the time that his close association with the team in the past drew him to Chicago and he wanted to help Papa Bear Halas win one more title. Later that year the Bears won their first NFL championship since 1946. "Joe was something special for me," Halas said when Stydahar died of a heart attack at 65 in 1977. "But more important than any of his football accomplishments, Joe Stydahar was a man of outstanding character and loyalty."

Stydahar was afflicted with alcoholism, but stopped drinking and stayed sober for some 13 years before he was inducted into the Pro Football Hall of Fame in 1967.

Left to right, Coach Ralph Jones (with hat), offensive lineman Link Lyman, Bronko Nagurski, Red Grange and Keith Molesworth in 1932. Jones promised George Halas he would give him a title within three years and with the likes of Nagurski and Grange on the roster, he came through. *Bettmann/Corbis*

"My belief is that a college team would have little, if any, chance of winning."
—*Red Grange, when asked in 1932 if a great college team could beat a good pro team.*

needed him.

Three different times in a variety of deals and stock purchases, McMillen produced cash for Halas when the team was in financial straits in the early 1930s. For decades afterwards, McMillen was listed in the team directory as a club vice president. In addition, Halas' mother Barbara, ponied up several thousand dollars

investing in the team.

Just reviewing these pleas for help, the resulting transactions, and the likelihood that the commitments were made to Halas more because of who he was rather than the value of what he was selling, it is no wonder that Halas came to prize the trait of loyalty above all others.

Yet for all of that assistance, on August 9, 1932, Halas still came within minutes (or hours depending on the account) of losing the Bears when he couldn't meet payment deadlines. He didn't have the money to pay Sternaman and, under the terms of their deal, if Halas couldn't pay, then Sternaman assumed control of the team. A banker named C. K. Anderson, whom Halas knew, but who learned of his plight from their mutual friend McMillen, telephoned Halas and offered

a $5,000 reprieve.

Halas raided his children's bank accounts and gave IOUs to players and coaches for back salaries. Many of these were for $500. The kind of money being talked about that affected the future of the team is not even meal money for players these days. The Bears are closer to a $1 billion property now. During this period, Halas, who was devoted to his wife Min, daughter Virginia McCaskey, who eventually took over the franchise, and son George "Mugs," worked 12-hour days and noted that money was not plentiful at home, either.

Two other factors contributed to the shakiness of Bear finances. Halas had been persuaded to start a professional basketball team in Chicago, as other football owners were doing, and it didn't take off. Also, C.C. Pyle's competing football league, which had borrowed Grange's services for a season, was an unwelcome distraction.

With these pressures and worries surrounding the franchise, and with Halas retired at 34, the Bears completed the 1929 season with an un-Bear-like 4–9–2 record. Halas relieved himself of the coaching job and sought a fresh face to be innovative, who would make the Bears a bigger scoring threat and who had a reputation as a good teacher. For the 1930 season, Halas turned to Ralph Jones, who had previously been an assistant football coach at the University of Illinois and the basketball coach, but at the time was the football coach and athletic director at nearby Lake Forest Academy Prep School. Jones was regarded as an offensive innovator and after the Bears had been out-scored 227–119, Halas liked the sound of that.

Halas rounded up the talent and the money to keep going and gave Jones, who was 50 and no novice, the freedom to run the game plan. It worked. In 1930, the Bears finished 9–4–1. Although Chicago bested Green Bay in the season's last game, there was no organized championship game in the NFL yet and the league awarded the title to the Packers. In 1931, the Bears were 8–5. In 1932, the Bears compiled the strange record of 7–1–6.

However, significantly, Jones thrust a new offense into professional football. He introduced the T-formation into the Bears' repertoire. What the T-formation offered was a more explosive offense, with plays that relied more heavily on the quarterback throwing the ball. More yardage would be picked up quickly. Instead of the three-yards-and-a-cloud-of-dust running style, the Bears played a more open game.

Halas said he turned to Jones, a surprising pick given that he was at a high school, because he knew Jones would be daring. "He believed it also took brains

to win games," Halas said. When hired, Jones promised that he would deliver a Bears championship within three years and the 1932 season was Jones' third year.

Most previous offensive structures lined up tackles, guards and ends with little room between them,

Red Grange dodges Joe Zeller's diving tackle in practice in 1934.
Bettmann/Corbis

BEATTIE FEATHERS'
PHENOMENAL 1934 RUSHING SEASON

Game	Attempts	Yards
Green Bay	8	41
Cincinnati	18	140
Brooklyn	14	132
Pittsburgh	8	101
Chicago Cardinals	15	97
Cincinnati	7	114
Green Bay	15	155
New York	8	55
Boston	11	80
New York	10	47
Chicago Cardinals	3	42

101 attempts, 1,004 yards,
average 9.9 per carry

the advantage gained by the defense of more space by emphasizing quicker backfield action.

Offensive formations had been static. Although there were rules in the books allowing the "man-in-motion" now familiar to all football fans, nobody used this tactic. Jones put Red Grange, who could run or throw, into motion. Quarterback Carl Brumbaugh was a sharp guy who mastered myriad plays spun off the T-formation. The Bears had more options than opponents had defenses and they executed them crisply. Grange said the new offense made playing football more fun than ever. Halas commented, "It broke the game wide open. Best of all, the public found our new brand of football exciting."

Actually, best of all, the new brand of football led to a championship on Jones' schedule. As the season ran its course, it became apparent that the best teams were the Bears and the Portsmouth Spartans (forerunners of the Detroit Lions) from Ohio. The final score of the Bears' first three regular-season games that season were 0–0, 0–0, 0–0. Then the Bears lost 2–0. Halas' favorite Cubs team should have had such pitching. The Bears were still seeking to perfect their new offense. Still, for all of the hullabaloo about the new-fangled offense, the Bears' defense put its stamp on the season. The team allowed just 44 points in 14 games. Only once did the Bears permit double-figure points to be scored in a game. That occurred in a 13–13 tie—with Portsmouth.

A championship game was scheduled for December 18 in Chicago. However, with howling winds, dropping temperatures and blinding snow, the blizzard that descended on the Windy City was appropriate for the Arctic. A game played at Wrigley Field would have left players with frostbite and been so inhospitable for fans that few would have come. The weather was similar a week before and only 5,000 had turned out to watch the Bears beat Green Bay, 9–0.

The decision to play in Chicago rather than Portsmouth had been made a week ahead of time. A new plan was hatched—play indoors at Chicago Stadium, home of the hockey-playing Blackhawks and roaring circus lions.

Points for creativity could have been awarded to decision-makers, though a postponement might have made more sense. While it was cozy, Chicago Stadium had the disadvantage of being too small for football. A field 80 yards long was designed and made of dirt and turf. In NFL lore this indoor title game came to be called "The Tom Thumb Game." There was no break in the weather as the teams lined up to play before 11,198 paying customers. It was 19 degrees outside and snow was piled in drifts around the building. Certainly no one at the time could have imagined that

virtually forming a protective cocoon, or wedge, for a back running up the middle. The quarterback called the signals, but the center hiked the ball to the player who was going to run on the play while the quarterback became a blocker. Jones' formation lined the quarterback up directly behind the center for all snaps, put more space between the linemen when they approached the line of scrimmage, and negated

60 years later there would be a popular modified football game called Arena Football played indoors.

Each year in November in the 2000s, the United Center, the building that succeeded Chicago Stadium for the Blackhawks and the basketball Bulls' home games, is turned over to the circus for more than a week. Coincidentally, when the Bears needed Chicago Stadium in 1932, the circus had just left town. Unfortunately, the animals had left behind souvenirs and it took some effort to improve the playing surface.

The Spartans played with one major handicap. Earl "Dutch" Clark, their quarterback, was unavailable— because of his other job. It would have been tough to call in sick since Clark coached the Colorado College basketball team and the club had a game against Wyoming on the same night as the Spartans' game.

Those familiar with Arena Football realize the indoor game encourages high scoring and that it is not uncommon for teams to score 50 points. Likewise, the Bears and Spartans were predicted to churn out touchdowns as if they rolled off an assembly line. But the unexpected occurred. Defenses adapted to the short field better than the offenses. Defenders cut off passing lines, brought their

formations in tight, squeezed the middle on runs, and sealed off the corners.

After three quarters, nobody had scored. The Bears were not helped when back Red Grange was knocked cold by a kick to the head in the first quarter. The Bears were all-too-familiar with 0–0 scores and did not want another on their resume. Fittingly, in the fourth quarter, Bears defender Dick Nesbitt intercepted a Spartan pass and ran it back to the Portsmouth 7-yard line.

The Bears' first offensive play of the subsequent possession was a hand-off to Bronko Nagurski and he steamrolled to the 1-yard line. The next play Nagurski was nailed for a 1-yard loss. Unfazed, the Bears handed off to Nagurski once more. Only this time, instead of putting his head and shoulder down to plow ahead, Nagurski stopped, jumped, and threw a pass over the middle to a now-wide-awake Grange in the end zone.

"I lined up as usual, four yards back," Nagurski said. "Red went in motion. The ball came to me. I took a

Red Grange shows a group of kids how to play football at DeWitt Clinton Park in New York City in 1934.
Bettmann/Corbis

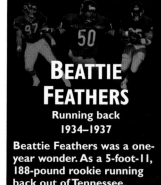

BEATTIE FEATHERS
Running back
1934–1937

Beattie Feathers was a one-year wonder. As a 5-foot-11, 188-pound rookie running back out of Tennessee, Feathers astonished Bears followers with his 1934 showing.

Football was a runner's game, but no one had accomplished the barrier-breaking Feathers put on his resumé. At a time when the Bears were the dominant team in the NFL, Feathers became the first back in history to rush for 1,000 yards in a season.

Feathers' final stats for 1934 were incredible. He gathered 1,004 yards rushing in 11 games. Even more impressively, he only carried the ball 104 times, so his average yards per carry was a stunning 9.9. Although it was not in vogue to throw to running backs, Feathers also caught five passes that season for 174 yards, again for an overwhelming 34.8 yards per catch. He finished with 9 touchdowns.

The bad news was that Feathers' season was cut short with a shoulder injury. Whether it was because he was never again the same physically, the most Feathers ever rushed for in a season again was 350 yards in 1936 at 3.6 yards per try.

When Feathers was asked years later how he produced such a magical running season, he speculated that at 25 he was older than the average rookie. Feathers said he had dropped out of and returned to school several times. Football kept him coming back. Without the sport he never would have stayed in school, Feathers said.

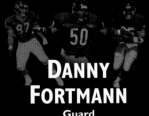

DANNY FORTMANN

Guard
1936–1943

When Dan Fortmann came out of Colgate University (where he earned 12 athletic letters) to play for the Bears in 1936 at age 20, he became the youngest starter in the league. Fortmann was a ninth-round pick in the Bears' first draft. Scouting was limited in those days and except for the most famous All-Americans, teams made other draft picks based on word of mouth recommendations or because a coach saw a player compete once. When the Bears reached the last round, Halas did not recognize a single available player. He chose Fortmann for a simple reason. "I like that name," Halas said.

Not the largest of linemen at 6 feet and 210 pounds, Fortmann made up for lack of size with tenacity and an unerring sense of how to figure out opposing team's play calls. Once he diagnosed the problem, Fortmann was a dead-on tackler. He brought much the same characteristic to his next career as a surgeon.

Even though Fortmann was All-NFL six times, playing football was his secondary interest. While competing for the Bears he attended medical school. Fortmann left the Bears for the service during World War II and did not return to football, settling in California to practice medicine. However, years later he rekindled a connection to football when old teammates coached the Rams.

When Fortmann was selected for the Hall of Fame in 1965 a description of his career referred to him as "One of the smallest of the great linemen."

Dan Fortmann had a Hall of Fame caliber career as a guard and later became a surgeon.
B. Bennett/Getty Images

> **"It takes two things above all others to make a 1,000-yarder. A back must be fortunate enough to avoid injuries and he must be fortunate enough to have good blocking."**
> *—Beattie Feathers, the first NFL player to rush for 1,000 yards, in 1934.*

step or two forward as though to begin the plunge everyone expected. The defenders converged, doubling up on the line to stop me. There was no way through. I stopped. I moved back a couple of steps. Grange had gone around the end and was in the end zone, all by himself. I threw him a short pass." Grange had been knocked down and actually made the catch while lying on his back. Touchdown, Bears.

Or not. Portsmouth coach George "Potsy" Clark, raced onto the field to protest. Under NFL rules at the time, it was illegal to throw unless the passer retreated five yards behind the line of scrimmage. Clark claimed Nagurski was too close to the line when he went up in the air. "Nagurski insisted he was [legal]," Halas said. "So did I. The referees agreed."

Without the aid of instant replay, there was no way that play was going to be overturned. Paul Engebretsen kicked the extra point and the Bears led 7–0. Engebretsen's boot landed deep in the stands. A few minutes later, Portsmouth punter Mule Wilson dropped the snap and the ball rolled through the end zone for a safety. The two points provided the 9–0 final score.

It was a commentary on the place of the NFL in the sports firmament that Chicago newspapers barely noticed a Bears championship. A Bears team advancing to the Super Bowl nowadays would be followed by around 20 reporters, photographers and editors from a single newspaper. In an era when there were far more newspapers, the coverage was minimal in some papers and non-existent in others. And that was for a home game played in extraordinary circumstances.

What the exciting and unusual game did do was prod the NFL into establishing two divisions and starting an official, season-ending championship game between the winners of each division in 1933. And it also engendered debate about the passing rule. The five-yard rule was eliminated and quarterbacks could throw from anywhere behind the line of scrimmage.

After the indoor Snow Bowl, Ralph Jones packed up his playbook. He had fulfilled his promise to Halas to win a title within three years. Jones became the athletic director at Lake Forest College where he stayed until retirement in 1949.

The successor coach to Jones was an easy hire. Halas returned to the bench, saying he would coach "for a few more years." He was only off by about three decades. In 1933, it became clear the Bears had solidified their status as the new NFL powerhouse. They finished the regular season 10–2–1 and with the league divided into Eastern and Western Divisions met the Eastern champ New York Giants in the title game. This is viewed as the first truly sanctioned championship decided on the field based on pre-determined rules, mostly proposed by Halas and Washington Redskins' owner George Preston Marshall.

Though little remembered as anything more than one in the series of championships captured by the Bears in the history of the franchise and first in the series of meaningful games played between the Bears and Giants, the game was an epic with a spectacular ending.

The city was once again Chicago, but the setting was normal, outdoors at Wrigley Field, on a 100-yard field in front of 30,000 fans. The Bears and Giants had met twice during the regular season offering few clues of supremacy. The Bears won the first encounter, 14–10, at home in October. The Giants won the second encounter, 3–0, at home in November. It was a pick-'em scenario. A clothing store on State Street took out a program ad pledging to give a new overcoat to the first Bears player who scored a touchdown that day.

The game figured to be close, but there is rarely any foreshadowing about games that turn out to be great. Pro football was a comparatively young sport and its organized history brief, but when the contest was over, with the Bears 23–21 victors, the game was hailed as "undoubtedly… the greatest game of football ever played." The Associated Press account of the game called it "a sensational forward passing battle" and said it "was a thrilling combat of forward passing skill, desperate line plunging and gridiron strategy." Other accounts talked about "the loosing of thrills" provided.

The scoring started slowly, with the Giants leading 7–6 at the half, but the lead changed hands six times in the 60 minutes. Too bad for Bears kicker Jack Manders that the overcoat offer was not worded to reward the first Chicago player to score, period, since he had two field goals. New York's Harry Newman, a quarterback rarity who looked to throw often, completed 12 of 17 passes for 201 yards. Manders kicked his third field goal to give Chicago a 9–7 lead. Newman kept leading his team down the field and each time the Bears fought back.

The Giants' touchdown had not been scored in a normal manner. A premeditated trick play where New York conferred with the officials before the game as a warning left viewers agape. Giants center

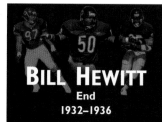

BILL HEWITT
End
1932–1936

You didn't need binoculars to see Bill Hewitt's distinguishing characteristic on a football field—he was the last National Football League player to compete without wearing a helmet. Hewitt did not forego head gear as an act of bravado. At least not in his words. He simply said that wearing a helmet bothered him and that it interfered with his play. Hewitt was a creative end, who drew up plays, as well as running impressive routes, and failure to wear a helmet didn't prevent him from being elected to the Hall of Fame.

Hewitt caught only 101 passes for 1,606 yards in his career, statistics that have been matched in a single season, but he played in an era when the quarterback was more likely to hand off or keep the ball himself instead of flinging it long. Hewitt was credited with 26 touchdowns.

Two offbeat nicknames were attached to Hewitt. He was called "Stinky" by some and "The Offside Kid," the latter not because he committed so many offside infractions, but because Hewitt shot off the line of scrimmage so fast he looked as if he was jumping offside.

Hewitt, who died at 37 from injuries suffered in an automobile accident, weighed only 185 pounds, but was all muscle and power. One Bears season he performed so superbly, Red Grange groped for words. "I never saw anything like it," Grange said. "I don't think he made a mistake all year."

Team founder George Halas coached the Bears from 1920 to 1967 with periodic interruptions, rain or shine, snow or hail.
Bettmann/Corbis

later and he got creamed, "I guess that was a one-timer, that play."

Eventually, on the Bears side, catching a jump pass 6-yard completion from Bronko Nagurski, end Bill Karr scored a touchdown. It won Karr the coat.

With less than three minutes remaining, the Bears trailed 21–16, but were advancing on Nagurski's power thrusts into the line. The Bears had the ball at the New York 36-yard-line. The circumstances were similar to the finish of the 1932 Portsmouth game. This time Nagurski faked a run, stopped, and threw a pass to Bill Hewitt.

Hewitt, the helmet-less hero, made 14 yards, but as he was about to be tackled, he flipped a lateral to the Bears' other end, Karr, who raced past. Karr ran the last 19 yards into the end zone and the touchdown gave the Bears the lead, the game, and the title. It came out afterwards that this was a scripted play, for emergencies, Halas said. A mural was painted of Hewitt on the play and displayed at the Pro Football Hall of Fame in Canton. And for many years, Halas called the finish and the win his greatest thrill in football. Grange remembered it just as fondly. "It was the greatest game I have ever seen," Grange said 40 years later.

The match-up was the first of many high-profile games played between the Bears and the Giants over the following decades. Not only were the teams fated to meet often when the stakes were high, but peculiar and spectacular things occurred during the games. While players came and went, the Bears remained in the hands of George Halas and the Giants remained in the hands of the Mara family. Founding owner Tim Mara had two sons, Jack and Wellington, who had a keen interest in football from the time they were youngsters. Wellington stayed involved with the franchise for eight decades.

Still, the Bears' greatest rival remains the Green Bay Packers. The Packers were around the NFL from the beginning, too. They were built by a cantankerous coach named Curly Lambeau, who remained with the team for more than 30 years, and since they were in the same division as the Bears, they were always competing head-to-head in two regular-season games each year and for the right to represent the West in the championship game. There was also proximity. Illinois and Wisconsin share a border and Chicago and Green Bay are located only a few hours' drive apart.

Maybe it was because they were two very strong personalities, demanding of their teams, and they lived and breathed football, but Halas and Lambeau did not get along. That added spice to the games as the years passed. The bragging rights were a little bit sweeter.

Mel Hein snapped the ball to Newman, but Newman handed it right back to him, and faded back as if to pass. As Newman stumbled and was going down on his own, Bears defenders smothered him. Meanwhile, Hein tucked the ball up his jersey and started walking towards the end zone. When he realized he was in the clear he ran. Bear defender Keith Molesworth read the play and tackled Hein after a 30-yard gain. The wild play set up the first TD, though Hein has said the Giants tried the same trick on the Bears a year

> **"(Bronko) could have been an All-American at 11 different positions."**
> **—Clarence Spears, Bronko Nagurski's coach at the University of Minnesota.**

After the 1933 Bears championship, Chicago Tribune sports editor Arch Ward, who also suggested the creation of the major league baseball all-star game, urged that a special football game be played annually to raise money for Chicago charities. The plan put together the cream of senior college all-stars on one team, during the summer before they joined their pro teams, as an opponent for the reigning NFL champ. The game was a hit and lasted through 1976. The Bears played in the first one before nearly 79,432 people at Soldier Field and the pro teams won the series 31–9–2.

Halas could not have gleaned more pleasure from the Bears' 1934 season-opening 24–10 win over the Packers. The pleasure was doubled in mid-season when the Bears triumphed over Green Bay again, 27–14. This was a grand season for the Bears. They were defending NFL champions. Rookie Beattie Feathers flourished in the backfield, his 1,004 yards making him the first player to gain more than 1,000 yards on the ground in a single season. And the team finished 13–0 in the regular season.

The championship game opponent was the Giants again, victims of the Bears by scores of 27–7 and 10–9 during the regular season, with a record of 8–5, so nothing that had transpired since the preceding December indicated New York had the goods to win.

This year the December 9 title game was in New York, at the Polo Grounds, but New York had borrowed the same type of frigid weather from Alaska as the Bears regularly did. There was a coating of ice on the ground because the temperature dropped to 9 degrees after four days of rain had turned the field to mud. That made the footing poor for football players dressed out in cleats. During pre-game warmups, Ray Flaherty, a Giants star end, tested his shoes on the turf and said out loud, "Too bad we don't have sneakers instead of these things." He remembered playing a game in college where his Gonzaga team switched to basketball sneakers and trounced the slipping and sliding opposition. Giants coach Steve Owen agreed that sneakers would be a good idea, but had no idea how to procure them on a Sunday afternoon on short notice.

Trainer Gus Mauch had connections to the Manhattan College basketball team, made a few phone calls, and the Giants sent Abe Cohen, a part-time clubhouse attendant who was a tailor by profession, to the campus. Cohen returned with a couple of dozen pairs of sneakers. Owen did not have his players put the rubber-soled shoes on yet. He watched how the game unfolded and felt he could use them as a secret weapon if needed. When Giants players began putting on tennis shoes one by one, Halas didn't perceive the threat. On his first play in basketball shoes, Ken Strong booted his first kick out of bounds. Halas laughed.

By the end of the third quarter, the Bears led 13–3. The Giants broke out more basketball shoes and they worked as magically as Judy Garland's footwear when she clicked her heels together in *The Wizard of Oz*. Suddenly, the Giants were running over, under and past the Bears. Not only had Halas stopped laughing, he ordered his players to use their spikes to step on the Giants' feet. The Giants scored 27 points in the fourth period to win 30–13.

Nagurski said the Bears had to tip-toe and they felt helpless while the Giants ran full out. "It was a freakish way to lose, but it was legal and it cost us the championship," Halas said. Ken Strong scored 17 points yet in the locker room afterwards he said the Most Valuable Player was Abe Cohen. "Abe, you were the real hero of this game," Strong said. "We never could have done it without you."

George Halas (left) is all smiles as he watches Sid Luckman ink a contract with the Bears for the 1939 season. Halas viewed Luckman as his savior quarterback and he was right.
Bettmann/Corbis

BRONKO NAGURSKI

Some of it was the name. Bronko. It was perfect. The toughest football player of his generation had a name that was the same as the description of a wild horse. That was Nagurski in a nutshell—untamed. He was fierce and rugged, possessed of remarkable power. At 6-foot-2 and 235 pounds he was bigger than most and stronger than everyone in the game in the 1930s.

Nagurski was a legend almost before he was a player. The story goes that he was working on the family farm in International Falls, Minnesota, when the University of Minnesota coach stopped to ask directions. When the young man lifted up the plow to point, the Gophers coach signed him on the spot. The story was humorous, but apocryphal; not even Nagurski claimed truth in that one.

Another eye-widening Nagurski story is that he head-butted the brick wall at Wrigley Field and left a crack—in the wall. Because the stadium was built for baseball it was shaped awkwardly for football and in one corner the wall was only about five yards from the end zone. It was believable that Nagurski's head was harder than a brick wall. "I made a 40-yard run and when I got to the end zone, I couldn't stop," Nagurski said. "I did hit. I fell into the baseball dugout afterward. All that is true, but I never did check the wall for a crack."

If Red Grange's name and fame helped put the Bears on the map, Nagurski's bear-like physique, growl, and inhuman might personified the cultivated Bears image. He was the second coming of Hercules, except that he knew how to block, tackle and run with the football. He had

colossal hands, as if he had been born cupping a sledgehammer and the fingers grew around the tool. He used those enormous hands to cradle a football and throw would-be blockers out of the way with a single heave. Nagurski was an All-American at Minnesota and was another player George Halas knew he had to have. He knew Nagurski was the right fit to share a backfield with Grange.

By the time Nagurski left the Gophers he had already written some history. In 1929, he was chosen as an All-American at two positions in the same season. One of his college teammates at Minnesota, George McKinnon, said it was clear that Nagurski would be a special player for the Bears. "He stood out above everyone else," McKinnon said. "Oh, when he'd hit you, he'd hit you."

Starting in 1930, Nagurski was good for about 500 yards a year as a fullback, but also made what seemed like 5,000 tackles and 50,000 blocks leading the way through the line for such beneficiaries as Grange or Beattie Feathers in 1934 during his breakthrough 1,000-yard season.

The way Nagurski ran with a football was counter-intuitive to what defenders expected. The defensive man was supposed to deliver the hits. But Nagurski was so big and so tough that he could often brush aside would-be tacklers. "The way I used to run, if a tackler was coming at me, I'd just put my shoulder down and put on the gas before we hit," Nagurski said. "I'd have the leverage on him. I'd just keep going."

Bronko Nagurski, in a stiff arm pose in 1935, was considered to be the strongest man in football.
B. Bennett/Getty Images

Nagurski's given name when he was born in Rainy River, Ontario, was Bronislau and he told friends he really did have his name shortened because he reminded people of a bronco. Most of the time he preferred fishing near his virtually life-long home of International Falls, instead of being in the spotlight for the Gophers or the Bears. But if he seemed gentle to some in conversation he was a physical man who didn't mind contact. Nagurski thought Halas should have paid him more than $6,000 so, after the 1937 season, he became a professional wrestler. Still, when summoned back because the Bears needed him due to a player shortage during World War II, Nagurski returned for the 1943 season.

Some considered Nagurski the greatest football player of all time. The legendary sportswriter Grantland Rice wrote that a team of 11 Bronko Nagurskis would easily defeat a team of 11 Red Granges or 11 Jim Thorpes. That may or may not be true, but the 11 Granges or Thorpes would certainly be nursing bruises by the end of the game.

Don Hutson, the Green Bay end out of the University of Alabama, who was a pioneer wide receiver from the moment he stepped on a professional football field for a game, said his welcome-to-the-NFL moment was facing Nagurski. "In college I'd been known as a good defensive end," Hutson recounted of a play his rookie year with the Packers, "so I played Nagurski the way I'd play a Kentucky fullback. On first down they gave him the ball, and he ran straight over me. I mean he ran me down and kept going without breaking stride."

It was no wonder that defensive players actually grew too frightened to try to tackle Nagurski one-on-one. When they collided with him, defenders felt as if they had been in a train wreck and they hadn't even brought the guy down. Red Grange, who was on Nagurski's side, nonetheless had to practice against him and many times said "running into him was always like getting an electric shock. He was the greatest player I ever saw and I saw a lot of them in my lifetime."

Grange was 77 when he made that comment about his old teammate.

Nagurski was a key figure as the Bears rose to prominence in the 1930s, but he wrestled much longer than he played football, then he ran his own gas station back in International Falls and raised cattle. Bronko Nagurski always preferred the country and after retiring from football and wrestling he did little mingling with the old-timers at sports events. Paul Bunyan had returned to the woods for his final years.

Bronko Nagurski in 1933. *Getty Images*

Smiling Bronko Nagurski, hard-nosed Bears fullback and linebacker regarded as one of the toughest of players from the early era and one of the most famous. *Bettmann/Corbis*

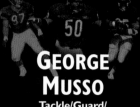

GEORGE MUSSO

Tackle/Guard/
Defensive tackle
1933–1944

George Musso was definitely a George Halas bargain hire. Musso signed with the Bears initially for $90 a game plus $5 expenses. By his fourth season he was team captain and Musso became the first NFL player selected All-Pro at two positions, offensive tackle and guard.

The son of a Pennsylvania coal miner, Musso was called "Moose" by some, and because he was easily the heaviest guy in the lineup, "Big Bear" by teammates. Musso attended Millikin College in Decatur, Illinois, and played against future president Ronald "Dutch" Reagan of Eureka College. Reagan used to mention the time he went up against the 270-pound Musso who out-weighed him by 100 pounds. In a 1981 interview, Reagan, whose team lost 45–6, said it had been "a very busy evening" trying to avoid Musso.

Musso, elected to the Hall of Fame in 1982, said he learned to move off the line of scrimmage swiftly when blocking for Mack-truck-like fullback Bronko Nagurski. "If you didn't open the hole, he'd hit you in the back," Musso said, "and the next time you'd either open it or get out of the way quick."

Once, Musso screwed up a play and pulled the wrong way for the running back. He bumped into and knocked down fellow lineman Danny Fortmann. Musso looked down at Fortmann and said, "What's the matter, Danny? Haven't you learned the signals yet? I knew it was my mistake, though. Danny was a Phi Beta Kappa."

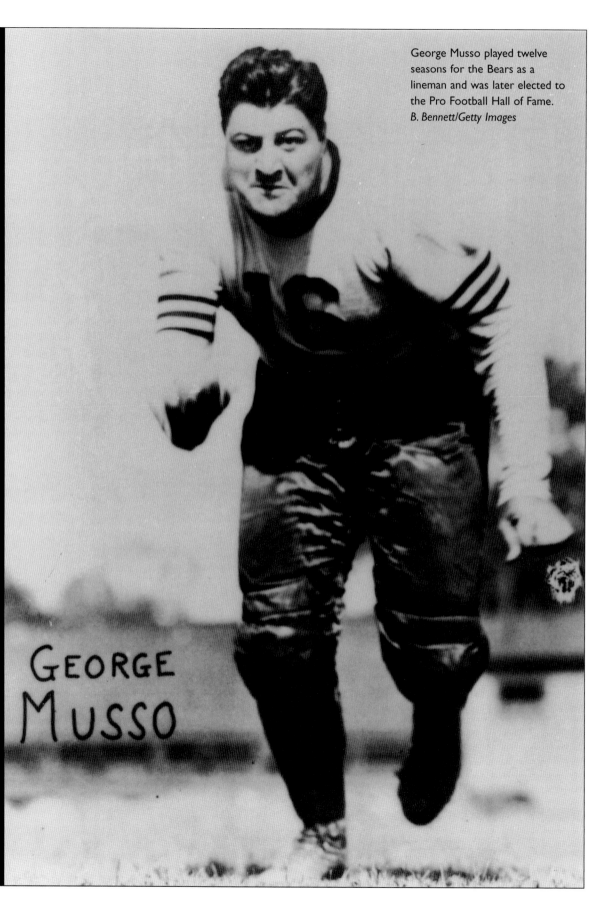

George Musso played twelve seasons for the Bears as a lineman and was later elected to the Pro Football Hall of Fame.
B. Bennett/Getty Images

The frustrated Bears experienced transition over the next years. Grange retired. So did long-time Hall of Fame center George Trafton. The team won more than its share of games, but did not return to the title game until 1937 when a fresh league power, the Redskins, emerged. The Redskins were new to the nation's capital. George Preston Marshall had put up with meager crowds in Boston for years. But after drawing just 5,000 fans to a win over Pittsburgh at Fenway Park that provided the Redskins with a division title in 1936, Marshall moved the championship game from Boston to New York. The Redskins never went back to Boston.

The Redskins added a tremendous rookie to their team in 1937. Fresh from an All-American, record-setting career at Texas Christian, Sammy Baugh may be the greatest football player of all time. Not only would he be the premier quarterback in the NFL, but he was all-league as a defensive back and set records for punting. By the time the Redskins faced the Bears for the 1937 championship, Baugh was already the league's leading passer and he had a complementary running back in Cliff Battles, who gained 847 yards. Washington's coach was Ray Flaherty, the same fellow whose fine idea about footing led the Giants to the sneaker attack in 1934.

Once again, the NFL title game was scheduled for Wrigley Field in December and once again the day dawned more appropriate for dog sledding than football. It was 15 degrees with a 12 mph wind and fewer than 16,000 fans rooted on a 9–1–1 Bears team hungry for another championship.

It seemed every time Chicago showed up for a championship game there was some kind of flukey drama. This was another back-and-forth game with Bears running back and kicker Jack Manders, the league's leading scorer, trying to overcome Baugh's brilliance. Although the Bears did lead at times, Baugh always brought the Redskins back and they prevailed, 28–21. Baugh completed 18 of 33 passes for 335 yards and 3 touchdowns, an unheard of airing it out for the 1930s. As a rookie, Baugh served notice that the rest of the league better get used to such weaponry.

The 1937 championship game was close, but the difference-maker was clearly Baugh. Halas and the Bears had passed up Baugh in the draft, selecting Ray Buivid out of Marquette. Buivid's career resumé ended up considerably shorter than Baugh's. He caught one pass a season for two years in 1937 and 1938 and was gone. "What we would have achieved if we had had Baugh!" Halas reflected years later.

Even as Baugh spoke with his arm, the Packers were formulating their own superior passing game.

1930s CHICAGO BEARS YEAR BY YEAR

Year	Record
1930	9–4–1
1931	8–5
1932	7–1–6
1933	10–2–1
1934	13–0
1935	6–4–2
1936	9–3
1937	9–1–1
1938	6–5
1939	8–3

The combination of quarterback Arnie Herber and end Don Hutson contributed mightily to opening up the game. Hutson was far ahead of his time as a receiver and set every conceivable pass-catching record, though only for the briefest of times during their long existence were the Bears known for passing. More often the Bears were the brutes on the field, who moved foes out of the way with power in the offensive and defensive lines and grind-it-out running backs.

Halas recognized how important Baugh was to the success of the Redskins. He wanted his own Baugh. Players, leaders, talents like Baugh, came along once a decade, perhaps, but Halas understood the significance of a signal caller who all looked up to and who could perform in-game miracles. He was not going to pass up a Baugh a second time.

Halas eventually found his man. It took some wining, dining and convincing, but Halas saw something special in a young quarterback from Columbia named Sid Luckman. In 1939, Luckman became the Bears' field general and the career of the greatest quarterback in Chicago Bears' history was under way.

THE 1940s:
THE MONSTERS OF THE MIDWAY

For decades, the University of Chicago football team was known as "The Monsters of the Midway." The fearsome description was applied because part of the school was located on the Midway Plaisance, the site of the 1893 World's Columbian Exposition. The event was better known as the Chicago World's Fair. The Maroons were a football power for a time under the leadership of famed coach Amos Alonzo Stagg, but after the 1939 season the school determined that its mission lay in quality higher education and not on the gridiron and dropped the sport. Soon, with the fresh rise of the Bears as a dominant NFL powerhouse, the phrase was applied to the professional franchise. Following the demise of the Maroons, the Bears also

George McAfee runs around left end against the Washington Redskins in the 73–0 Bears slaughter in 1940.
Bettmann/Corbis

appropriated the famous "C" that still adorns team helmets.

The disappearance of the Maroons from the Chicago sports landscape and the coincidental ascent of the Bears to the top of pro ball was fortuitous timing for the perpetuation of "The Monsters of the Midway" nickname. Most teams operate in cycles, with high points, peaks, low points and valleys. Personnel shifts and injuries affect outcomes and the mix of talent rotates in and out. Yet there was no more propitious time than 1940 for the Bears to re-christen themselves with a moniker that included the word "Monsters."

With George Halas putting financial worries behind him and the Depression difficulties overridden by an increasingly prosperous economy, all his focus was on football. Under the direction of quarterback Sid Luckman, whose good looks and slick play endeared him to Bears fans for all time, the 1940s became one of the best decades in the history of the team.

The Bears set just the right tone in their first game of the 1940 season, crushing the rival Green Bay Packers, 41–0. A season could not be judged a success solely by one-on-one results with the Packers, but a thorough beating of the enemy always left Bears fans aglow. Later, the Bears bested Green Bay, 14–7. Going 2–0 against the Packers in a season was almost enough

to send Bears supporters home happy for the year. But that was mere foreshadowing. The Bears were the best team in the West, going 8–3, and setting up a championship showdown with the Washington Redskins.

In mid-November the Redskins beat the Bears, 7–3 in Washington. The re-match for the title was also scheduled for the nation's capital on December 8. As a team the Bears were improving, forming the tight-knit, hard-nosed group that would become the NFL's class of the Forties. The Redskins were confident because they had already notched the regular-season victory and the game was set for Griffith Stadium.

The Bears felt Washington's was a hollow win, however. On the last play of the game in Washington, the Bears were on the Redskin 6-yard-line. A pass into the end zone hit fullback Bill Osmanski in the chest and bounced away. The Bears complained that Washington should have received an interference penalty. The protest was ignored and the Redskins won. And Halas threw a tantrum at the refs that was long and loud.

That was the backdrop. What transpired in the title game has never been seen again, or even approached, in the annals of professional championship football. Every analogy comparing the results to a massacre, to a scorched earth thumping, truly applies. The Bears emerged not merely as champs, but as the message

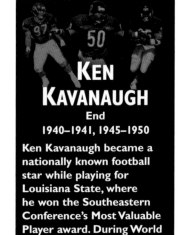

KEN KAVANAUGH
End
1940–1941, 1945–1950

Ken Kavanaugh became a nationally known football star while playing for Louisiana State, where he won the Southeastern Conference's Most Valuable Player award. During World War II, Kavanaugh was decorated for service as a pilot in Europe, flying 30 missions.

When he was in Chicago, Kavanaugh contributed to the Bears' cause in many ways. During the 1947 season, Kavanaugh led the team in scoring with 78 points. In 1940 and 1946, Kavanaugh was the squad leader in pass receptions and three times he led the team in receiving yardage.

This was a period when the Bears fielded one of their most potent offenses ever, and the 6-foot-3, 207-pound Kavanaugh was a key figure. He scored 13 touchdowns in 1947, and when the Bears needed first downs, he had the knack of picking up yardage in big gulps. Aided by 100-yard-dash speed of under 10 seconds, Kavanaugh's career yards per catch was an impressive 22.4 and in 1941 he averaged 28.5 yards per grab. He caught 50 touchdown passes in his Bears career.

Kavanaugh was one of the players introduced to pro ball in the college all-star game and he said it was a rude awakening trying to block a 6–6, 240-pound tackle named Baby Ray. "He just beat the living heck out of me," Kavanaugh said, adding that Ray just sat on him "like a wrestler."

Coach Halas being carried into the locker room after the Bears trounced the Redskins 73–0 in 1940. *Bettmann/Corbis*

Future Hall of Fame lineman Joe Stydahar, diving for a fumble in the 1940 Bears 73–0 rout of the Washington Redskins, a game with the largest margin of victory in NFL history that gave Chicago the title.
Bettmann/Corbis

"Was he drunk when he said that? If we were throwing the game, we wouldn't throw it 73–0."
—*Washington Redskins guard Clyde Shugart, reacting to quarterback Sammy Baugh's comment nearly 60 years later that players were mad at owner George Preston Marshall and might not all have played on the up-and-up.*

bearers of the most humiliating defeat of all time. The 73–0 result stunned fans and players on both sides. It was not merely a rout, but an annihilation. Teams have

good days and the Bears had a phenomenal one. Teams have bad days and the Redskins had an atrocious one. Rarely do such extremes collide in the cosmos in such dramatic fashion.

In the type of pre-game publicity long ago shelved because of political correctness, there is a bizarre *Washington Star* photograph of the Redskins showing a group of players going through the motions of a drill in sweatclothes while wearing Indian headdresses.

Redskins owner George Preston Marshall was working hard to promote his team, fresh from its recent move from Boston, and without TV to help he lobbied newspapers within a 100-mile radius to send sports writers to cover the game at his train fare expense. It turned out not to be the best advertisement of his product.

The close loss three weeks prior stung the Bears, and they were determined to carry the championship trophy back to the Midwest. There was a lot of mouthing off in Washington, from Marshall on down. Marshall called the Bears "strictly a first-half ball-club." The Bears were perplexed to be called cry-babies and furious about the label. In the locker room, rather than exhort his troops to fight hard, play hard, and get revenge for the regular-season loss, Halas eschewed speeches. Instead he brought out copies of the D.C. newspapers where insults were printed. He pointed to a paper and said, "This is what the people in Washington have to say about you." The understated approach was effective. The Bears were already fuming and regardless of who said what to whom, they were going to take out their emotions on the field.

Afterwards, Halas said, "I can assure you I had no difficulty whatsoever preparing the Bears' mentally for the return match."

Washington kicked off and the Bears started the game's first series on their own 25-yard line. On the first play from scrimmage, George McAfee gained 7 yards on a fake reverse. On the second play, Luckman handed off to fullback Bill Osmanski. Bears right end George Wilson led the interference and threw a turf-clearing block that sprung Osmanski. He dashed 68 yards for a touchdown and two plays into the game the Bears had a 7–0 lead. Wilson, said Luckman, "made one of the greatest blocks in the history of football. He blocked out two men."

That quieted some of the 36,034 Redskin rooters, but they remained optimistic. That outlook faded soon. The Redskins looked fairly sharp moving the ball into field goal range, but the kick was missed on a play following a dropped pass.

The Bears answered with a 17-play, 80-yard drive that culminated with a 1-yard Luckman touchdown and a 14–0 lead. It was still the first quarter, but the game was essentially over. Washington's next possession ended with a partially blocked Sammy Baugh punt. Chicago took over on the 42 and on the first play Joe Maniaci dashed around left end and down the sideline. It was 21–0 Bears and Chicago spent the rest of the day scoring any which way it wanted.

With a 28–0 lead, Luckman sat out the second half. Second-stringer Bob Masterson played into the fourth quarter, third-stringer Sollie Sherman followed, and then fourth- stringer Bob Snyder quarterbacked the rest of the way. The Bears added 26 points in the third quarter and 19 in the fourth. The result was humbling for the Redskins, invigorating for the Bears, and shocking for the country.

Afterwards, thinking back to the critical dropped pass, a sports writer asked Baugh if he thought things might have turned out differently if the ball was caught. Baugh, realistically assessing the thoroughness of the devastation, and remembering the missed field goal, said, "Yes, the score would have been 73–3."

Luckman said the Bears had become expert at tweaking the T-formation and using the man-in-motion rule. Every time Chicago had one of its speedy backs in motion, it spread the other teams' defense, he said. The Bears were also pretty good. They had six future

Preparing to meet the Chicago Bears in the 1940 championship game, Washington Redskins players (left to right) Frank Filchock, Andy Farkas, Sammy Baugh and Dick Todd dress the part.
Bettmann/Corbis

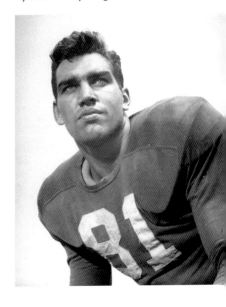

George Connor in 1947
Hy Peskin/Getty Images

BIGGEST NFL WIPEOUT EVER

DECEMBER 8, 1940

CHICAGO BEARS 73, WASHINGTON REDSKINS 0

SCORING SUMMARY

Chicago Bears	Osmanski 68-yard run, Manders extra point	**7–0**
Chicago Bears	Luckman 1-yard run, Snyder extra point	**14–0**
Chicago Bears	Maniaci 42-yard run, Martinovich extra point	**21–0**
Chicago Bears	Kavanaugh 30-yard pass from Luckman, Snyder extra point	**28–0**
Chicago Bears	Pool 15-yard interception return, Plasman extra point	**35–0**
Chicago Bears	Nolting 23-yard run, extra point fails	**41–0**
Chicago Bears	McAfee 35-yard interception return, Stydahar extra point	**48–0**
Chicago Bears	Turner 20-yard interception return, extra point fails	**54–0**
Chicago Bears	Clark 44-yard run, extra point fails	**60–0**
Chicago Bears	Famiglietta 2-yard run, Sherman pass to Maniaci for extra point	**67–0**
Chicago Bears	Clark 2-yard run, extra point fails	**73–0**

Bill Osmanski (left) is tackled by Redskin Willy Wilkin but it didn't matter much in the Bears' record-setting 73–0 1940 title win.
Bettmann/Corbis

"It was just one of those games where we did everything right and the other team did everything wrong."
—Bears coach George Halas after his team dismantled the Washington Redskins 73–0 in the 1940 NFL championship game.

Hall of Famers among 33 players on the roster, plus a Hall of Fame coach on the sidelines. Counting owner Marshall and coach Ray Flaherty, the Redskins had five Hall of Famers involved.

Baugh threw three interceptions for touchdowns in the game, an uncharacteristic showing. "I just have to think the Bears executed as well as anyone ever has that day," Baugh said years later.

Near the end of his life, Halas said the 73–0 win was the event that gave him the most satisfaction in his football career. "It was like a miracle," Luckman said.

A strange byproduct of the frequent Bears touchdowns occurred in the second half. Fans kept the balls (the only worthwhile souvenir of the day if you were a Washington supporter) booted as extra points into the stands and if the Bears had scored too many more times officials would have run out of footballs. The final few extra points were not kicked, but run into the end zone. That was additional embarrassment. If there was any crying after that game, it took place in Washington.

The 73–0 triumph was satisfying, exciting, and as if they really needed it, a confidence booster for the Bears entering the next season. Many suggest that the 1941 "Monsters of the Midway" were better than the 1940 edition. There is no incredible, famous game to dwell on, but the argument is well-supported by the numbers.

The Bears of 1941 rushed through the campaign with a 10–1 record, out-scoring foes 396–147. By edging the Packers in the opener, 25–17, and losing to them, 16–14, at the end of the regular season the Bears were tied with Green Bay and forced into a playoff. The occasion was scheduled for Wrigley Field and, despite frigid weather, more than 43,000 came out. This time the Bears were their growling, snapping, monstrous selves, running up 24 points in the second quarter on their way to a 33–14 victory. The convincing win propelled the Bears into the championship game against the New York Giants.

Surprisingly, even with the draw of the Giants, the December 21 championship game did not bring in a good crowd at Wrigley Field. It was unusual to play a major sporting event close to Christmas in those days and there was speculation that the timing may have held the gate to 13,311, especially since it was a rare warm-weather title game, with the thermometer hitting 47 degrees.

The reception was chilly for the Giants, though. In the early going, the Bears relied on the foot of Bob Snyder, who kicked three first-half field goals for a 9–6 lead. Behind breakaway runners George McAfee and Norm Standlee, the Bears turned up the heat in the second half and, using every player on the roster, sprinted to a 37–9 win.

The league still had not caught up to the Bears' modifications of the T-formation that provided so much freedom to the offense. It was tough enough for Bears players to master the nuances of the offense, never mind opponents who saw it only once or twice a year at a time when studying upcoming teams by film was in its infancy. Halas was an early proponent of that advance scouting method. He called the game films movies.

"We had 2,300 plays in the playbook," said Ken Kavanaugh, who broke in with the Bears in 1940. "I counted them up when I was a rookie. Now that's counting a play in which a guard pulls one way and a separate play that is basically the same except that the guard pulls the other way."

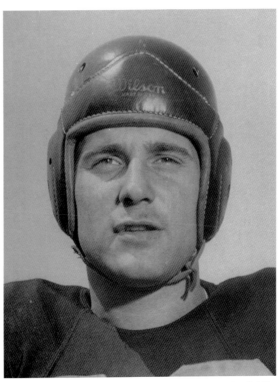

Johnny Lujack set a single game NFL passing mark of 468 yards in 1949.
Hank Walker/Getty Images

JOHNNY LUJACK
Quarterback
1948–1951

George Halas hoped Johnny Lujack would be the next Sid Luckman. Because he spent three years in the service during World War II, Lujack got a late start as a pro. He won the Heisman Trophy in 1947 at Notre Dame and led the Irish to three straight national championships. In four seasons quarterbacking the Bears, he was selected for two Pro Bowls.

Lujack's best season was 1949 when he threw for 23 touchdowns, completed 162 passes, and 2,658 yards to lead the league in all those categories. Lujack's career completion rate was 50 percent and he threw for 468 yards in one game. Always versatile, the 6-foot, 186-pound thrower also played defensive back for the Bears.

There have been remarkably few stretches when the Bears could count on reliable quarterbacking and Lujack was in the mix during the grand-daddy of quarterback controversies. Lujack arrived from the draft as the quarterback of the future in 1948. Bobby Layne, who later led the Detroit Lions to championships, came in the same year. In 1949, George Blanda, a future Hall of Famer, arrived.

Halas did not handle his embarrassment of riches well. Luckman developed health problems and retired. Layne was traded. Blanda languished on the bench and Lujack, who also hurt his shoulder, abruptly quit at 27 because he and Halas could not get along, especially on money matters.

The early retirement of Lujack haunted the Bears for years.

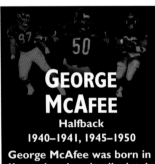

GEORGE MCAFEE

Halfback
1940–1941, 1945–1950

George McAfee was born in Kentucky, played collegiately at Duke and was a superb all-around offensive and defensive player for the Bears, though his career was interrupted by Navy World War II service.

McAfee was a very versatile weapon. Besides being the number one running option for the Bears during their 1940s glory days, McAfee intercepted a career total of 25 passes and scored 234 points. This multi-talented threat was initially drafted by the Philadelphia Eagles, but Papa Bear Halas made an immediate trade to obtain McAfee. Sometimes McAfee rushed (474 yards for a 7.3 average per carry in an all-pro 1941 season), sometimes he caught passes (32 in 1947) and sometimes he intercepted them (6 in 1941 and 6 in 1949).

Halas worried about McAfee at first because he weighed only 165 pounds, but then he realized McAfee had no intention of running over tacklers, just around them. In the first game of his rookie season McAfee ran back a kick-off 93 yards for a touchdown. In the same game, he threw a touchdown pass. Making it all the sweeter, the Bears trounced the Packers, 41–0.

After watching McAfee run with a football tucked under his arm, the legendary Red Grange was impressed. "The most dangerous man with the football in the game," Grange said. McAfee was such a whiz that years later Halas said, "The highest compliment you can pay a ball carrier is just to compare him with McAfee."

The Bears were at the apex of their power and felt poised to dominate the NFL for years to come with superior talent and a sophisticated strategy. It was not difficult to envision the Monsters piling up several championships in a row. But that outlook became moot when world events overtook sporting events. The Japanese bombing of Pearl Harbor on December 7, 1941, dragged the United States into World War II and made the results of professional sports seem insignificant. When a war—true life and death—intruded, the sports realm seemed reduced to the equivalent of playing with toys.

Major league baseball took its cue from President Franklin Delano Roosevelt when he said it would be

good if the games continued as a form of entertainment for the home-front population. Other professional sports took their cues from baseball, the acknowledged national pastime. "Sport is the very fiber of all we stand for," FDR said. "It keeps our spirits alive."

The National Football League kept playing, but there was only a vague pretense that it was business as

> **"I used to think that I could handle anybody that they could put in front of me."**
> —Bears all-star center Clyde "Bulldog" Turner.

usual. Yes, teams played a regular schedule culminating in a championship game. But they did not play with their usual complement of players. Many players were drafted into the service. Many volunteered. Personal circumstances affected who stayed and who went, but no team was the same.

Two of the league's most historic and popular franchises took the drastic step of temporarily merging in 1943. The Philadelphia Eagles and the Pittsburgh Steelers lost so many players who couldn't be replaced that they connected their operations. Officially, the team was called the Eagles–Steelers. Unofficially, people referred to the team as "The Steagles."

Immediately after the 1941 season, a poll of players who felt they would be enlisting or be drafted indicated that 16 Bears did not expect to play the next year. The same situation was faced around the league, but many key Bears, including Luckman, played on. The overall quality of play was reduced league-wide, but the Bears were able to retain their mastery.

After two superb seasons there seemed no limit to what havoc the Bears could wreak on the rest of the league. In 1942, the Bears rolled to an 11–0 regular-season record that included pummeling the Packers 44–28 and 38–7, and handling the Giants 26–7. Chicago and Washington did not meet during the regular season. The Bears were unstoppable, scoring 376 points, and stopping everyone else, giving up just 84 points while recording four shutouts.

Things were far from normal, however. After five games, George Halas relinquished the coaching reins and re-joined the Navy as a lieutenant commander, asking to be sent overseas to fight. Commanding the Bears at home were co-coaches Heartley "Hunk" Anderson and Luke Johnsos. Anderson supervised the defense and Johnsos the offense. Halas, who was 47, attended the November 1 game against the Lions in his military uniform. Halas was far more than just a coach. He also ran the entire Bears operation. In his

Sid Luckman shows his versatility as he punts from his own goal line during the annual charity game against the College All Stars in 1942. Luckman is better known for his lifetime passing achievements—including the Bears' record of 137 touchdown passes. *Bettmann/Corbis*

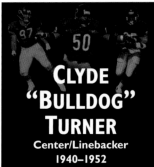

CLYDE "BULLDOG" TURNER
Center/Linebacker
1940–1952

Bulldog Turner believed that there was no one he couldn't block after he hiked the ball to quarterback Sid Luckman. And pretty soon everyone around the league agreed with him. As a 6-foot-2, 235-pound lineman Turner also surprised opponents with his speed.

Redskins great Sammy Baugh went to the same high school as Turner and, even though Baugh was a quarterback and defensive back, Turner later used to taunt him, suggesting Baugh knew Turner could out-run him. Turner was from tiny Sweetwater, Texas, but weighed only 155 pounds in high school and didn't grow, start, or star until he played collegiately at little-known Hardin-Simmons. The first-string Hardin-Simmons center got injured and the coach called on Turner. "Right then and there I knew I had found my place," said Turner. Even that didn't occur until Turner had taken a year off working as a cattle trader and his body finally filled out. Yet for all the setbacks, he was a Bears No. 1 draft pick.

Turner was nearly as effective on defense and he led the NFL in interceptions with eight in 1942. He was all-league six times and helped the Bears to four championships. Any short list of the league's greatest centers has Turner's name on it. He might have been a great fullback where, like Nagurski, Turner could have run his own interference, but he loved the center position.

Turner was inducted into the Hall of Fame in 1966.

Bill Osmanski runs in the clear against the Philadelphia Eagles for 8 yards in a 1941 game.
Bettmann/Corbis

place he appointed team secretary Ralph Brizzolara, already the watchdog of the purse strings, to make front-office decisions.

When the Redskins emerged as the Eastern Division champs and were slated to meet the Bears for the 1942 title, wounds from 1940 were still fresh. It didn't take a long memory to recall the 73–0 shellacking. Players and fans alike figured the Redskins were in for it again. For Washington, players still angry over their humiliation, being scheduled to play the Bears was more like a battle cry of "Remember the Alamo!" Due to their undefeated record, their three-year domination of the league, and the results from 1940, the Bears were heavily favored.

Halas was able to obtain leave to fly into Washington to see the game but it's possible he wished he had stayed away. Instead of unleashing their usual force on offense, the Bears played as if in a quagmire all day. The Redskins prevailed, 14–6, after the Bears had taken a 6–0 lead, but missed the extra point. The rest of the day belonged to Sammy Baugh, who played all 60 minutes.

This was another freezing day for football, so cold that the tarpaulin was stuck to the field before the game's start. The grounds crew, it was reported, had to

peel it off like a band-aid being ripped from "a hairy leg." It was also reported that the Bears met and argued for four hours about playing in the upcoming December 27 scheduled all-star game that would partially conflict with Christmas. It was unimaginable Halas would have let player dissension go on as a distraction from the main task.

Although the score was nothing of the proportion of the 1940 Bears romp, the Redskins were in charge most of the day. When the game ended, the capacity crowd of 36,000-plus that had witnessed the nadir of Redskin franchise history, ran onto the field and ripped down the goal posts in celebration. "Half of us are going into the service in a couple of weeks," Redskins coach Ray Flaherty, himself included, said to his team afterwards. "Hit the enemy just as hard as you hit the Bears today. Do that and this war won't take long to finish and we can get back here pretty quick."

A reporter asked him who played the best game and Flaherty wouldn't single out anyone. "Best game?" he repeated. "Hell, every one of those guys played brilliant games. Nobody played the best game except the Redskin team."

The eight-point margin felt like 73 to some. One newspaper account read, "The once mighty football empire of the Chicago Bears was forever crushed and ground beneath the feet of the disbelieving Washington Redskins yesterday in one of the super upsets of all time." The Bears were muted at the finish, in many cases dressing without commenting on the streak-ending defeat. However, guard Danny Fortmann said, "It had to come sometime. The law of averages was working against us." Winning was the most important thing, for sure. The playoff check to the winners amounted to just $327 apiece.

What became clear very soon, though, was the equivalent of what author Mark Twain noted when his demise was reported in a newspaper. "Reports of my death are greatly exaggerated," he said. The same went for the Bears.

The war was just beginning and it would be years before the United States and the National Football League returned to peace and normalcy. As an organization, the NFL made financial contributions to domestic agencies, running fund raisers at games and elsewhere. In 1942, it was estimated the league gave

$680,000 to war relief groups. The quality of play was diluted and clubs struggled to field solid teams, but the league kept playing.

Despite the absence of Halas, despite the mentally crushing defeat, the Bears were not a team to write off. In 1943, after completing the regular season 8–1–1, they were back in the title game. The opponent was once again the Washington Redskins.

The football manpower shortage was growing more acute. The league had been reduced from 10 teams to 8 and rosters were capped at 28 players, down from 33. With some exceptions, if you were healthy enough to play football you were healthy enough to fight the Germans in Europe or the Japanese in the Pacific. Just fielding teams was a challenge for some clubs. As players disappeared one by one, teams became innovative in their pursuit of replacements. Conducting open tryouts, the Bears gave anyone and everyone a chance to play professional football. Johnsos, the co-coach, commented of those times that the Bears "signed up

Philadelphia Eagles halfback Russ Craft tries to crawl to the goal line as Bears defenders close in during a 1947 game.
Mike Freeman

anybody who could run around the field twice." Some of those anybodys were in their forties.

Bronko Nagurski had retired in 1937, but stayed in shape through professional wrestling. Nagurski rejoined the Bears for the 1943 season following a special appeal from Anderson. Nagurski, then 34, came back on two conditions. The first was that Halas, who was stationed in the South Pacific, be told that it was a one-year-and-done arrangement. And secondly, that he would be paid $5,000.

A step slower and perhaps not as invulnerably strong, Nagurski helped fill holes in the lineup, mostly blocking and tackling, not so much running anymore. Nagurski had actually warned Anderson that he would "need a sundial to time me in the 100." Still, the mere mention of the words "Nagurski" and "comeback" in the same sentence unsettled the rest of the league. Sammy Baugh said he still had nightmares from playing against Nagurski. Giants center Mel Hein said, "God save us all."

The 1943 season was Luckman's greatest. He was at his peak and in the manner of a modern-day Peyton Manning or Tom Brady, he delivered week after week on Sundays. His teammates looked to him for leadership and he led. He was asked to produce and

he did. When the Bears were trailing, which did happen a few times during the regular season, Luckman was the cocky field leader who marched his guys to the goal-line.

In mid-November, against the New York Giants, Luckman demonstrated that his last name should have been something else because luck had little to do with things. The Bears crunched the Giants, 56–7, and Luckman threw for seven touchdowns, setting an NFL record for a single game that has been tied, but never eclipsed.

The country was deep in a war that had spread beyond the home continents of the primary combatants. There was tank warfare in Africa. The Allies were flying missions into Germany and bombing Hamburg and Berlin. There was no indication the war would end soon, but there were indications the United States and its allies were taking the strides that would produce victory.

At the time, Luckman was enrolled in the Merchant Marine and was able to use weekend leave to participate in Bears games. He could have been deployed overseas at any time but was available for the championship game, facing the Redskins once again. The Redskins had delivered the Bears' only regular-season

Opposite: Chicago Bears team portrait September 1, 1948. *Hank Walker/Getty Images*

Members of the Bears (left to right) Dante Magnani, Harry Clarke, Bronko Nagurski and Sid Luckman discuss their upcoming NFL title game against the Washington Redskins in 1943. *Corbis*

SID LUCKMAN
QUARTERBACK 1939–1950

Nearly 60 years after he retired, Sid Luckman remains the best quarterback in Chicago Bears' history. He was a player ahead of his time and his records have endured long after he left. In the 1940s, Luckman was George Halas' good-luck charm. He was lucky he had him in the lineup in the first place and it was talent more than luck that positioned Luckman to lead Chicago to five NFL title games in the '40s and four championships.

Luckman grew up in Brooklyn, more of a hotbed for baseball players than football players, and with plenty of smarts he enrolled at Columbia University. During the 1930s, Halas' friendship with Clark Shaugnessy, then the University of Chicago coach, led to the Bears installing a sophisticated version of the T-formation offense. The most important player was the quarterback, who was the focus of the action. Halas needed a savvy leader who was athletic. Someone tipped him off about Luckman.

Halas traveled to New York to watch Luckman play. He liked what he saw. Columbia's prominent coach Lou Little added his own endorsement. Luckman had just gotten married and with his Ivy League education had good job prospects with a packaging firm in New York. Halas virtually forced himself into a dinner invitation at Luckman's apartment and swayed the newlyweds with fast talking and an offer of $5,000. Halas informed Luckman that the only other person he would pay that kind of money to was Jesus Christ.

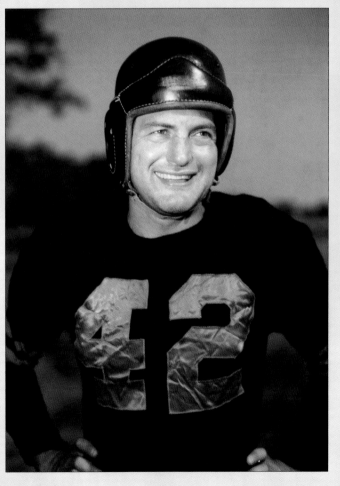

Smiling Sid Luckman, Bears quarterback star of the 1940s.
David McLane

Luckman, who was Jewish, thanked Halas for putting him in that company.

Then he went out and earned the check. Perhaps even more daunting than being the helmsman for the Bears' 1940s championship rides, was maintaining good relations with Halas. It helped that Luckman had genuine affection for Halas, but in Halas' 60 years of involvement with the Bears, Luckman might have been the owner's favorite player. There were few others the owner felt so strongly about, including Mike Ditka and Gale Sayers. "Halas was a tough disciplinarian," Luckman said, "but a human being beyond anyone's imagination, a best friend. He was, and always will be, the NFL. He made it. His dreams and visions came true."

Halas' eye for talent and his vision of what Luckman could be made the partnership between the player and coach work. Halas knew what he wanted out of the T-formation on offense and he needed someone with both brains and ability as the unquestioned leader. Luckman had been a tailback in college, not a T-formation quarterback. He had to study hard to absorb the lessons of the offense. Much later, after Luckman had retired, Halas said the player deserved all the credit for making himself a star. Luckman said it wasn't as easy as people thought. "The signal calling was diametrically opposite," Luckman said. "The spinning was very difficult because you had to be so precise and so quick. We had counter plays and double counters and fakes."

With Luckman as quarterback, the Bears defeated the Washington Redskins in 1940, the New York Giants in 1941, the Redskins in 1943 and the Giants in 1946 to capture four NFL titles. They also reached the title game, but lost to Washington, in 1942. Luckman was the mastermind of the unbelievable 73–0 rout of Washington in 1940 during which 10 different Bears scored. Earlier in the season the Redskins had won a close, low-scoring game from the Bears. Afterwards, the Bears were shocked to read in newspapers that Washington players were dismissing them as important threats and saying they were cry-babies. The cry-baby line got to the Bears, made them stew and steam.

The Bears traveled by train to D.C. for the championship game and Luckman said they were the most focused group of people in the universe. The Bears spent the hours on the train brushing up on coaches' advice, Redskin tendencies and anything they thought might give them an edge. There was no card playing, no joke telling. There was only one book being read and it was not the bestseller of the moment, it was the playbook. "That was the most amazing thing, that train ride," Luckman said. "There weren't five words spoken on the whole train trip. Not one guy wanted to talk. That game was the greatest thrill of my lifetime."

Luckman threw for 28 touchdowns in 1943 and set a team (and league) record with seven TD passes against the Giants in one game. The bushel of touchdown passes came when he was being honored in the Polo Grounds in his home territory on "Sid Luckman Day." It was also one of the few times his mother watched him play in person. The performance gave the 6-foot, 195-pound future Hall of Famer the Most Valuable Player award. Luckman still owns the Bears' single-season top quarterback rating and the team's record for career yards gained passing. He threw 137 touchdowns for the Bears.

In 1946, a group of businessmen were putting together a new professional league to compete with the NFL. One strategy was to steal high-profile talent by paying top dollar. Luckman was offered $25,000 to defect to the fledgling Chicago Rockets, but said no. "How could I ever possibly have taken it?" Luckman said, citing his longevity and special relationship with the Bears. "How could I quit a club that has done so much for me?"

After playing, Luckman came back as a Bears' assistant coach working with quarterbacks. But that mild team involvement was not Luckman's sole livelihood. Luckman made more money in private business. Still, he stayed in touch with Halas until the old coach died in 1983. Only a couple of months before that Halas sent Luckman a flattering letter about where the one-time young quarterback rated in his thoughts. In the May 1983 letter, Halas wrote, "I love you with all my heart. My friend, you have a spot in my heart that NO ONE else can claim."

Sid Luckman (middle) makes a 16-yard run in the Bears 1943 championship triumph over the Washington Redskins.
Corbis

loss, 21–7, in November (the Bears had also tied the Packers 21–21 in the opener). With this and after their upset the year before, the Redskins were viewed as favorites, the team that had the Bears' number.

As had been shown in their previous two championship showdowns of the decade, anything resembling an assumption was discarded when the Bears and Redskins kicked off. The great Sammy Baugh suffered a slight concussion early in this encounter and missed more than half the game. Luckman was in the finest big-game form of his career. On a day that so many predicted would belong to the Redskins, Luckman threw five touchdown passes and the Bears overwhelmed Washington, 41–21. The Monsters of the Midway patrolled their home territory with vigilance. "You can't have a better day than Sid had out there," Anderson said.

Perhaps the Bears had extra vigilance that day. Brizzolara, as acting president, acted precisely the way he felt Halas would in a given situation. Redskins owner George Preston Marshall, seated in the stands, decided to work his way to the field in the second quarter. When Marshall emerged from Wrigley Field's grandstand, he first stood behind the Bears, then took a seat at the end of the bench. Brizzolara was informed Marshall was on the Bears' bench, saw Marshall hovering in the area and became incensed when Marshall refused to move. Marshall, a vociferous, officious owner, did not accept his removal quietly and he yelled at Brizzolara and, accusing Marshall of trying to steal the Bears' plays, Brizzolara yelled back at him. An usher asked Marshall for his ticket. Brizzolara tried to have the protesting owner turned over to police for an escort back to the stands. Instead, Marshall headed towards a baseball dugout. It was very easy to imagine Halas getting into the same type of confrontation. Despite his presence he took no part in the incident because he was upstairs in the press box.

Nagurski left football again the minute the final gun sounded. "I'm retiring again," he said. "It's not a game for a 35-year-old. And besides, I can't listen to George Halas' songs all my life." Nagurski had listened to the siren song of the Bears one last time. And Halas left Wrigley Field likely whistling his favorite tunes. That didn't stop him from telling anyone who would listen that he was sure Nagurski would play just one more year in 1944. One

Luke Johnsos (left), Bears coach, looks at a play on film with team owner George Halas in 1947.
Bettmann/Corbis

> **"That was the first time I had carried the ball this year."**
> —*Quarterback Sid Luckman after a 19-yard run that helped give the Bears the 1946 title.*

person who never believed that was Nagurski's Hall of Fame teammate and close friend, tackle George Musso. "You are the greatest player who ever lived," Musso told Nagurski as they left the stadium.

Of the 28 men on the Bears' squad that day, 19 left on service duty. Luckman's Merchant Marine unit was shipped to Europe and he participated in the D-Day invasion. Chicago still fielded a football team called the Bears in 1944 (6–3–1) and 1945 (3–7), but it did not resemble The Monsters of the Midway. Anderson and Johnsos were caretakers, trying to make the most of a little, making sure the franchise stayed alive. The next time most of the Bears were together again was the 1946 season. George Halas was back as coach. Sid Luckman was back as quarterback. And the Bears, well, the Bears were back as the Bears. They completed an 8–2–1 season, won the Western Division and competed for the championship against the New York Giants in New York.

As family reunions go, this was a heck of a party. The Bears bested the Giants, 24–14, and on a day of unfortunate surprises for the hosts, notched one touchdown on a rare Luckman bootleg scramble for a 19-yard touchdown. As a quarterback Luckman had a great arm. He was as likely to run as attempt to swim downfield. To say that the Giants didn't expect his sneak play would be like saying Luckman's next move would have been declaring for president.

Yet that was not the biggest surprise or unlucky happening for the Giants on championship day. Before the game, it came out that two members of the team had been approached by a gambler to take bribes to throw the game. Quarterback Frank Filchock was quizzed, but allowed to play. Fullback Merle Hapes was suspended by Commissioner Bert Bell.

The incident had to bother the Giants. The Bears gained the early advantage with touchdowns scored after a fumble recovery and an interception. The Giants fought back and the score was 14–14 at the start of the fourth quarter. That was when Luckman made his sensational run for the decisive points. "About the 10-yard-line I saw some red shirts moving in on me," Luckman said. "I was hit, lost my balance, but stumbled on across the goal line."

The Bears had captured their seventh National Football League title, fifth since playoff games were

1940s CHICAGO BEARS YEAR BY YEAR

Year	Record
1940	8–3
1941	10–1
1942	11–0
1943	8–1–1
1944	6–3–1
1945	3–7
1946	8–2–1
1947	8–4
1948	10–2
1949	9–3

added. The victory was a grand toast to the tradition of the Bears, but it marked rather the beginning of the end of the Bears' position of NFL dominance, not the beginning of a new march to glory.

Luckman had just played in his final championship game. Halas had coached in his last championship game for a long time. The 1940s, despite the horrors of war and upheaval across the globe, had been good to the Bears. But for most practical purposes, for the Chicago Bears, the decade ended in 1946.

The winning continued in 1947 (8–4), in 1948 (10–2), and in 1949 (9–3), and there were many fine moments. Johnny Lujack was being eased in as Luckman's replacement at quarterback. The Bears beat most teams they played but didn't reach a championship. Halas knew, in a post-war America that was booming, where young families were sprouting and spreading to the suburbs, where the automobile was taking over, that he too would have to change. The Bears greats of the 1940s were either retired or headed to retirement soon. George Halas had to rebuild for the modern age of football. The slow-paced era of grind-it-out professional football was over. The TV age of wide-open football was dawning.

Bears player Norm Standlee at officer candidate school in 1943 preparing to fight either the Japanese or the Germans in World War II.
Bettmann/Corbis

CHAPTER 4

THE 1950s:
TIMES OF CHANGE IN CHICAGO AND THE GAME

When George Halas returned from the Navy and his men returned home from war, they were older, more mature, but in most cases eager to resume their football careers. At first, the post-World War II Bears were much like the pre-war Bears but, after recording the 1946 championship, one by one the former greats became old and retired.

As much as Halas loved Sid Luckman, he knew his favorite quarterback could not play at a high level forever. By the end of the 1940s, Halas was drafting for the future. He stock-piled good quarterbacks with potential, including Johnny Lujack, George Blanda, and Bobby Layne. By 1950 Luckman was in his final season and was the back-up to Lujack. Luckman threw just 37 passes that season.

Lujack was not quite the field general that Luckman was, but he was more than able. He directed the Bears to a 9–3 season and tied the Los Angeles Rams for the Western Division title. After a four-year absence, the Bears were back in the post-season, one game removed from another championship contest but they never got there. The Rams won, 24–14, and it was Chicago's final playoff game until 1956, an eternity by Halas' standards.

The Rams displayed the superior offense. This was the era when Los Angeles Rams were neck deep in a quarterback controversy. The team featured Bob Waterfield, except when it featured Norm Van Brocklin. The 83,501 fans attending in the Los Angeles Coliseum expected to see Van Brocklin open because Waterfield, sidelined by the flu, had not practiced all week. Waterfield was strong enough to kick a field goal

for a 3–0 lead in the first quarter. But assuming the strong medications he had to be taking mixed well with his adrenaline, Waterfield relieved Van Brocklin behind center.

Waterfield threw for three touchdowns and 280 yards in the victory. The key play occurred shortly before half-time with LA leading 10–7, Waterfield found end Tom Fears for a 68-yard bomb to boost the margin to 17–7. Waterfield and Fears combined for a 27-yard touchdown pass in the third quarter. The Bears piled up more yards, 422 to 371, but the critical statistic on the day was turnovers. The Bears lost three interceptions and two fumbles.

The game really marked the end of an era for one group of Bears. As the team's record slipped to 7–5 in 1951, 5–7 in 1952 and a lousier 3–8–1 in 1953, Halas worked on rebuilding through the draft. The next generation of Bears was on the way.

The Bears still prided themselves on playing stiff defense. They clung to "The Monsters of the Midway" nickname, even if their play did not match the standard. Ed Sprinkle, who came out of Hardin-Simmons, was one of the hard-nosed holdovers whose career straddled the war years into the mid-1950s. He played a little bit of offensive end, but a lot of defensive end and linebacker. Sprinkle did not sprinkle his hits, he unleashed them in torrents. He was 6-foot-1 and weighed 206 pounds, but played bigger. His desire and heart were larger than his body. Sprinkle hit hard enough to cause opponents memory loss and after a time he was labeled a dirty player. Clean or dirty, when Sprinkle hit you he caused pain and he was nicknamed

Green Bay Packer Veryl Switzer, 27, breaks into the clear chased by Bears defenders Jerald Weatherly, 60, and McNeil Moore in a 1954 game.
Casey Migon

"The Claw." The appellation grew from the manner in which Sprinkle often decked quarterbacks and running backs, his arm sweeping across their heads and bodies. "If playing tough football makes one dirty," he said, "I guess I am."

The biggest change in pro football in the post-World War II era was the new order. Men with money wanted in on the National Football League, but the league was not expanding sufficiently to accept all applicants. The rival All-America Football Conference began and competed for talent. No one in the NFL, least of all Halas, took the AAFC threat very seriously.

But the new league hired its share of big-time players and the fledgling Cleveland Browns, completely under the authority of coach Paul Brown, was the class of the conference. Brown was an innovator on the level of Halas. His teams were well-drilled and he recognized football ability. Brown, born in 1908, was originally from Norwalk, Ohio. His family moved to Massillon when he was nine. After high school, the 145-pound Brown went out for football at Ohio State, but soon transferred to Miami of Ohio. Eventually, he returned to his home town as the school's football

> **"I didn't know anything about pro football. It didn't take me long to catch on to what the feeling was with the Packers."**
> —*Receiver Harlon Hill.*

coach and began to construct a reputation for genius on the gridiron. Under Brown, Massillon finished 80–8–2. When the Buckeyes needed a football coach they turned to a player who couldn't make his playing mark on the team. Brown coached Ohio State for two years, but World War II dragged him away from his post.

Halas evaluated Brown as "the most promising coach" outside of the pro ranks. Pretty soon Brown demonstrated what he could do in the pros, as well. Brown agreed to coach the new Browns in 1945 and he did legendary work with a team that starred quarterback Otto Graham, fullback Marion Motley, end Bill Willis, and eventually, perhaps the greatest football player of all, Jim Brown. Brown's Browns stampeded

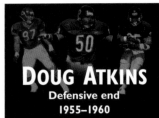

DOUG ATKINS
Defensive end
1955–1960

Doug Atkins was THE Monster of the Midway. He stood 6-foot-8 and weighed 280 pounds, making him one of the largest players of his era. The Hall of Famer was also blessed with remarkable athleticism. Atkins was a big guy who played basketball and high-jumped at the University of Tennessee.

And although he did not lift weights (it was not part of football's standard training repertoire at the time), Atkins was generally considered to be the strongest man in the NFL. Atkins' strength was legendary. Sometimes Atkins picked up puny blockers like halfbacks and simply threw them out of the way as he charged in on the quarterback.

Atkins enforced his own rules. Once, when the Bears were still conducting pre-season camp in Indiana, Atkins was annoyed with a rookie playing a radio on the floor above him in the dormitory. When the player did not respond to the suggestion that he turn down the sound, Atkins took out a pistol and shot a bullet through the ceiling. That produced silence.

Verbal battles between Atkins and George Halas were epic. Often, they were over salary and, angered because he rarely won those skirmishes, Atkins got back at Halas in small ways. Ordered to run laps after practice, Atkins returned to the field naked but for a football helmet and took his jog.

Ultimately, Halas sent Atkins to the expansion New Orleans Saints, where he played the final three years of his career.

"You got to know those guys since sometimes you lived in the same neighborhood. It was just a situation where we wanted to prove that we were better than they were."
—Defensive back J. C. Caroline on playing the Chicago Cardinals.

through the All-America league, winning all four of its titles and losing only four games in all. But stubborn NFL higher-ups refused to recognize that some of the teams were on par with their own. That miscalculation was on display as soon as the AAFC folded and the Browns joined the NFL. While George Halas sought newcomers to rebuild his Bears, Paul Brown's charges took control of the league by winning five titles in a row.

Halas possessed the same shrewdness he always brought to the game and was restocking the Bears with stars like linebackers Bill George and Joe Fortunato, lineman Stan Jones, fullback Rick Casares, receiver Harlon Hill and a host of quarterbacks. The Bears finished 8–4 in 1954 and 8–4 in 1955, but no

one could get past Cleveland. "It seemed like we were in it every season during those years," Sprinkle said, "but could just never get over the top."

When the Chicago Bears were born, radio was an electronic medium in its infancy. After World War II, television, with its free pictures beamed into millions of homes, was the electronic medium in its infancy. Just as the 1950s were beginning, the first discussions were conducted about televising pro football. By then the Bears had a 25-station radio network. Hearing the product and seeing the product were vastly different ideas in Halas' mind, however.

Radio broadcasts would whet the appetite of a fan to see a game in person. TV broadcasts would amount to giving the product away for free and undermining fans who paid for their ticket. Yet Halas relented once. The Bears were the marquee franchise in Chicago, but there was always curiosity about how the Bears and Cardinals would fare against each other. In 1949, the game between the two Chicago clubs was the first Bears game televised. The game was sponsored by Standard Oil of Indiana, sponsor of the radio shows.

This TV showing also whetted the appetite of fans, but Halas had no intention of making Bears performances a regular part of over-the-air fare. He

Larry Morris, better known as a linebacker later in his career, also practiced hiking the ball.
Bettmann/Corbis

was vilified by critics. He admitted that he was accused of being guilty of every and any sin, including being unconstitutional. As a compromise, the Bears filmed their Sunday games, allowed them to be edited into half-hour highlight films and shown on TV on Tuesdays.

Dan Reeves, owner of the Rams, tried the opposite tactic. He permitted all Rams games to be televised, but had a clause in his contract providing payback for lost revenue if ticket sales dropped. They did and he was paid $300,000. Halas considered this the clinching argument that televising home football games was a bad idea. Before the end of the decade, though, Halas recognized the potential value from nationwide telecasts and became a vocal proponent of the NFL working with the TV networks.

Halas was sometimes so rooted in the past and in tradition that he might as well have been a redwood tree. Other times he was creative, an innovator, and saw the future as clearly as if he was peering into a crystal ball. His jutting jaw seemed to precede him into a room by a step or two and he was never shy about making his point. Some thought of Halas as hard-bitten and cynical, but Halas was consistent, always doing what he thought was best for the Bears in looking for any edge, but also supporting the common good of the league.

No one in the early 1950s was going to suggest that the game had passed George Halas by. He may have been present at the NFL's conception, but he could still piece together winners. George Connor, one player who made the transition from the 1940s to the 1950s and later was a long-time Bears broadcaster, was of the type of ferocious tacklers that appealed to Halas.

Connor, a well-known banquet speaker in retirement, wore a 15EEEE shoe size that he liked to say was good "for tripping ends." Connor was very good at that task and always had been. Before the war he was an All-American for Holy Cross. When the war ended the New York Giants drafted Connor and the San Francisco 49ers of the All-America Football Conference were interested in him. But the 6-foot-3, 240-pound lineman chose to finish college. He enrolled at Notre Dame and became an All-American there, too. He won the Outland Trophy as the nation's best lineman and Halas traded for his rights, and scooped him up. They were an odd pair. Halas was considered plain old mean by many and Connor was gregarious, funny, and made friends easily. His comment on Halas: "Halas was a helluva guy. I liked him."

Not everyone thought so. Sprinkle said that before a Bears–Green Bay game in 1955, Halas took note of a Packer player with a thin mustache that Sprinkle

described as "cute." He offered a $5 bounty to any Bear defender who delivered a hair torn from that player's face. Halas was a maniac on the sidelines, often swearing at referees. He yelled, he stomped, he paced. Once, in protest of a penalty call, Halas yelled, "You stink!" to an official. The referee promptly marched off a 10-yard bonus penalty and replied, "How do I smell from here?"

Entire generations of football fans have grown up not realizing that the Arizona Cardinals, which used to be the St. Louis Cardinals, were actually for many years the Chicago Cardinals. In theory Chicago was a large enough city to support two professional teams, but

Future Hall of Famer George Blanda, who made his reputation later with the Houston Oilers, demonstrating his pass throwing form in 1954.
Bettmann/Corbis

Bidwell and Halas were friends, but Halas showed no mercy when it came to beating the Cardinals on the field.

Bidwell always had more wealth than Halas—during the Bears tough financial times in the 1930s he loaned Halas money—but Halas always had the better team—except for 1947 and 1948 when the Cardinals, who had signed the great halfback Charlie Trippi, twice prevented the Bears from advancing into the playoffs. The Cardinals won their only title in 1947 and lost in the title game in 1948. After Bidwell died, however, Halas feuded with the new management and the era of cooperation between the two Chicago teams ended. Not completely so for the players, though.

J. C. Caroline, the University of Illinois star who joined the Bears in 1956 and played both offensive and defensive halfback, said Bears and Cardinals players fraternized at nightclubs and hung out together, particularly the black athletes. Caroline said he was tight with Ollie Matson, the great Olympic track star who excelled in the Cardinals' backfield. "Ollie was a close friend of mine," Caroline said. "We got to know those guys. You've got the two teams in the same town. After the game we would socialize together. We would go to some of the same affairs."

Bears owner George Halas holds up the trophy honoring him as the outstanding pro football coach in 1956.
Bettmann/Corbis

the Bears always overshadowed the poor relative. The Cardinals were originally called the Racine Cardinals when the NFL began. Charlie Bidwell, a local millionaire, was the Bears' team secretary, but when the Cardinals went up for sale, Halas facilitated Bidwell's purchase during a cruise on Lake Michigan.

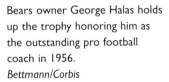

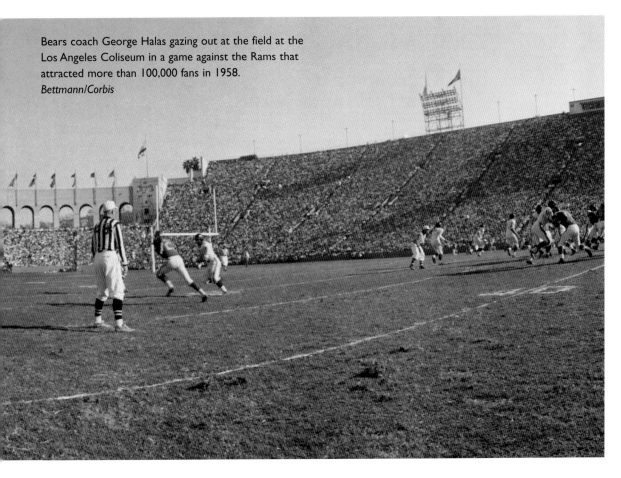

Bears coach George Halas gazing out at the field at the Los Angeles Coliseum in a game against the Rams that attracted more than 100,000 fans in 1958.
Bettmann/Corbis

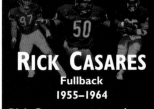

RICK CASARES
Fullback
1955–1964

Rick Casares possessed throwback toughness and modern speed. He was a Monster of the Midway who ran up the middle and never flinched at hits. In an 11-year NFL career, mostly with the Bears, Casares rushed for 5,797 yards, an impressive 4.1 yards per carry. But what distinguished him at the time was his agility as a 6-foot-2, 226-pound man, who was supposed to block for his halfback and quarterback, in catching passes, too. Casares not only rushed for 1,126 yards in a season, he caught more than 20 passes in a season four times and he scored 60 touchdowns in his career. "Rick Casares, people didn't realize what an extraordinary athlete he was," said Bears quarterback Bill Wade.

Casares liked to have a good time. He liked good music and he liked to go out at night. Teammate Mike Pyle called Casares "one of the funniest men who ever lived." Coach Halas required weekly weigh-ins at maximums he set. Casares always had trouble making weight. So Casares got in the habit of going out drinking the night before and totally dehydrating himself before stepping on the scale.

Once, on Thanksgiving, Halas, who was not above hiring private detectives to follow his players, showed up in a bar planning to chastise Casares. However, Casares hadn't had a drink. He was with his steady girlfriend and ate the holiday meal with her parents. There was nothing Halas could say.

The United States reached new levels of prosperity in the 1950s. The decade has been called the vanilla decade, but social change was afoot in many areas. The Korean War was an undeclared war and Americans at home were more focused on buying their first car, purchasing their first homes, moving to the suburbs and raising families. Television viewing skyrocketed. The new American pastime was sitting in front of the tube.

When the Baltimore Colts defeated the New York Giants on television, 23–17, in overtime in 1958, the television era of the NFL dawned. Colts–Giants was the water-cooler buzz the next day. Johnny Unitas became a bigger star than Sid Caesar. That compelling game that some say is the best ever played, instilled a demand for more football. Long-time commissioner Bert Bell had been innovative and shepherded the league through its tribulations fending off the All-America Football Conference, but he died of a heart attack in October 1959. The man who replaced him, young, vigorous, enthusiastic and visionary Pete Rozelle, proved himself a marketing genius. On Rozelle's watch between January 1960 and November 1989, the NFL became the TV networks' favorite programming and during his reign billion-dollar TV rights contracts were signed.

Just before Bell died and just before Rozelle took over, the Chicago Cardinals fled to St. Louis. George Halas was very happy about it. He had the Chicago market, with its growing value in a TV-juiced economy, all to himself.

After the 1955 season, Halas decided to "retire" again. In reality it was another leave of absence. To coach the Bears this time he turned to his old trusted teammate and friend John "Paddy" Driscoll. Driscoll was good enough as a baseball player to receive the opportunity to play in the majors. He was born in Evanston, just north of Chicago, and in 1917 he spent 13 games as an infielder for the Chicago Cubs. Batting .107, Driscoll proved to be only a hit or two better than Halas. He was a better quarterback and punter than hitter.

Driscoll played ball for Northwestern and served in the Navy during World War I. At the Great Lakes Naval Training Station he played football with Halas and after his discharge joined Halas in the Decatur Staleys venture. He shifted to the Chicago Cardinals, but in 1926 was traded to the Chicago Bears.

Driscoll had been a long-time assistant Bears coach and assumed command of the team on the field at a fortuitous time. Much of the talent assembled by

GEORGE CONNOR

Tackle/Linebacker
1948–1955

If George Connor became an actor he probably would have had a star for his name in the cement outside Grauman's Chinese Theatre in Hollywood. He was a star everywhere he went. Not too many football players were All-Americans at two colleges, Holy Cross and Notre Dame (before and after World War II). In addition, Connor, a born and raised Chicagoan, was selected for the Pro Bowl four straight times in the early 1950s with the Bears.

Connor was 6-foot-3 and 240 pounds, which made him a natural for the line. But he moonlighted as a linebacker, using speed to complement size. The Bears' 1953 media guide referred to Connor as "the most versatile player in the NFL" because he played tackle, guard, end and linebacker. He was exceptional in all roles, and earned acceptance into the Pro Football Hall of Fame.

As one of the typical linemen who rarely get noticed when they are playing well during a game, Connor cited a flashy play he made on defense during his last season as his favorite. In a game against the Detroit Lions, Connor scooped up a fumble and ran 48 yards for a touchdown. In the 1952 Pro Bowl, Connor displayed all his multiple talents in one series of defense for the West. In succession, he made a tackle for a loss, a solo tackle, sacked the quarterback, and batted away a fourth-down pass. It was a personal highlight.

BEST BEARS DRAFT PICKS OF THE 1950s

1951	No. 2	Bill George	Wake Forest
1952	No. 1	Jim Dooley	Miami (Fla.)
	No. 5b	Fred Williams	Arkansas
	No. 6	Ed Brown	San Francisco
	No. 7	Joe Fortunato	Mississippi State
1953	No. 2	Zeke Bratkowski	Georgia
	No. 5	Stan Jones	Maryland
1954	No. 2	Rick Casares	Florida
	No. 3	Ed Meadows	Duke
	No. 15	Harlon Hill	Florence State
1956	No. 5	Willie Galimore	Florida A&M
	No. 7	J. C. Caroline	Illinois
1957	No. 1	Earl Leggett	Louisiana State
	No. 8b	Bob Kilcullen	Texas Tech
	No. 9	Bill Brown	Syracuse
1958	No. 1	Chuck Howley	West Virginia
	No. 2	Willard Dewveall	SMU
	No. 4	Erich Barnes	Purdue
	No. 12	Johnny Morris	Cal-Santa Barbara
1959	No. 2	Richie Petitbon	Tulane
	No. 9	Maury Youmans	Syracuse
	No. 15	Roger LeClerc	Trinity (Conn.)

"He was good in his day. When football changed, Coach Halas didn't change too much. They [in-house old-timers] worshipped Mr. Halas."
—Hall of Fame defensive end Doug Atkins.

Halas in the first half of the 50s was in its prime. The biggest confusion during that time period, following Luckman's retirement, was who to play at quarterback. Bobby Layne was a hell-raiser who hated following rules and wrote his own, so he and Halas never became bosom buddies. Layne became a Detroit Lion. For some reason, Halas disliked George Blanda and rarely took advantage of Blanda's tremendous potential, except as a place kicker. In only one season, 1953, during the decade Blanda was a Bear, did he run the offense full-time.

It was a strange miscalculation by a coach generally right on personnel calls. Misjudging and misusing Blanda might have been the biggest mistake of Halas' career. Halas tried to ruin Blanda's career, running him out of football for the 1959 season. What saved Blanda was the creation of the American Football League in 1960. He was handed the reins to the Houston Oilers' offense and in 1961 threw 36 touchdown passes. Moreover, Blanda assumed the Oilers' kicking job, then went on to tremendous success with the Oakland Raiders, played pro ball until he was nearly 50 and retired as the leading NFL scorer of all-time, a record he held for two decades.

That flair did not do the Bears much good in the 1950s when Blanda lived on the team bench. Halas kept trying. He drafted Zeke Bratkowski out of Georgia in 1954 and while Bratkowski had a lengthy career, most of it was as a back-up. Blanda seemed better. "George, he's incredible," said Bears fullback Rick Casares. "He's one of the greatest competitors I ever played with. We had an inside joke. We would say, 'Poor George. He went to Houston and he only won the championship and got a basket full of money.' Halas liked Bratkowski."

Along came Ed Brown, also in 1954. Brown was the starter for the middle years of the 1950s, but he was no Luckman and, more importantly for the Bears at the time, he was no Otto Graham. Brown could run an offense, but he did not have the arm strength or accuracy to complete more touchdown passes than interceptions. But Brown was good enough to supervise a talented team's 1956 run to the NFL championship game under Driscoll. In his finest performance, Brown completed 57 percent of his

passes that year, and connected on 11 touchdowns. Brown and the Bears were blessed with an outstanding receiver in Harlon Hill, who had the sticky fingers to make receptions and the elusiveness to go a long way after he caught the pass.

Just as significantly, Brown's passing arm was complemented by Rick Casares' legs. Casares grew up in Tampa, Florida, and played collegiately at the University of Florida. He was drafted by the Bears in 1955 and as a rookie rushed for an exceptional 5.4 yards per carry. The Bears only trusted him with the ball 125 times on the ground that season but after reviewing the final statistics decided that Casares was ready for more—much more. Casares was the focal point of the offense during the 9–2–1 1956 season, rushing 234 times for 1,126 yards. At nearly 230 pounds, he was a power runner, a bull of a back who sometimes could not be downed on the turf without the assistance of three tacklers.

The championship game in 1956 marked the fifth time the Bears and New York Giants fought it out for the title. Usually, the Bears had had the upper hand. The only time the Giants took home the trophy was in 1934, the Sneaker Game. But this was a magnificent Giants team. They were loaded at every position. Frank Gifford was the flanker, Alex Webster the fullback. Roosevelt Brown was a tackle on his way to the Hall of Fame. And the defense was a stone wall with linebacker Sam Huff, defensive linemen Andy Robustelli and Rosy Grier, and defensive backs Emlen Tunnell and Jimmy Patton protecting against all assaults. Even more impressively, among head coach Jim Lee Howell's assistants were Tom Landry, soon to take over the expansion Dallas Cowboys and create legends in Texas, and Vince Lombardi, soon to take over the Green Bay Packers and make myths in Wisconsin.

If Halas didn't know what to do about his quarterbacking half the time, the Giants developed an answer for how to play two men at once. Howell started Don Heinrich each week and then, after letting him watch the action unfold, he inserted leathered Charlie Conerly.

Gene Filipski ran the opening kick-off back 53 yards to excite the 56,836 fans at Yankee Stadium as the Bears' coverage team stumbled. Running back Mel Triplett scored the first Giants touchdown on a 17-yard run four plays later and the Giants never gave up their lead. It was 13–0 New York after one period and 34–7 at the half. Heinrich had exposed a few openings and Conerly, mixing the run and pass, exploited them. The Bears' only touchdown came on a 9-yard run by Casares. In the end the Giants squashed Chicago, 47–7.

HARLON HILL
End
1954–1961

Harlon Hill was one of George Halas' greatest finds. Scouting is super-sophisticated now. High school players in remote precincts make video tapes of their exploits in hopes of winning a scholarship. Stars in NCAA Division II or III are well known to pro teams. That was not true in Hill's time. He grew up in small-town Alabama in the 1930s and 1940s before television beamed the NFL across the world. When it came time to choose a college, Hill selected Florence State Teachers College, the school that is now known as North Alabama.

One thing Hill could always do was snatch a football out of the sky if it was thrown near him. And he could run like a deer. In the 1950s, the NFL draft lasted 30 rounds. Teams often picked players who were simply names on rosters with little insight into the likelihood of their success. Halas got a tip that Hill was worth a look-see and Hill was so far below the radar no one else would select him.

The Bears took Hill with the 15th pick and he became an instant sensation. Starting as a rookie, Hill caught 45 passes for 1,124 yards, for a stunning 25.0 average, and 12 touchdowns. The average and touchdowns led the league.

In a career cut short because he said he did not take good care of his body, Hill's 20.4 average per catch still rates as one of the best in team history.

Even worse than the magnitude of the slaughter was the way it happened. History repeated itself. This turned into Sneaker Game II. Just as in 1934, the field was icy, the day was frigid, and the Giants out-smarted the Bears on footwear. Before the game, Howell sent two Giants players onto the field to test the firmness of the ground. One player, Ed Hughes, wearing standard football shoes, fell down. The other player, Filipski, wore sneakers and his footing was fine. Howell told his players to put on sneakers. Not yet being

sponsored by Nike, or any other sports shoe maker, the Giants sought a different solution. Andy Robustelli, a 230-pound defensive end on his way to the Hall of Fame, owned a sporting goods store and not surprisingly he had some white sneakers for loan.

The equipment disparity produced one of the most frustrating games in Casares' career. "Our guys were sliding all over the place," Casares said. "Filipski had traction and our guys were sliding by him. We changed our cleats and they still weren't gripping.

For the 1956 championship game on an icy field, the New York Giants chose their footwear more wisely than the Bears. Note the sneakers on Frank Gifford.
B. Bennett/Getty Images

We were three-point favorites going into the game, but they ruined it."

Harlon Hill, the marvelous end, said Halas did not always keep up with the weather forecast and operated on the assumption there would be a muddy field. When the field turned icy, with lower temperatures than expected, the Bears were ill-prepared. Hill said the difference between the Giants' sure-footedness and the Bears' skidding "knocked us for a psychological loop." And sent the Bears right back to the Loop with an "L" on their record.

Driscoll coached the Bears again in 1957, but that was a lean 5–7 year. Then Halas came out of retirement once more to resume coaching the Bears. Driscoll became a Halas assistant again and then in the 1960s took the position of team director of planning and research, a job he held until his death at age 73 in 1968. That was the Halas loyalty at work for his long-time friend and partner. A job for life.

In 1958 the Bears finished 8–4. They posted the same record in 1959. But things were changing in the

> **"I liked it. I got a lot of satisfaction out of it because we had some good runners. It was rewarding."**
> *—All-Star defensive lineman Stan Jones after becoming an All-Star offensive lineman.*

Western Division. The despised Packers were on the rise. For decades, Halas and Lambeau, two pioneers who built the NFL brick by brick, were heated rivals. But Lambeau departed from Green Bay in 1949 (and next ran the Chicago Cardinals for two seasons) and the team's fortunes on the field declined dramatically.

The 1950s were just as cold and windy in Green Bay as ever, but it felt a little bit chillier with the beloved football team faltering. Between 1950 and 1958, the Packers did not have a season where their winning percentage was better than .500. Most years it was far inferior.

STAN JONES
Tackle/Guard/
Defensive tackle
1954–1965

Jones was the rock. Whether he played the offensive line or the defensive line, Stan Jones was the immovable foundation. He was 6-foot-1 and many were intimidated by his 252 pounds, though the men who play Jones' positions now weigh 300 pounds or more. Jones jokes that an NFL team now would turn him into a tight end.

Jones knew little about pro football growing up and when he joined the Bears he was impressed by the fans. "They seemed so enthusiastic, loyal," Jones said. "I hadn't really expected that in the pro game. I thought they'd just come out like they were going to see an exhibition or something. I didn't think they'd have the spirit."

Maybe Jones just had the look of a tough guy because he generally wore his hair in a buzz cut that seemed as if his stylist was a Marine and he discovered weight lifting to make his muscles bulge long before most athletes. At the peak of his career, however, Jones, a seven-time pro all-star who was national college lineman of the year at the University of Maryland, nearly quit. Players might make less than $10,000 and George Halas was not known to be the most generous of owners at contract time. Jones taught school in Maryland each off-season and he almost decided to forsake football for the cash rewards of teaching. But he stayed with the Bears and switched to defense for variety and eventually a championship.

The Bears knew how to play, too, with this fun for all sizes exercise. Ed Rutsch, a 270-pound All-American tackle drafted by the Bears in 1958, tries out a Hula Hoop with 97-pound cheerleader Ann Sneeringer at George Washington University, the college he attended. *Bettmann/Corbis*

BILL GEORGE AND THE INVENTION OF MIDDLE LINEBACKERS

Bill George was the first in the line of linebackers who for more than 50 years have defined Chicago Bear excellence on defense. Until George brought an innovative style to the way he positioned himself, the key man in the center of the defensive alignment was called the middle guard. Using his agility—mental and physical—the 6-foot-2, 237-pound George diverged from the script. Instead of always charging ahead at the offensive center, he sometimes dropped back to participate in pass coverage.

By retreating from the line of scrimmage, the middle guard in a five-man front became a middle linebacker and essentially created the 4–3 defensive formation that remains in vogue today. By performing the tasks of this new role so expertly, the eight-time NFL all-star paved the way for others.

And, their birthright from being present at the creation of this role, no team has produced more superstar middle linebackers than the Bears. George was voted to the NFL's 1950s all-decade team. Although he played a final season with the Los Angeles Rams in 1966, George left the job in more than capable hands. He was succeeded by the stupendous Dick Butkus, a carnivorous middle linebacker who some consider the greatest defensive player of all.

The next great Bears middle linebacker, another Hall of Famer, was Mike Singletary, who was the spiritual leader of the 1985 Bears' Super Bowl champions. And since 2000, the heart and soul of the Chicago Bears defense has been middle linebacker Brian Urlacher, an NFL defensive player of the year.

The riches at linebacker do not stop there for the Bears. Under the 4–3 alignment, defenses deploy three linebackers at once. During the best years of the 1960s, George was flanked

by Joe Fortunato and Larry Morris. In more recent years, other Bears linebackers of note were Doug Buffone, Rosevelt Colvin, and Lance Briggs. Playing linebacker for the Bears—especially middle linebacker—is one of the glamor roles in the game.

It all started with George. George was from Waynesburg, Pennsylvania, a coal mining community where high school football was king. Mike Ditka, a decade younger, was from the same area and later said George was the first friend he made on the Bears when the older man took him under his wing. "He definitely was one of the all-time great players," Ditka said much later of George, who has been listed among the 100 greatest NFL players.

George attended Wake Forest and was a second-round draft pick of the Bears, beginning his career with the big club in 1952. George wore the closely cropped hairstyle in vogue in the 1950s, and played the game with a ferocity that made opponents drop the ball around him. Described by *Sports Illustrated* as "the meanest Bear ever" (and there has been plenty of competition), George recovered 19 fumbles in his career and intercepted 18 passes. When members of the Green Bay Packers and the Detroit Lions glimpsed George's number 61 bursting into the scene out of the corners of their eyes, they shivered. George had long arms and the strength of a real bear, useful tackling attributes. "Somebody once said he had the cross-build between a pelican and a gorilla," said teammate Stan Jones.

The idea for changing his approach to his position occurred to George during a 1954 game against the Philadelphia Eagles. As a middle guard, George's assignment on obvious passing downs was to hit the other team's center when the ball was snapped, then backpedal. Invariably, by

Bill George of the Chicago Bears chases down a runner in a 34–23 win over the San Francisco 49ers on October 23, 1955, at Kezar Stadium in San Francisco, California.
NFL/Getty Images

the time George retreated, the quarterback had completed a pass over his head into the empty zone.

George was playing alongside Bears left-side linebacker George Connor and complained about the situation. "Hell," George said, "I could break up those passes if I didn't have to hit that offensive center first."

Connor, the defensive captain, instructed George to adapt. "What are you hitting him for then?" Connor said. "Why don't you go for the ball?"

It was not clear who was more surprised the first time George attempted the maneuver, he or the Eagles' quarterback since the pass flung in his direction hit him directly in the belly. The second time George assessed the situation as a passing down he clogged the previously abandoned zone and intercepted a pass.

The style distinguished George from other middle guards, brought him great acclaim and led to his induction into the Pro Football Hall of Fame in 1974. In 1964, before George completed his Bears tenure, Chicago fans celebrated a "Bill George Day" at Wrigley Field. He was presented with a car, TV set, and other gifts. Then he promptly tore up a knee and missed the season's last six games.

George had a colorful career in many ways. For a game in the late 1950s, Halas, the famous control freak, installed a radio receiver in George's helmet so the coach could broadcast defensive instructions to him during the action. Commissioner Bert Bell banned the device, forcing Halas to rely on George to call defensive signals—probably a better move.

After he retired as a player, George returned to the Bears as an assistant coach for a little while. He was killed at the age of 52 in an automobile accident in 1982. George's death came less than a decade after he was chosen for the Hall and enjoyed the ceremony in Canton, Ohio. There he heard one-time Bears coach Abe Gibron, one of the player's chums, discuss his career. "Bill George was the first great middle linebacker," Gibron said. "He brought all the romance and charisma to the position. He was like having Clark Shaughnessy (the famous coach) on the field. He called all the plays and he had a special knack for it."

Bill George also had a special knack for innovation and his legacy endures in the National Football League.

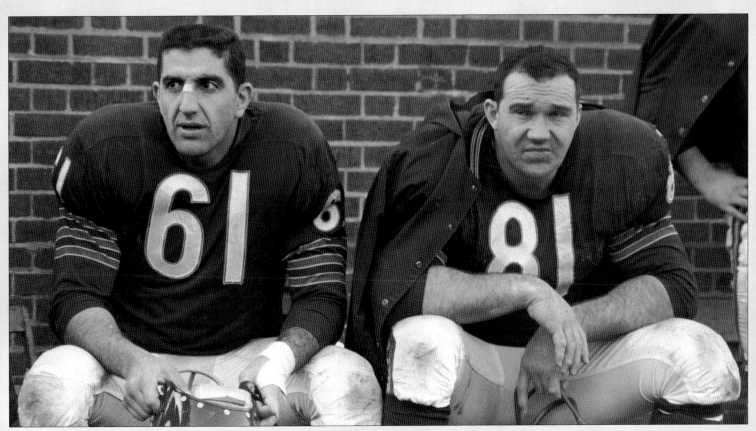

Defensive lineman Doug Atkins (right) and linebacker Bill George. *Getty Images*

Green Bay was still a circled game on the Bears' schedule, more for old times' sake and tradition than for its meaning in the standings. Green Bay was trying to stay out of the cellar. The Bears were trying to win division titles and championships. Halas never let the importance of beating Green Bay slip too far into the background, however. "The Packers were the game of the year," Casares said. "Halas instigated the preparation and intensity for the Packer games and we played good games against them."

Casares said that the Bears would often come up with a special play that worked in practice and then keep it secret. "We'd mothball it and say, 'We're going to save that for the Packers game,'" he said.

Like any good rivalry, results of the Bears–Packers match-ups of the time period do not necessarily indicate where teams were located in the standings. In 1955, Casares' rookie year, the Packers beat the Bears early, 24–3, then the Bears retaliated later in the season with a 52–21 thumping.

The Bears swept in 1956, the year they reached the title game and the teams split in 1957, a bad year for Chicago all around. The Bears swept again in 1958. The teams split in 1959, too. But that year marked a change in Green Bay's status. The Packers were pushovers no longer. Their former glory under Lambeau was being restored by Vince Lombardi, in his first head coaching job after working in college ball and for the Giants.

The phrase, "Winning is the only thing," has been attributed to Lombardi as a method of briefly describing the man's incredible desire to succeed. At the least, the sentiment was correct. Lombardi, one of the famed "Seven Blocks of Granite" as a lineman at Fordham, a disciplined coach under Earl Blaik at Army, and the architect of the Giants' offense, could match Halas in intensity. His demands for discipline and hard work, and his ability to fill the roster with talented players who meshed, helped Lombardi give the city of Green Bay the most glorious years in its long love affair with its football team. The firm-handed Lombardi introduced himself with a 7–5 record in 1959. A year later the Packers won the Western Division and lost to the Philadelphia Eagles in the NFL championship game. In 1961 and 1962, the Packers won titles.

Lombardi took on nearly mythological status as the epitome of a football coach. His players, from superstar halfback Paul Hornung, a Heisman Trophy winner out of Notre Dame, quarterback Bart Starr and middle linebacker Ray Nitschke admitted to both loving and fearing the old man, who played the dual roles of doting and stern father.

Much of the Packers' success came at the expense of the Bears. They were in the same division and while

1950s CHICAGO BEARS YEAR BY YEAR

1950	9–3
1951	7–5
1952	5–7
1953	3–8–1
1954	8–4
1955	8–4
1956	9–2–1
1957	5–7
1958	8–4
1959	8–4

Green Bay dominated Chicago languished. There was only room for one team at the top in the West. The rivalry took on its fiercest proportions in years. "When I came in," said Hall of Fame lineman Stan Jones, who made his Bears' debut in 1954, "they [the Packers] had kind of gone downhill. Then when Lombardi came in, of course they had a good team. You wanted to beat the best and they were the best." The Bears had won more than their share of championships since the National Football League was formed and they were not used to admitting that someone else was the best.

Halas was always proud that Green Bay made it as an enduring franchise. He liked the town and its people even if he hated the players and coaches while the Bears were trying to beat them. There was something special in having a smaller city like Green Bay mingling with the major cities of the country and holding its own. To prove his loyalty—there it was again—to the community that had backed the team since the league's beginnings, in 1956 Halas made public appearances in Green Bay to help raise money for a new stadium.

With that gesture, Halas demonstrated that the Bears and Packers might feud on the field, try to kick one another's teeth in for 60 minutes twice a year, but that beneath it all they were blood relations in the brotherhood of the National Football League.

Opposite: New York Giants receiver Kyle Rote makes a key catch in the defeat of the Bears in the 1956 title game. Chicago defender Doug Atkins is in the background.
Kidwiler Collection/Getty Images

CHAPTER 5

THE 1960s:
GLORY AND DESPAIR

The arrival of Vince Lombardi in Green Bay changed the dynamics of the National Football League's Western Conference and, as the team swiftly morphed into a powerhouse, the entire league. As television interest expanded, Packers players from Paul Hornung to Henry Jordan, from Max McGee to Fuzzy Thurston, became household names.

For George Halas, it was a challenging time on the field because the Packers were in an up cycle and had eclipsed his team's capabilities. But from the first moment Halas became involved with pro football, sitting in that crowded Hupmobile showroom, he was equally concerned about the fortunes of the league as a whole.

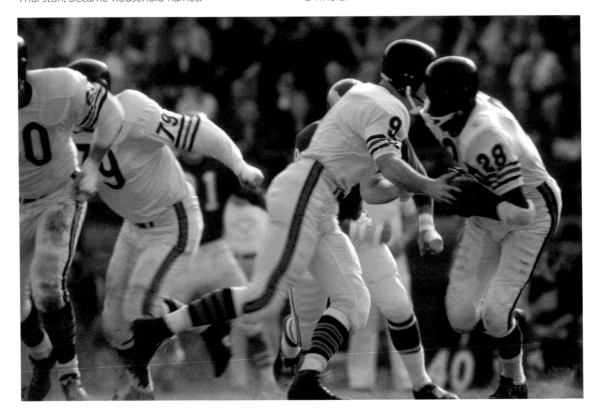

Quarterback Bill Wade hands off to Willie Galimore in a game against Philadelphia in November 1961. Galimore died tragically in an automobile accident during training camp in 1964.
Robert Riger/Getty Images

"People kept telling me I would become muscle-bound. I decided not to worry about being narcissistic and just worry about keeping my body in shape."
—Hall of Fame lineman Stan Jones on being an early proponent of weight-lifting.

The owner who had been vociferously against televising too much football in the 1950s, was heartily in favor of the tool of television boosting the pro game in the 1960s. Although he was commander-in-chief of a franchise in one of the largest markets in the country, Halas was a vocal proponent of making sure that all TV proceeds were equally divided among the big city teams and the small city teams. He innately understood that a level playing field was the league's strength and that a greedy approach would likely run some teams out of business. The team most jeopardized by a plan that distributed income by city size would have been the Packers. In this manner Halas sacrificed a larger slice of the pie for the common good.

It was that fair and novel approach that enabled the NFL to grow steadily and make certain that its teams retained a rough parity over the ensuing decades. The formula of equal shares has never been tampered with.

One of the great Bears of all time arrived in the draft in 1961 and forged a special relationship with Halas at first. Mike Ditka might have become just another offensive lineman if he had been drafted by another team, but Halas saw the player, thought about how his skills might best be used and turned the tight end position into more of a hybrid taking advantage of Ditka's receiving ability, too. "Mike just likes to get the ball and bowl over people," George "Mugs" Halas Jr. said. In no time at all Ditka had been anointed with a shortened version of the Monsters of the Midway description. Some just called him "Monster."

That still did not help Halas assemble a team that could best Green Bay, riding high under Lombardi's forceful personality and demanding style. The Bears finished 8–6 in 1961 and lost to the Packers twice. The Bears finished 9–5 in 1962 but lost by scores of 49–0 and 38–7 to the Packers. Halas was determined, and with a team that was anchored by seasoned veterans of great talent like Stan Jones, Rick Casares, Bill George, Joe Fortunato, defensive back Rosey Taylor, and the

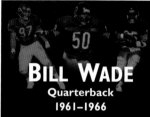

BILL WADE
Quarterback
1961–1966

After playing musical quarterbacks in the 1950s, it was soothing when Papa Bear Halas settled on Bill Wade as his regular signal caller. Many of the Bears who lived through the disappointing 1956 title game loss were running out of time. Wade helped them jell and led the group to the 1963 championship.

Wade had an interesting pedigree. He was born in Nashville, Tennessee, where his father had been a Vanderbilt football captain. Wade grew up dreaming of playing for the Commodores. He was on an elementary school team that played as part of half-time entertainment the first time he took to Vanderbilt's Dudley Field. As a 15-year-old in high school, in workouts there Wade impressed Vanderbilt's coaches with his throwing arm.

In college Wade made a splash by appearing on the cover of *Look* magazine and Wade said that when the issue came out Georgia Tech fans shouted "Hey, glamor boy" during a game. Most Valuable Player of the Southeastern Conference, Wade showed well in college all-star games and the Rams drafted him in 1952. The Bears obtained Wade in 1961—he was the right man for the quarterback job at the right time.

During the 1963 title season, Wade threw for 2,301 yards and 15 touchdowns. Wade was religious, but said he didn't care how spiritual his teammates were as long as they were ready on game day. "I was hoping on Sunday they would be in a fighting mode," he said.

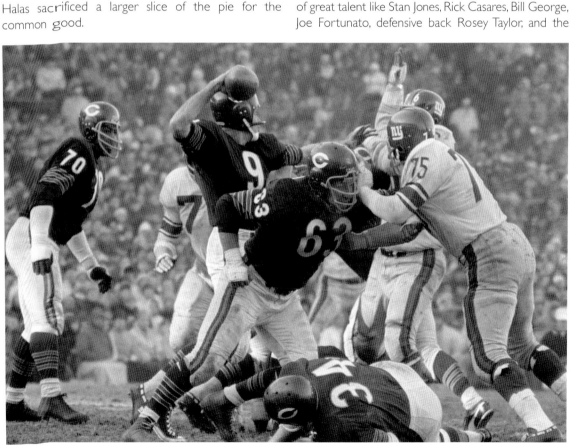

Bill Wade cocks his arm, ready to throw against the New York Giants in the Bears 14–10 victory for the 1963 championship. *Bettmann/Corbis*

"All week the coaches were muttering, 'Sayers, Sayers.' So they put in what we called the 'Chicago defense.' I was never involved in anything like that before or since."
—San Francisco lineman Charlie Krueger after Gayle Sayers scored six touchdowns against the 49ers in 1965.

The Packers did not expect to be handled in such a manner and were surprised when the Bears won so easily. "We gave 100 percent, but the trouble was the Bears gave 150 percent," said Green Bay linebacker Bill Forrester. The Packers were two-time defending world champions and they felt they were just as good, if not better, in 1963. They were prepared to win it all again. But the Bears shut them down.

"If I were to answer for my ego, I would have to say no… the Bears are not a better team," said Packer

young Mike Ditka, he had the core of a group that responded well to humiliation. They had great pride and they refused to accept Green Bay's domination.

Halas always aimed for championships. Winning it all was always a goal talked about in training camp, but he emphasized that it was important for the Bears to beat Green Bay, too. He drummed it into the heads of players who saw the rivalry, especially with the Packers' supremacy, as something etched into the DNA of the franchise and the fans of Chicago. "Halas loved that rivalry," Ditka said. "He drilled it into us. 'You gotta beat the Packers.' Before Lombardi got there, Green Bay's mission was to beat the Bears. Period. We started to climb the ladder to get even with them."

Once in a while Lombardi would telephone Halas directly to talk trades. Halas was wary of dealing with Lombardi given the state of the rivalry and no matter how much charm Lombardi oozed. Sometime after the 1962 season, Lombardi posed a few hypotheticals to Halas. It seemed he was looking for some defensive help, perhaps All-Pro Doug Atkins or the other defensive end Ed O'Bradovich. Halas turned down everything then glowered and let loose with one of his infamous temper tantrums. "The gall of that guy," Halas said. "I want to kick his ass."

During that same off-season, Halas and legendary defensive coordinator Clark Shaughnessy had a falling out and Shaughnessy left. Halas gave George Allen the job. This was the beginning of a beautiful partnership that later erupted into flames. But Allen was the forerunner of the 2000s football coach who thought nothing of working incredible hours and sleeping in the office if he must. It may have been his fine-tuning that turned the Bears from runners-up to champs.

The moment that Ditka talked about—drawing even with Green Bay—arrived in the 1963 season. The Bears and Packers met on opening day in September and the Bears prevailed 10–3. The Bears intercepted Green Bay quarterback Bart Starr five times—good revenge for the two thrashings the year before. When the teams met again in November, the Bears won 26–7.

defensive tackle Henry Jordan. "But looking at the scores, I can't say anything but yes... the Bears are better."

There was a new sheriff in the NFL West. The Bears completed the regular season with an 11–1–2 record, the team's best since 1942's 11–0, and the victories put the Bears into the league title game for the first time since 1956. It was a season of great satisfaction, especially for long-time players who had earned many individual honors, but whose only taste

of championship play was a sour one given the failure against the Giants.

The Bears defense was loaded with prime-time players, but what set the team apart from other recent versions was the depth on offense. Ditka was the best tight end in the business. In Bill Wade and Rudy Bukich, Halas had two solid quarterbacks. Flanker Johnny Morris was a deep threat and halfbacks Ronnie Bull and Willie Galimore complemented Casares well. Galimore, a speedy back from Florida A&M, was

Bill Wade prepares to deliver a pass in a game against the Baltimore Colts during the Bears' 1963 championship season.
Robert Riger/Getty Images

expected soon to blossom into a superstar. He had suffered a knee injury and missed much of the 1962 season, but was regaining his speed slowly.

Morris, who a year later would catch 93 passes for 1,200 yards in his best season, caught 47 in 1963 and he was only 5-foot-10 weighing 180 pounds. "I thought Johnny Morris was a great football player," Wade said. "Without any question I felt there were times when he could get clear against anybody in the business."

The image of Casares as a tough guy was not limited to opponents. Angelo Coia, a receiver on the 1963 team, likens Casares to the big players of the current era and recalls a game when Casares got clobbered on a play. He told Coia he thought he had broken ribs. But Casares stayed in the game and caught a pass for a 7-yard gain on the next play. "He goes out of the game and he has two broken ribs," Coia said.

"Some people can't even breathe with a broken rib and he's playing football."

In 1963, the Bears won their first five games, lost to San Francisco, won four more in a row, tied two in a row, and won the last two. The offense tallied 301 points and the defense surrendered only 154.

As usual, the great Doug Atkins did things his own way—he loved to test Halas because of his grudging feeling that he was being paid too little. One day in training camp, Atkins missed the start of practice. All of a sudden, well into the activities, Atkins burst out of the locker room, ran around the field for about 20 minutes, ran right past Halas, and then ran back inside. The other players, who never would have tweaked Halas like that, but who appreciated the renegade who did, asked what the heck Atkins was doing. He replied that he was breaking in his new helmet.

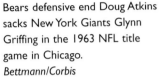

Bears defensive end Doug Atkins sacks New York Giants Glynn Griffing in the 1963 NFL title game in Chicago.
Bettmann/Corbis

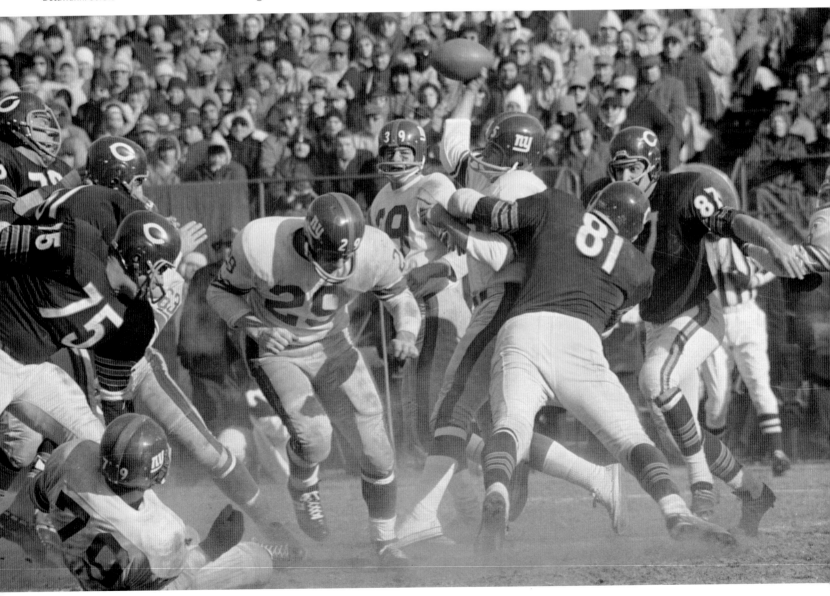

Mike Ditka came out of the University of Pittsburgh to the Bears and revolutionized the tight end position.
Robert Riger/Getty Images

MIKE DITKA
Tight end
1961–1966

Mike Ditka gained such prominence as the Bears coach in the 1980s that some people forgot how great a football player he was when he joined the team in 1961 out of the University of Pittsburgh. Ditka was the NFL's rookie-of-the-year and became a Hall of Fame tight end who, combining his speed and power to block and catch passes, revolutionized the importance of the position.

As a 6-foot-3, 230-pounder, Ditka resembled an interior lineman more than a wide receiver, but he brought the receiver's skill set of good hands and sharp route-running to the job. One sportswriter said Ditka was built like a cross between a rhino and a battering ram.

"I just like to play football and I only know one way to do it," Ditka said in a 1963 interview. That way usually involved running into and over defenders. Ditka relished the contact and his style typified the manner in which the Bears liked to think of themselves, that they represented a blue-collar city in a blue-collar sport.

Syndicated sports columnist Milton Gross recounted an exchange between Ditka and rugged Green Bay linebacker Ray Nitschke. "Ditka, you're a dirty player and I'm going to get you," the Packer player said. "Too bad you feel that way," Ditka answered. "But you'd better get me first." A perfect Chicago Bear, extolling toughness, refusing to be pushed around, and standing up to a Packer no less.

Halas could be harsh. He was the only NFL coach who made his teams practice on Sundays when they had played on Saturdays. In pursuit of perfection, he loudly let his teams know if their actions on the field displeased him whether they won or not. You could be benched for scoring a critical touchdown if you had disobeyed orders.

One time defensive back J.C. Caroline got Halas' goat, apparently without really trying. Halas did not like the way the Bears had to survive a close encounter with the Baltimore Colts, so the next morning before breakfast he lectured the team about its shortcomings. As time passed, the players' stomachs began growling. Supposedly, Halas completed his speech and asked, "Are there any fucking questions?" Caroline raised his hand and asked, "When are we going to eat, coach?" "J.C.," Halas said of the Indian activist known for his fasts for social change, "Mahatma Gandhi went 40 days and nights without any bread and water. The least you

can do is wait five extra minutes for breakfast." Caroline turned to another player and asked, rather loudly, "What team did Mahatma Gandhi play for?"

Long an all-pro on the offensive line, Stan Jones crossed over to the other side and played defense during the 1963 run. He said he did not know the plays and the only way he absorbed them in time was reviewing alignments written out on cards by Allen.

The season was approaching the home stretch when President John F. Kennedy was assassinated on November 22, 1963. The shooting of a popular president whose youthfulness had invigorated Washington politics, stunned the nation. The country was shocked and paralyzed by the news emanating from Dallas. All television stations immediately went to round-the-clock news broadcasts.

Most normal activity in the United States ceased that Friday. Regularly scheduled events were postponed by the score. Most professional sports

Above: Dick Butkus, the Bears' star linebacker, was a terror on the field. Here, in a 1966 game against Baltimore, he's blocking a pass thrown by fellow Hall of Famer Johnny Unitas. *Bettmann/Corbis*

Right: Members of the Chicago Bears get instruction during National Guard training, including Dick Butkus (left) in 1966. *Bettmann/Corbis*

"It was a great honor to play for Halas. George has to be the No. 1 man in professional football. He held on to the Bears' franchise when many people, including myself, thought he was nuts."
—Red Grange speaking at a sports banquet in 1968.

leagues suspended action. NFL commissioner Pete Rozelle, who said he consulted with JFK's press secretary Pierre Salinger, announced that he was told the president would want the football games to go on. It was easily the most disputed decision Rozelle made during his long and successful career in NFL leadership.

Two days later, on Sunday, November 24, as suspect Lee Harvey Oswald was being shot down by Jack Ruby in the basement of a Dallas police station, the Bears prepared to play the Steelers in Pittsburgh. Bears players were not necessarily opposed to playing. Center Mike Pyle and Ditka both said it was their job and if the game was scheduled they should play it. Ditka said he believed JFK would have said to play. Halas told the players that they were playing "to get people's minds off the assassination." That may or may not have been what Rozelle told Halas and it may or may not have been why the games went on. But nothing else happening in the world that weekend was going to take American citizens' minds off of the shooting death of their president, or the First Lady's blood-stained pink suit.

The Bears played on without either television or radio coverage. They did not play especially well and could easily have lost. Ditka, who was visiting Pittsburgh for the first time since leaving college, made a huge catch and 63-yard run near game's end to prevent defeat. The tie was an unsatisfactory conclusion to an unsatisfactory event. It was only after the game ended that the Bears learned of Oswald's murder. After that game Halas told reporters that Ditka "is going to be one of the greats of the league, if he isn't there already. What desire and determination that young man has."

When the Bears clinched the Western Division they were pitted against their old nemesis, the New York Giants. The Giants still featured many of their top guns from the 1956 team, but now had Y. A. Tittle, the great quarterback on his way to the Hall of Fame, behind center. The game was widely seen as a confrontation between the Bears' defense and the Giants' explosive offense. "There was a feeling of having something to settle with them," said Jones, who had

Dick Butkus with George Halas.
Bill Eppridge/Getty Images

DICK BUTKUS
Middle linebacker
1965–1973

Dick Butkus played defense as if someone was trying to steal his children's lunch money. He hit so hard that running backs wanted to know the license plate of the truck that ran over them. The 6-foot-3, 245-pound linebacker combined force and speed to create fear in enemy ball carriers silly enough to venture into his territory—and the scariest part was that his territory was about as large as Alaska. Butkus came into prominence at the University of Illinois and made an instant impact with the Bears in 1965 as part of the same remarkable draft that brought the team runner Gale Sayers.

Although limited by knee problems, Butkus stated his case for being called the best-ever by recovering 25 fumbles and grabbing 22 interceptions. He was a seven-time NFL all-star in an injury-shortened career.

Butkus' appearance, usually leading with a frown, and topped by closely cropped hair, added to his fearsome reputation. He later admitted he invented some of that persona. "When I went out on the field to warm up," Butkus said, "I would manufacture things to make me mad. If someone on the other team was laughing, I'd pretend he was laughing at me or the Bears."

After an overpowering game during the 1969 season, Butkus provoked Pittsburgh Steelers quarterback Terry Hanratty to gush with superlatives. "I think he's the greatest football player I've ever faced," Hanratty said. "He's the total defensive player."

Brian Piccolo breaks free in a 1967 game
running against the St. Louis Cardinals.
Diamond Images/Getty Images

"Bill George's 35-year-old body looks like an experimental laboratory for a medical school. There are stitch reminders here, operation scars there and cleat wounds almost everywhere."
—*Sportswriter Brent Musberger in the Chicago American in 1966.*

played in the 1956 loss.

The Bears' defense won. It was another cold day at Wrigley Field in late December for the title match and Chicago made Tittle, who had completed 36 touchdown passes that season, look ordinary. With pressure from the front four converging on him and hurrying his throws, Tittle tossed five interceptions. Relying on passing in 8-degree temperatures didn't help. The interceptions helped give the Bears a 14–10 triumph.

The Giants actually scored first on a Tittle to Frank Gifford 14-yard touchdown pass. But the Bears tied the game in the first quarter after a Tittle pass aimed to back Phil King was intercepted by Chicago linebacker Larry Morris whose run produced the most Bears offense of the day. Morris was hauled down on the 5-yard-line and Wade nosed it in from the 2 soon after.

A Don Chandler 13-yard field goal in the second quarter gave the Giants a 10–7 lead at the half. When the Bears retaliated in the third quarter on another short run by Wade for a touchdown, set up by another interception, this one by Ed O'Bradovich, no one thought it would be the end of the scoring. But that was it. The Bears hardly moved the ball all day, accumulating only 93 yards rushing and 129 passing but when the Giants broke through at all, the Bears stole the ball.

When the game ended, Bears players presented the ball to defensive coordinator George Allen. Morris was rewarded with an automobile as the game's Most Valuable Player, but Allen said he would cherish the ball more. Joe Fortunato said that the Giants did exactly what Allen had predicted they would do. "We followed that chart," the linebacker said, identifying the tendencies Allen had highlighted. "We called it [the screen pass O'Bradovich intercepted] in our huddle."

Morris revealed that he and defensive teammates Fred Williams and Bill George joked around before the game that if one of them won the award they would split it three ways. "I had to give Fred and Bill $1,000 each," Morris said.

It was the Bears' first championship in 17 years and

68-year-old George Halas, choking up, said it meant more to him than any other win since the 73–0 destruction of the Redskins in 1940. There was some feeling that Halas, who had stepped away from coaching twice already before, might make his retirement from the sideline permanent after this significant win. However, Halas was going nowhere fast. He felt he had the troops coming back to repeat. After the high of winning a championship, there isn't a team in any professional sport that doesn't believe it can repeat the next year. Nobody's leaving because of graduation and as long as players stay healthy they figure they can do it all over again. But this attitude does not take into the account the unforeseen, whether it be the encroachment of age, decisions to retire, or opposing team improvement that is now peaking.

What happened to the Bears leading into the 1964 season was none-of-the-above. It was much worse. During the championship year, the 6-foot-1, 187-pound Willie Galimore out of Florida A&M, had rushed for 321 yards and caught 13 passes. He was a spot player who made important contributions on occasion, but for 1964, he was being counted on as the top running back, fully functional again after his knee problems of 1962. John Farrington, nicknamed "Bo," was a 6-foot-3, 217-pound wide receiver from Prairie View A&M who caught 21 passes during the title season and made the most of them, averaging 16.0 yards per catch.

In those days, the Bears spent the hottest part of the summer at a training camp in Rensselaer, Indiana, using the facilities of St. Joseph's College. On the night of July 26, after practice, the two players went out. They were driving home in the dark in Galimore's Volkswagen and, perhaps because a directional sign was missing, they missed a turn, the car flipped, sailed over a ditch, and both were killed. Galimore was 29, Farrington 28—neither was wearing a seat-belt. Farrington was thrown from the car. Galimore suffered a broken neck. The players were in the prime of life and in the primes of their careers. Their shattered lives destroyed the spirit of the 1964 team. The Bears did not concentrate well after that, played poorly, and the defending champions started the season 2–7 and finished 5–9. The players were not themselves. They mourned their dead teammates outwardly at first and inwardly afterwards.

When tragedy strikes suddenly, it is absorbed and processed differently by each human being. Outward gestures, to the public, to families, are important, but big, rough, tough men are not allowed to cry in public, and especially in the 1960s were not expected to voice lingering feelings. They were supposed to gather their

JOE FORTUNATO
Linebacker
1955–1966

Joe Fortunato is one of the legion of great linebackers the Bears have been fortunate to have, but who because he was not a middle linebacker was not as glamorized. If he had played for another team, Fortunato might be hailed as the greatest linebacker in that club's history.

Fortunato was originally from Mingo Junction, Ohio. He became a star at Mississippi State and spent 11 years with the Bears. He was drafted in 1952, but his entry to the NFL was delayed until 1955 because of military service.

Fortunato made five NFL pro bowls. He had a special ability for knocking the stuffing out of ball carriers and then recovering loose balls. In all, he recovered 22 fumbles in his career. In addition, Fortunato intercepted 16 passes.

The hard-hitting 6-foot-1, 225-pound outside linebacker played a huge role in the Bears' 1963 championship season. Fortunato had been a participant in the 1956 title game loss to the New York Giants and when the Giants were the opponents for the 1963 championship, he was glad. "We wanted them to feel badly about losing to us," Fortunato said. "So we were all really fired up going into the game."

After retirement, Fortunato stayed with the Bears as an assistant coach for two seasons. He later started an oil services company in Natchez, Mississippi, where he is also an avid fisherman. Fortunato is a member of the Mississippi Sports Hall of Fame and the National Italian-American Sports Hall of Fame.

emotions and move on. It did not seem like they did.

As a symbol, and a common one when a team is afflicted by a death, the Bears played out the season wearing black armbands on their uniforms. It is a sign of respect for the departed and to those who know what a team goes through. Tackle Bob Wetoska said the armbands in some ways just contributed to the overall sense of gloom. "The whole year was a reminder instead of trying to move on," he said.

Although it was not publicized until much later, Halas paid for the college educations of Galimore's three children. His son Marlon played basketball at Florida A&M and son Ron became an NCAA champion gymnast at Iowa State and qualified for the 1980 Olympics.

There was also disgruntlement and hurt feelings among players who believed Halas had not adequately financially rewarded them for producing the 1963 title. The Bears of 1964 in no way resembled the Bears of 1963 except in team name and the names of returnees on the roster. But not in style of play.

It was time for a Bears makeover. The method of acquiring talent had changed dramatically since Halas founded the Bears. In the 1920s, Halas rounded up people he had heard of, knew, had played with, or felt would fit in well. The NFL draft began in the 1930s as a way of distributing players more equally to the haves and have-nots. In the late 1940s, NFL teams had to fight off All-America Football Conference teams who tried to land the best players, but that challenge did not last long and the best teams were accepted into the older league. The situation was different in the mid-

Giants defenders practically rip Gale Sayers jersey off in their attempts to tackle him during a 34–7 loss in 1967.
Corbis

1960s. The American Football League was throwing big money around. From its chronic shortage of cash at its founding in 1960, the league had collected millionaires with deep pockets as owners who were not used to losing at anything they tried.

The AFL was aided by the same ally that the NFL was—national TV. There was more demand for football on the tube and networks which didn't have NFL games, could take AFL games. The infusion of money was much needed and the owners who made fortunes in oil, in silver, in the stock market or real estate not only considered signing established NFL players, they threw their bucks behind signing hot rookies. By 1965, the AFL seemed likely to stick around. The price of landing top-ranked rookies was rising. When the New York Jets' Sonny Werblin signed Alabama's Joe Namath to a

$400,000 contract before he played a down it was clear the rules had changed and that it was going to take big paydays to sign big names.

The player wars were highlighted by organized "baby-sitting" operations. People affiliated with the AFL, the NFL, or certain teams, would keep watch on a draft pick and try to prevent him from even meeting with representatives of the other side. At a time when James Bond was breaking into the movies and copycat spy pictures were the rage, there was almost as much cloak and dagger action in the pro football world. Diversionary tactics with automobiles, and stashing prospects in hotel rooms and wining and dining them were commonplace.

Halas was old-fashioned and despised such ruses. He liked to play upon one of the NFL's strengths—that it was the established league with a long history and that it wasn't going anywhere while the AFL could fold any day. Still recalling the Depression days when he was so poor he had to take out loans just to hang onto the team, Halas was appalled at the six-figure contracts being offered to untried rookies.

It was a miracle that Halas managed to draft Gale Sayers and Dick Butkus in the same draft, but signing them while AFL bloodhounds chased after them, too, was an against-the-grain achievement. Halas had to spend more money than he wanted to, had to reward rookies who hadn't played for him, and pay them more than veterans who had won him a championship. He signed Sayers out of Kansas and Butkus from his alma mater, the University of Illinois. They lived up to their reputations and became two of the greatest Bears players of all time. However, both men had careers cut short because of knee injuries and they were never surrounded by the needed talent to enjoy the team success of their immediate predecessors.

If Bill George invented the position of middle linebacker, Butkus fine-tuned it. The best defensive players made their presence felt on the gridiron in ways that put the fear of the Almighty into opponents. They were assigned positions, but made the entire field their personal fiefdoms. Running backs and ends knew that if they carried the ball they might meet up with Butkus anywhere without advance notice and have their bells rung.

Bill George was gone. He wanted to play one more season and he signed with the Rams for 1966. He had played the 1963 season with neck pains after an automobile accident, never knowing another car accident would take his life in 1982. "The minute that guy [Butkus] walked into camp, I started packing my gear," George said. "There was no way he wasn't going to be great."

Sayers raced for 22 touchdowns as a rookie, still an

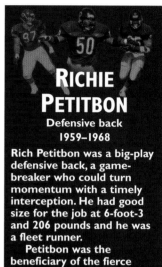

RICHIE PETITBON

Defensive back
1959–1968

Rich Petitbon was a big-play defensive back, a game-breaker who could turn momentum with a timely interception. He had good size for the job at 6-foot-3 and 206 pounds and he was a fleet runner.

Petitbon was the beneficiary of the fierce Bears pass rush. When Doug Atkins hurried the quarterback, sometimes the throw missed the receiver by a mile and landed in Petitbon's hands. It was as if he had radar. In his long career he intercepted 48 passes, including six for return yardage of 212 yards in 1962. Petitbon led the Bears in interceptions three different seasons. His 101-yard touchdown return with an intercepted pass in 1962 was a career highlight. And when he wasn't intercepting passes, Petitbon also showed off his gift for pouncing on fumbles.

A key member of the 1963 championship team, Petitbon came out of New Orleans and played his college football at Tulane. After his playing days ended he became a long-time assistant coach, and eventually, head coach, of the Washington Redskins.

Petitbon always marveled at how important the Bears seemed to the fans of Chicago. The city was one of the biggest in the country, was more sophisticated than most, but fans seemed to have a special place in their emotions and commitment to the Bears, ranking them above the community's other professional sports franchises. "I think Chicago has always been a Bears town," Petitbon has said. "The Bears have always seemed to capture the heart of Chicago."

Bobby Douglass was one of the greatest running quarterbacks in NFL history, but here he opts to let his star running back, Gayle Sayers, do the work against Cleveland on November 30, 1969.
Tony Tomsic/Getty Images

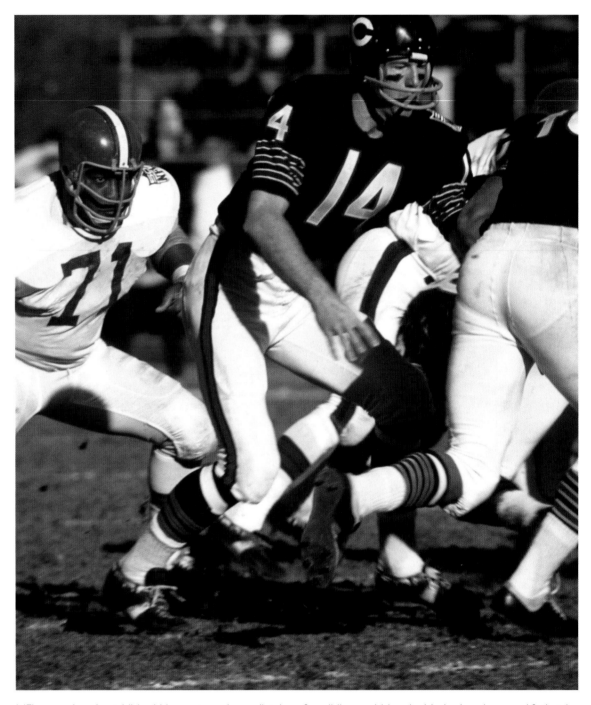

NFL record, and established his greatness immediately. Butkus was his equal on the other side of the ball and Halas found himself lobbying for those around the league to vote for both of them for co-rookie of the year. Butkus' persona was evident quickly. He was not a big talker usually, but spoke more eloquently with his body slamming ball carriers to the turf. His intentions were clear. "I want to be recognized as the best, no doubt about it," Butkus said. "When they say 'All-Pro middle linebacker,' I want them to mean Butkus."

Butkus, of Lithuanian heritage and the youngest of five siblings, said he decided when he was 10 that he would become a pro football player, but separated his determination from other kids' fantasy. "A lot of kids say that," Butkus said. "But I don't really believe they're really serious about it and willing to devote their whole energy to doing it."

His hits were so vicious that he swiftly gained a reputation as a player no one wanted to cross and some reporters delighted in describing him with details that made him sound more animal than human. After a while, Butkus took exception. Nasty, fierce, killer, angriest—all of the descriptions seemed so negative to him. "It makes me sad sometimes," Butkus said. "Nobody thinks I can talk, much less write my name." Butkus could do that and more, though more diverse sides of him emerged after retirement when he started acting in Hollywood.

There was no play acting on the field when Butkus was around. He took his job seriously, had trained for it since he was a youth, and was being proclaimed the best in the world. Things went fine in 1965, a good recovery from the heartbreak of 1964. The problem was that Butkus could not be a one-man defense. And the other problem was that Sayers could not be a one-man offense.

The slide into mediocrity began in 1966 and reached its depths with a 1–13 season in 1969, the worst in team history. Off-field problems, including medical bulletins on what Sayers and Butkus could or could not do on their rapidly deteriorating knees, dominated the news.

After a 7–6–1 season in 1967, in 1968 Halas announced his retirement from coaching. It was the fourth time, counting his World War II absence in the Navy, that he excused himself from the Bears bench. This time it sounded permanent. Halas read his retirement statement three different times to groups of different reporters. "The time has come for me to retire as head coach of the Bears," Halas said 48 years after he founded the team. "I have made this decision with considerable reluctance, but no regrets. There was a strong temptation to coach for another season, but looking at the practical realities, I am stepping aside now because I can no longer keep up with the physical demands of coaching the team on Sunday afternoons."

His voice was fine, but Halas was 73 years old, walking with a cane and suffering with an arthritic hip that made it difficult to chase referees and yell at them. There was no suggestion that Halas was mellowing, just physically slowing down.

A few years earlier it seemed certain that Halas' successor would be George Allen, the brilliant defensive mind and workaholic who was another on the short list of football men close enough to Papa Bear to be considered family. Allen was very ambitious, anxious to become a head coach, and at 43 (or 47 depending on contrasting reports) impatient not to wait longer. Allen said Halas promised he would be the next Bears coach, but Halas wasn't retiring. Although he was under contract to the Bears as an assistant Allen felt he should be allowed to accept the opportunity to become head coach of the Los Angeles Rams. He was stunned when Halas filed a breach of contract lawsuit against him. And, although Allen led the Rams to an 8–6 record, he had to fight the bitter

Bears coach Jim Dooley pacing the sidelines in a 1968 game.
Bettmann/Corbis

Vince Lombardi, after he moved on to the Washington Redskins, coaches an exhibition game against the Bears in 1969.
Corbis

GALE SAYERS MADE MAGIC WITH HIS FEET

It is not recorded anywhere that the first time Gale Sayers ran around his family home as a toddler that he made observers gasp with awe. But that was certainly true later whenever he showed up in a new venue wearing football gear.

Being fast is one thing, but being as wispy as the wind, being as difficult to pin down as the atmospheric conditions because of that innate sense of elusiveness top-notch running backs possess when they are twisting out of danger is what made Sayers special. Catch him if you can. Almost no one could when he was right.

Sayers grew up in Omaha and his family was far from wealthy. In post-football years he has been an avid fisherman, but as a youth he was a hunter. Often, he shot rabbits. "I can shoot," he said. "A lot of times that's all we had to eat."

In college, Sayers was known as the "Kansas Comet," startling the foes of Kansas University football each time he raced past them or around them. Sayers was selected by the Bears in the first round in 1965, right next to Dick Butkus in the draft, a George Halas coup that might never be matched.

At the time the NFL was at war for talent with the upstart American Football League. Sayers was also drafted by the Kansas City Chiefs. Years later he reflected that he made the right choice. "I'm so glad I chose the Bears over Kansas City," Sayers said. "I met a man named George Halas. He was like a father to me."

From the moment he made the minute-and-a-half transition from college to professional football, Sayers was a highlight film on two

Superstar back Gale Sayers in the open field on his way to a 96-yard touchdown run against Minnesota in 1965. *Bettmann/Corbis*

quickly churning legs. And from the moment the young black man from Nebraska met the aging patriarch of the Bears—then 70—theirs was a most unlikely friendship. Their respect and fondness for one another transcended most of Halas' owner–player relationships. "He was the first man on the field and the last one to leave the field," Sayers said in an autobiography, *My Life and Times*. "He was just a great individual. That inspired me, just seeing him on the field."

It didn't matter if the footing was solid, or slippery, Sayers was one step ahead of defenders. As a rookie, during a 14-game season, Sayers scored 22 touchdowns. He proved he could run from scrimmage, make yardage on pass receptions in the open field, run back kicks and punts. As a kick-off returner, Sayers routinely averaged more than 30 yards a run-back. In a December 1965 game against the San Francisco 49ers, Sayers scored six touchdowns. After that performance, Halas was as stunned as any other witness, calling Sayers' achievement, "the greatest exhibition I have ever seen by one man in one game."

Sayers said fans always ask him about that game, but he doesn't brag about it. Thinking back to the muddy field, Sayers said simply, "I was the only one who didn't fall down."

Everyone assumes that is his favorite game as a pro, but it is not. Sayers chooses a game played less than two months earlier. In an action-packed contest, the Bears out-lasted the Minnesota Vikings,

45–37, and Sayers scored four touchdowns. Unlike the 49ers game, which was a 61–20 rout, each six points Sayers added to the Chicago total against the Vikings was meaningful. "That was my best game," Sayers said.

Sayers, whose playing vitals were 6 feet and 198 pounds, was forever linked to Dick Butkus once they were drafted by the Bears together. They had never met before a college all-star game and then Sayers met Butkus the wrong way—being tackled by him. "After that ballgame, I knew why they drafted him," Sayers said. "When you talk about middle linebackers, he's No. 1. He knocked the crap out of people."

Although it did not always seem so, Butkus did remember that he and Sayers were on the same side, calling him "cool" and saying they had a "great relationship. Gale was really something to watch."

In a question-and-answer session in 2001, Sayers was asked who was the player who hit the hardest when he was playing. He mentioned Packers linebacker Ray Nitschke, Rams defensive end Deacon Jones, and Lions linebacker Joe Schmidt. Then he injected Butkus into the conversation. "I've said many times that my teammate Dick Butkus hit me as hard in practice as anybody in a game," Sayers added.

Sayers and Butkus figured to be the foundation of a new Bears dynasty, but it didn't work out. They became friends, but they also had one thing too many in common. Both of them suffered serious knee injuries that forced them into early retirement. Sayers ripped up one knee first, bounced back from surgery, and then ripped up the other knee.

Retired by 1971 at age 29, Sayers became the youngest player inducted into the Hall of Fame at 34. He was elected in his first year of eligibility and that was unexpected because of the shortness of his career. "I only played in 68 ballgames, in four-and-a-half years," Sayers said. "And I got in on my first time. No doubt that was the highlight of my career."

After his playing days, Sayers switched to athletic administration. He became an assistant athletic director at Kansas and then athletic director at Southern Illinois University. Then he moved back to the Chicago area and started an extremely successful computer services company.

In 1994, the Bears held a ceremony at Soldier Field appropriately retiring Sayers' No. 40 jersey and Butkus' No. 51 jersey on the same day.

Sayers, who still follows the Bears closely and attends home games, sometimes makes autograph signing appearances in the Chicago area. The fans who seek his signature remember his super nova burst across the pro football landscape, or they just want to meet the legend they have read about.

Sayers breaks free from the Baltimore defense during a 13–0 victory over the Colts on December 5, 1965.
Diamond Images/Getty Images

Gale Sayers' 6-Touchdown Game

December 12, 1965

Bears 61, San Francisco 49ers 20

Sayers 80-yard pass reception from quarterback Rudy Bukich

Sayers 21-yard run

Sayers 7-yard run

Sayers 50-yard run

Sayers 1-yard run

Sayers 85-yard punt return

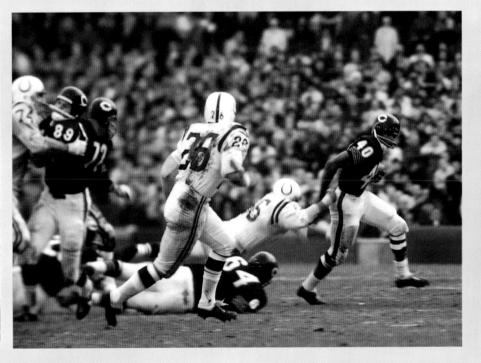

Linebacker Dick Butkus
intercepts a Miami Dolphins pass
in a 1969 exhibition game in the
Orange Bowl.
Bettmann/Corbis

war with Halas in court. The court ultimately said Halas was right, but Halas merely wanted to prove a point, not remove Allen from his job.

When the teams met in Los Angeles in September of 1966, the Rams won 31–17. During warmups on the field, Allen walked towards Halas, but Halas turned his back and walked away. Later, Halas said he had yelled over his shoulder that he had to catch up with his team and would come back. But he never returned. There was no post-game handshake at midfield, either.

Allen's version was that he was going to ask Halas to pose for a picture and that he had also tried to shake hands, but was refused. "I'll trade that handshake

for a victory any day," Allen said. "Winning any game is very satisfactory. But to beat the Bears and Halas is something special." It was a sad ending to a relationship that had seemed to promise good things ahead for the Bears when Halas left the bench.

The season of 1966 turned out to be Mike Ditka's last year playing for the Bears. He thought he deserved more money—which was probably true given what younger AFL-pursued players made. Halas held fast in not paying Ditka big bucks. Harsh words were exchanged and Ditka was shipped to the Philadelphia Eagles and then on to the Dallas Cowboys where he began his coaching career. But that was later and it was another unfortunate parting from the Bears. A player who seemed to be the perfect Bear, one who was a man after Halas' own heart, was dumped.

Jim Dooley, the respected wide receiver, and one of the stable of Halas' fine assistant coaches, succeeded the boss as head man in 1967, but his four-year tenure was a disaster, ushering in one of the longest, most painful stretches of losing in Bears history.

While the Bears were becoming the league's favorite soap opera story, peace broke out between the NFL and the AFL. In 1965, Lombardi's Packers were back on top, champs again. In 1966, they repeated. And they made it three titles in a row in 1967. Most significantly, when the first NFL-AFL, take-all-the-marbles game took place in January of 1967, the Packers made history by defeating Kansas City. A year later the Packers bested the Oakland Raiders. By then people were calling this annual contest "The Super Bowl."

But there was nothing super about the way the Bears played after Halas stepped aside.

Not for years.

A frustrated Dick Butkus (center) and fellow Bears defensemen argue with an official during a 31–14 loss to Minnesota on November 2, 1969. It was Chicago's seventh-straight loss to open the season.
Bettmann/Corbis

1960s CHICAGO BEARS YEAR BY YEAR

Year	Record
1960	5–6–1
1961	8–6
1962	9–5
1963	11–1–2
1964	5–9
1965	9–5
1966	5–7–2
1967	7–6–1
1968	7–7
1969	1–13

CHAPTER 6
THE 1970s: A HARD ROAD TO WALTER PAYTON

When aging George Halas stepped down as Bears coach because his body was falling apart, he didn't expect his team to fall apart, too. But the late 1960s through the early 1970s were some of the most frustrating times in team history.

Halas had pulled off one of the greatest player acquisition coups in NFL history by plucking Dick Butkus and Gale Sayers from college campuses in the only draft that produced two Hall of Famers for one team. But he could never piece together the important support pieces around them and their repeated knee injuries diminished their effectiveness.

Athletes the caliber of Butkus and Sayers look at themselves as invulnerable. They have ridden the wave to success because they could do things better than anyone else. Their bodies are their vehicles to glory. The first time Sayers injured a knee (and he ruined both of them) he was in denial. His rehab thrust him into depression. He thought he would never be the same again. Indeed, he had lost some speed, lost some of god's gift that enabled him to cut so abruptly and duck tacklers. But he rebuilt, overcame, rushed for more than 1,000 yards again and led the NFL in rushing. Twice was too much and after a demoralizing training camp and playing just two games Sayers retired following the 1971 season. Sayers, Halas, the fans, had every right to feel cheated. Sayers departed with class, with dignity and some sadness. The Gale Sayers era ended before it truly got started, leaving flashes of memory, a small collection of film testifying that his greatness was genuine, not the product of imagination.

Butkus' departure was messier, more complicated, but in essence for the same reason, the hinges that held his legs steady were failing. The knees that enabled him to roam the field from sideline to sideline were battered into submission, afflicted with rips and tears. Butkus took shots, pain pills, all types of artificial aids so he could continue playing with a deteriorating arthritic knee.

Far right: Dick Butkus (left) and George Seals (67) shut down Green Bay Packer Donny Anderson in a 1970 game. *Bettmann/Corbis*

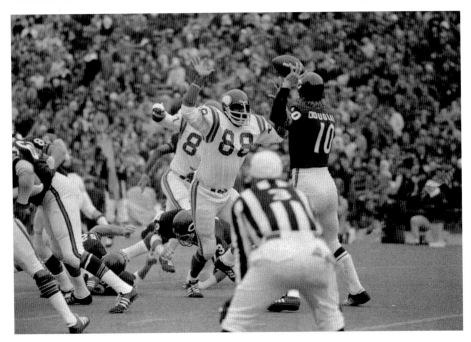

Above: Bears quarterback Bobby Douglass is about to get creamed by Minnesota Vikings defensive tackle Alan Page in a 1971 game. *Bettmann/Corbis*

Butkus' problems mounted over time. The hits were costly. At the start of the 1973 season he told a reporter he would continue playing "until I can't do a pretty good job anymore." "Pretty good" was not an expression in Butkus' vocabulary normally. He was an all-or-nothing guy. For Butkus football was about greatness, being the best. He expressed concern that when he retired "I'll have to have something done to it [his knees] in order to walk right."

Butkus had been a warrior his entire career and it looked as if he was going to be carried out on his shield. By this point in his career, however, Butkus, who did not shy away from the persona of "The Monster of the Midway," was feeling misunderstood, feeling his image was distorted and exaggerated. He was appalled that newspaper stories portrayed him in such extreme language that he might have been mistaken for someone on the Most Wanted wall at the post office rather than a face in the football program.

Butkus' reputation had ballooned to cartoonish magnitude. In an NFL players' poll, he was chosen the meanest player in the league. He was referred to in print as The Animal or Mr. Mean. He was accused of biting an official. He was portrayed in the media as the second coming of Godzilla, a man bent on destruction regardless of who got in his way. A sampling of headlines included: "Never Met Man He Didn't Hate." "Butkus: Man or Monster?" "Butkus a Robot of Destruction."

"I went through all the stuff for the Bears here [in Chicago], the bad years, but the fans embrace you. They say, 'Stay. This is your town.' The memories are so great, playing at Wrigley Field, playing at Soldier Field."
—Doug Buffone, Bears linebacker 1966–79.

"Butkus Named No. 1 NFL Meanie." "Human Bulldozer." The man possessed a more intimidating glare than Sonny Liston just before a heavyweight bout. Accurate or hyperbolic, there was no denying that Butkus was the king of sanctioned Sunday violence.

Yet, in a 1971 *Miami News* story, the reporter said Butkus was back-tracking from the image of ferocity. "He is sub-human, see, something the Chicago Bears uncage on Sundays and the occasional Monday. It is an image he helped create, but now he begs off." At the time, Butkus said, "I'm not promoting that animal stuff. People put that on you and it stays with you." Butkus had fostered the image early in his career, once famously saying that he would never deliberately plan to hurt someone "unless it was, you know—important—like a league game or something."

DOUG BUFFONE
Linebacker
1966–1979

Despite a long career with the Bears Doug Buffone had the unfortunate timing of being born too soon or too late to be a member of any championship team. He was a highly skilled, hard-nosed linebacker who made an impact with losing teams during a grim period in franchise history, though late in his career he was part of two playoff teams.

Buffone may not be as well known for his exploits as some other former Bears linebackers, but he had some remarkable games and remarkable seasons for Chicago. In 1972, Buffone recorded 158 tackles and he topped 100 tackles in seven seasons. In a 1974 game against New Orleans, Buffone had 11 solo tackles. In his career, Buffone collected 24 interceptions and during the 1968 season he nailed quarterbacks for sacks 18 times.

Buffone grew up in Western Pennsylvania, the son of Italian immigrants, and he played collegiately as a center and linebacker at Louisville, where he led the team in tackles three years in a row. Buffone was a fourth-round draft pick of the Bears and was also selected by the AFL's San Diego Chargers.

After retiring, Buffone remained a fixture on the Chicago sports scene through his involvement with the old Chicago Bruisers Arena Football League team and more prominently through broadcast work. Buffone hosted his own show for 14 years on Fox Sports Net Chicago, is a morning sportscaster on WSCR and helped produce other local sports figures' broadcast efforts.

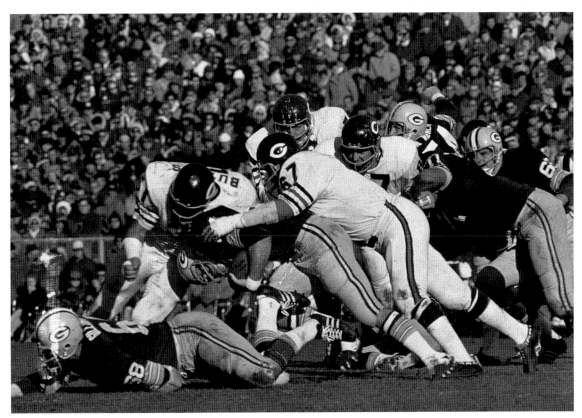

"I have left game strategy to the coaches, although it has been most difficult at times not to interfere."
—George Halas in 1974 when his team was playing badly.

In 1970, Butkus had said he didn't like anyone on the field, so he didn't get involved with other players. Within a year or so he was saying he didn't want to see anyone get hurt on the field since he knew so many players well. Before you knew it, in one of the unlikeliest couplings since Cupid twanged a bow, Butkus was making a recording of Shakespeare's sonnets. The pairing did not shoot to the top of the charts.

The image of indestructibility was unraveling. Hobbling some of the time, Butkus could no longer make the same plays that made him famous. He could no longer strike fear into the hearts of men of equal size and speed who might be looking for a little payback, as well. For some time Butkus suspected that

treatment he received for his failing knee was going to have long-term repercussions. He wanted more doctors' opinions, not just to rely on the word of the team physician. There is often an uneasy peace between sports teams' hired doctors and the athletes they treat. Although the doctors have a responsibility to their patients above all, they also work for the club, and the club wants to hear how soon the player can come back. The player works for the club, too, and he wants to hear how soon he can come back. The player also wants to be healthy when he returns to the field. He also wants the comfort of knowing that nothing he does right now will impact his life after retirement.

The ugly break-up of the Bears and Butkus played out in newspapers and on TV stations. Butkus charged that the team knowingly injected him with medication that gradually ruined his right knee, that he had been forced to play in 1972 and 1973 even though there was risk to his knee, that he would never be able to play football again, and that his knee might be wrecked for life. In May of 1974, only a few months after he played his last NFL game, Butkus sued the Bears for $1.6 million.

Bears defenders including 57, Don Rives and 60, Wally Chambers, try to stop the San Francisco 49ers in a 1974 game.
Bettmann/Corbis

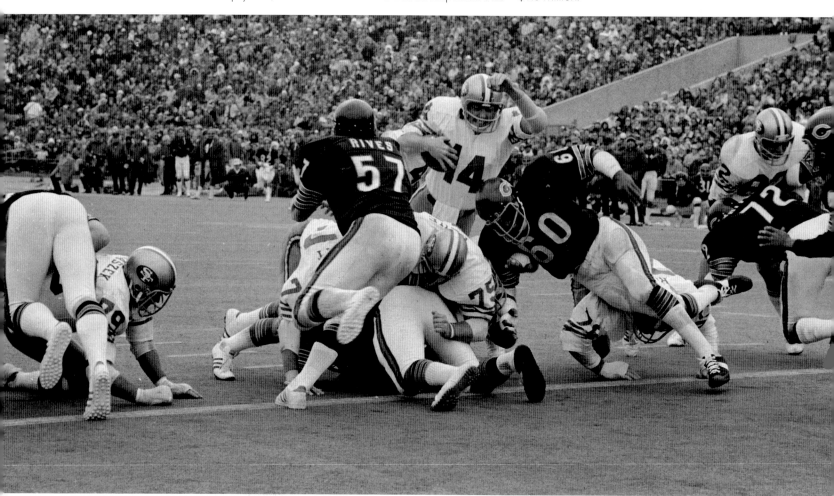

Before going to court, Butkus tried to settle with the Bears. When he filed the case, Halas was disappointed, saddened, and angered. Then he got nasty, saying Butkus' negotiations were a fraud. "It also seems eminently clear that all Dick is interested in is sitting in Florida and collecting his paychecks for the next four years," Halas said. Butkus eventually received a large payment from the team, but he and the Bears were estranged for years.

A major change for the Bears kicked off the 1970s. Because of a National Football League rule mandating the use of stadiums with a minimum seating capacity of 50,000, the Bears had to forsake their long-time abode of Wrigley Field and move to Soldier Field for the start of the 1971 season.

After a half century of playing at Wrigley on the North Side, the Bears had a home that was overlooking Lake Michigan in the downtown South Loop. Soldier Field had a long history as host of sporting events. The first football game of any kind in Soldier Field was a 1924 Notre Dame–Northwestern encounter. The 1927 Jack Dempsey–Gene Tunney heavyweight title fight took place there. Army met Navy in football at Soldier Field in 1926. When Notre Dame played the University of Southern California at Soldier Field in 1927, 123,000 fans attended. The Bears and the Chicago Cardinals met at Soldier Field in 1926, the first pro game played in the stadium. But even now,

Ed O'Bradovich was one of the Bears' most ornery defenders in the 1960s and early 1970s. Here he grabs a hold of San Francisco running back Doug Cunningham in a game in November 1970.
Tony Tomsic/Getty Images

Bears star running back Walter Payton dives over the top of Cowboys defender Thomas Henderson for a touchdown in a 1976 game.
Bettmann/Corbis

Far right: Quarterback Bobby Douglass throws under pressure against a Redskins pass rush during a game in Washington on December 15, 1974.
Nate Fine/NFL/Getty Images

Below: Walter Payton seems like a missile flying over the Green Bay Packers line for a first down in a 1976 game.
Corbis

the Bears have spent more time at Wrigley Field than at Soldier Field. Still, Wrigley was a baseball diamond first. That made for weird configurations. Football players being chased by tacklers fell into dugouts often enough for them eventually to be screened off with yellow police crime scene tape.

Around the time the Bears shifted to Soldier Field, there was a trend in stadium construction to build soulless, all-purpose municipal stadiums to be shared by football and baseball teams. Veterans Stadium in Philadelphia served the Phillies and Eagles. Three Rivers Stadium in Pittsburgh housed the Pirates and Steelers. So the Bears were moving counter to the trend.

Generations have followed not realizing that the Bears ever played at Wrigley Field, which has only grown in stature as a classic American ballpark in recent decades, but many historical Bears memories were made in that building. Sayers, for one, said he liked playing at Wrigley Field more than Soldier Field.

The saddest commentary on the Bears in the early 1970s was that they were making more news off the field than on. The perennial contenders were striving for mediocrity, cheering a 6–8 record in 1970 after the horrendous 1–13 of 1969. Once again the search for reliable quarterbacks took Halas everywhere but Afghanistan. Two decades had passed since Sid Luckman retired and at a time when the pro game was opening up and the passing game was taking on increased prominence, the Bears could find no one who challenged Luckman's statistics and leadership.

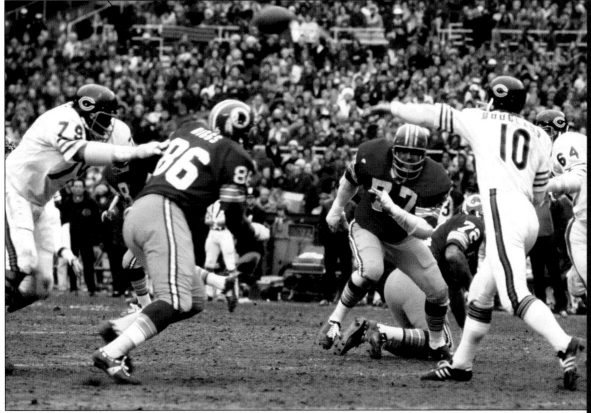

Bobby Douglass ran better than he threw. Jack Concannon, from Boston College, took over for half of 1969 and when turned loose as the No. 1 man in 1970 was OK. He completed 50.4 percent of his passes for 16 touchdowns, but he also threw 18 interceptions. Douglass was the main man again for the next three years.

The coaches (and they were turning over equally swiftly) gave Gary Huff a try in a 4–10 1974 season. He completed 50.2 percent of his passes, but huffed and puffed his way to 17 interceptions and only 6 touchdowns. From 1972 to 1974, the Bears were coached by the ever-expanding Abe Gibron, a one-time lineman whose playing weight of 243 pounds was a number from his distant past. Gibron was affable with the players, inviting them over for cookouts, but sharp with reporters. He had trouble keeping his pants up around his waist on the sideline.

Things were going badly and Halas didn't like it. His pride was affronted. Just because he couldn't coach didn't mean the Bears couldn't win. The man who prized loyalty so much it might as well have been one of his children, went outside the team to hire a new general manager. He brought in Jim Finks, a future Hall of Famer, and gave him orders to fix things. Finks fired Gibron, presumably not over dinner. Gibron announced that he was glad he was "one of the few

NFL head coaches, not one of the 50,000 sports writers."

In 1975, Jack Pardee, a one-time linebacker who spent most of his long NFL career with the Los Angeles Rams, became the third Bears coach since Halas' retreat to the front office. Bob Avellini, a Maryland product, replaced Huff behind center, but the team was still 4–10. It looked like more of the same. But the Bears improved to 7–7 in 1976. Somehow Avellini hung on to his job despite sub-par numbers.

Pardee, an accomplished defender, had improved the defense, but the other reason the Bears showed improvement on offense, despite passing deficiencies, was the addition of a prized running back in 1975. This rookie named Walter Payton looked like he might become something. Payton was only 5-foot-10 and at Jackson State he had not played in the toughest tier of college football. But on raw ability alone the scouts gushed about his potential. The Bears were bad enough to pick high in the draft and they did not waste their selection.

In Payton's first season he shared the running back slot with Roland Harper. He gained 679 yards on the ground and caught 33 passes. There were some growing pains, some adjustments, but by 1976 Payton was an all-star. He rushed for 1,390 yards and scored 13 touchdowns. As had been proven many times,

BOBBY DOUGLASS
Quarterback
1969–1975

Bobby Douglass was supposed to be the Bears' quarterback of the future when they selected him out of Kansas in the second round in 1969. But few players have experienced as a bizarre a career in Bears' annals as Douglass.

If there was one thing Douglass was not was a traditional signal caller and drop-back passer. He was 6-foot-3 and weighed 225 pounds, at the time more suitable for a fullback's role. Douglass was a hybrid, a quarterback who was a better runner than passer, a fullback who was a better runner than blocker. Basically, as a quarterback, Douglass was a good running back. He seemed sorely in need of coaching.

Douglass set records for quarterback running. In 1972, he rushed for 968 yards with a phenomenal 6.9 yards per carry and scored 8 touchdowns. The yardage mark stood for 34 years until Michael Vick ran for 1,039 yards in two more games. Douglass' lifetime rushing average of 6.5 was extraordinary. However, Douglass' passing accuracy hovered in the 45 percent range and in his career that included other stopovers, he threw for 36 touchdowns and 64 interceptions, which just wasn't good enough.

Gale Sayers contended that Douglass' undoing was throwing 90 mph whether he was aiming short or long. "Douglass threw the ball so hard that he had his Bears teammates ducking in practice because they didn't want to get hit by the ball," Sayers said.

GARY FENCIK
Safety
1976–1987

Gary Fencik graduated from Yale and definitely received a post-graduate education in football. Fencik, a rare Ivy League player in the pros, came along at a time when the club was down, but was one of the newcomers added through various drafts and trades who upgraded the lineup. Fencik, who was acquired from the Miami Dolphins, suffered through the Bears' difficult times, but had the satisfaction of staying around long enough to be involved, active and contributing when the good times returned and the Bears became Super Bowl champs in the mid-1980s.

Fencik put up such big numbers on stat sheets from his safety position he could have been mistaken for an offensive player. Fencik stood 6-foot-1 and weighed 194 pounds, but in the grand old tradition of the Bears, he smacked opposing players with disproportionate strength.

During his decade-plus with the Bears, Fencik intercepted 38 passes, recovered 14 fumbles, and as long as he was in the neighborhood anyway, recorded two quarterback sacks. Linebacker Doug Plank and Fencik as a pair were referred to as "The Hit Men."

A dashing figure, Fencik made his teammates envious by posing for the cover of GQ magazine in 1986 and being pictured in Playboy while shopping in Chicago with the Playmate centerfold. After he retired, Fencik worked as a sports commentator, particularly on football, and in the financial world in Chicago.

Bears coach Jack Pardee on the sidelines talking with Tom Hicks in 1976.
Michael Zagaris/Getty Images

there was no such thing as one-man teams in the NFL, but Walter Payton didn't come to Chicago to lose football games. In 1977, the Bears recorded their first winning mark in a decade, finishing 9–5 and qualifying for the playoffs.

It was as if the sun came out in Chicago after a 10-year solar eclipse. There was hope for the city's most beloved franchise again, especially since the Bears won six games in a row to end the regular season. Maybe the old man hadn't lost it completely, maybe the game had not completely passed him by. Halas could still put a team together and he just might make another run at a championship. It is that eternal optimism that feeds fan amnesia.

A certain amount of serendipity accompanied the advancement of the Bears into the playoffs at all. The Bears lost two of their first three games, four of their first six, and five of their first eight. They were poster children for treading water. Inconsistency was a trademark and there was little hint that the team would regroup and make the type of run it did to reach the playoffs. But all of a sudden, in what had become an alien concept in Chicago, the Bears started winning. They beat the Kansas City Chiefs, 28–27, in a morale booster. Then they ripped off wins against Minnesota, Detroit, Tampa Bay and Green Bay.

Going into the final weekend of the season, the Bears needed to beat the New York Giants. In other action, one team needed to beat another team by

"I'm just proud of my team. They stayed in there and played as hard as they could. The game meant a lot to them."
—Coach Jack Pardee after his Bears lost a 1977 playoff game 37–7 to Dallas in the team's first post-season appearance since 1963.

more than 30 points. And they needed one team to fare this way to set up a ripple effect that way. The number of tie-breakers lined up that could affect the Bears' future could only have been sorted out by Albert Einstein. "We had to weave our way through in order to get to the post-season," said 1970s tackle Dan Jiggetts.

The Bears might not have been able to figure out all the details without PhDs, but they knew they just had to win. That was no picnic, either. The Bears bested New York, 12–9 in overtime, before 76,626 fans, but when the game ended other teams were still playing and the Bears still didn't know if they were in or out. Players showered and dressed—and hung around. Some listened to the radio. Some watched TV. One by one the other games ended. Whatever the odds, everything fell Chicago's way. The Bears were in.

It was a satisfying year, but when the Bears got

Far left: Gary Fencik sets himself for the next play during an October 1979 game against the Buffalo Bills.
George Gojkovich/Getty Images

Defensive coordinator Buddy Ryan watches his charges while smoking his pipe at practice in 1978.
Jonathan Daniel/Getty Images

waxed, 37–7, in the first round of the playoffs, by a team led by Roger Staubach and Tony Dorsett, it was apparent that they still had miles to go. Avellini was intercepted four times and sacked three. Cowboy defensive back Charlie Waters picked off three. The

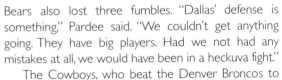

"The Chicago Bears of the late 1970s and early 1980s were not a particularly successful franchise. Actually, they weren't good at all. They lost more often than they won. They were occasionally humiliated by stronger opponents."
—*Hall of Fame running back Walter Payton, a rookie in 1975.*

Bears also lost three fumbles. "Dallas' defense is something," Pardee said. "We couldn't get anything going. They have big players. Had we not had any mistakes at all, we would have been in a heckuva fight."

The Cowboys, who beat the Denver Broncos to win the Super Bowl a few weeks later, had all of the ingredients. The poised leadership of Staubach, who had won a Heisman Trophy at Navy and turned pro late after serving in the Navy, was a primer in quarterback play. "Roger does everything so well," said Bears linebacker Doug Buffone. "He's the guy that beats you. He hits the right man for the defense we called, or he pulls it down and runs."

Even Payton was bottled up, rushing for just 60 yards on an average of 3.1 per carry. He was testy and out of sorts afterwards, smarting from a hit that knocked him partially senseless. "I got hit in the head and just don't remember," Payton said of game details. "I feel real bad. I wish you fellows would give me a break."

While the Bears were in the dumps, scuffling to escape their doomsday years, the NFL was growing, expanding, becoming more ingrained in the American psyche as THE sport. *Monday Night Football* took to the airwaves in 1970, a major opportunity for the league to change the viewing habits of TV watchers by intruding into prime time. Roone Arledge's brainstorm paid off happily for ABC and transformed the sleeping habits of millions on a work night. The NFL was becoming a hotter television property than *All in the Family*, *Happy Days*, or *Laverne and Shirley*. Not that anyone thought of the Bears as family fare at the time. Chances were you were not going to get a happy ending. And chances were that Archie Bunker or The Fonz were better known than anyone Chicago inserted at quarterback.

Pardee parlayed his success bringing the Bears into the playoffs into a new job as coach of the Washington Redskins, a team he had played for and Finks hired Neill Armstrong to coach the Bears. Not the Neil Armstrong who walked on the moon, but a Neill Armstrong willing to accept a task that could make

Bears coach Mike Ditka called Walter Payton the best football player of all time.
Ron Vesely/Getty Images

WALTER PAYTON
Running back
1975–1987

The Bears' No. 1 draft pick of 1975 came out of historically black Jackson State to become the NFL's all-time leading rusher. Nicknamed "Sweetness," the description did not fit Payton's on-field style. At 5-foot-10 and 200 pounds, Payton was hardly a behemoth, but rather than run around defenders he frequently chose to run over them. "Walter had that ability to deliver the blow, kind of get a stalemate, and keep on running," said Bears teammate Gary Fencik.

Payton rushed for 16,726 yards, a 4.4 yards per carry average, caught 492 passes and scored 125 touchdowns. Selected for nine pro bowls, Payton owned 16 NFL records when he retired. His jersey number 34 was retired by the Bears and he was elected to the Hall of Fame in 1993.

Payton was revered by teammates for his work ethic and sense of humor and they were shocked when he died at age 45 from liver disease. Mike Ditka, who coached Payton, refused to limit his praise to Payton's running capability, saying he might have been the best football player ever. Overlooked except by football insiders since fans don't watch for subtleties, was that Payton was also an exceptional blocker. "You have to look at the complete football player," Ditka said.

Bears linebacker Doug Buffone, who said he was fortunate to play four years with Gale Sayers and four years with Payton, loved watching Payton run. "Walter was terrific," Buffone said. "Walter would take three people with him."

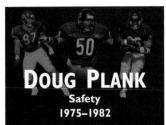

DOUG PLANK

Safety
1975–1982

Doug Plank was Dick Butkus' younger, smaller cousin when it came to making ball carriers grunt. Plank was not huge at 6-foot and 200 pounds, but he generated so much force that runners would swear they had been blind-sided by a rocket ship.

Plank attended Ohio State but was a late bloomer. He did not start at first as a Buckeye and did not think he had a chance to play pro ball. Plank also resembled Bronko Nagurski on the field, because of his relentless aggression and disregard for his own body. The Bears did not draft him until the 12th round but, displaying the type of heart not measured in statistics, Plank made the roster. Then he kept wreaking enough havoc on the field to get into the starting lineup.

When Buddy Ryan became the Bears' defensive coordinator he saw Plank as a kindred spirit. Plank became the symbol of the Bears' Super Bowl-winning "46" defense. Plank liked to say that the defense was named "46" after he went to Ryan's house, fixed his water softener, and endeared himself to Ryan's wife. Then Plank backed down and said it was just because his position happened to be in the middle of the formation and Ryan called all the players by their numbers when they watched film. Whatever the genesis, it worked.

Although Plank's career lasted just eight years, he has stayed in the sport, coaching teams in the Arena Football League and working as a commentator.

him just as big a hero in Chicago.

The cupboard was not bare when Armstrong took over—after all he could rely on Walter Payton, who rushed for 1,395 yards and 11 touchdowns in 1978. The Bears' running game was terrific. Complementing Payton was Roland Harper, who added 992 yards rushing. His 4.1 average was just behind Payton's 4.2. Payton also caught 50 passes coming out of the backfield and that led the team. Harper was second in receptions with 43.

That all proved the Bears had the same old basic problem. They didn't have a deep passing game. Avellini was still in charge and he completed 53.4 percent of his passes—the short game helped that average. But he tossed just five touchdown passes. Finally, the Bears traded for Mike Phipps, the one-time Purdue All-American and a No. 1 draft pick, with the hope that he would be the missing link on offense.

Once Payton displayed his greatness, the personality of the Bears changed. No longer was their dominant characteristic the defense. Payton could be vocal, but not exceptionally so. He had an off-beat sense of humor punctuated by a high-pitched giggle, but that was a side of himself he rarely showed to the public.

Payton was a package of dynamite on the field,

waiting to explode in one way or another. After his feel-it-out year in 1975, he emerged as the dominant figure on the team. He was a first-class guy who made his linemen feel appreciated and they loved him in return. Just watching him spring loose, taking advantage of their hard work in the trenches, thrilled them. Teammates saw how hard Payton worked despite all of the honors he earned and accolades he collected, and they respected him more. They understood that he had a gift, but they could see first hand how hard he worked to enhance it. Payton was no dilettante. He suffered for his art. He talked to reporters, but it was not "Me, me, me." He had supreme confidence, but he didn't brag. That made him an excellent teammate.

On any good team, there is likely to be a franchise player, the one go-to guy who is such a star that the others who follow in his wake view him as a certain kind of royalty. The rest of the players know what is good for the goose is good for the flock. The better the big guy does, the more likely they all are to get noticed, to win, to collect championship rings. The Alpha dog is the leader of the pack. He shoulders the responsibility of coming through in the clutch, making the big run, the big score, the big shot. It was that way for Larry Bird with the Boston Celtics. It was that way for Jim Brown with the Cleveland Browns. It was that way for Peyton Manning with the Indianapolis Colts. Walter Payton was that guy for the Chicago Bears.

There is a tendency to compare Payton to Gale Sayers, just because both of them were superb Bears runners and played the same position. But their running styles were dramatically different. Sayers liked to say that if he had 18 inches of daylight, he was gone. He was like a fuel dragster, erupting off the starting blocks just going faster and faster. Payton could make the cuts, too, but if Sayers' object was never to be touched by the defense, Payton didn't care. He seemed to relish the contact. Just being the object of the defense's pursuit didn't make him shy. Deep down he must have thought he was a fullback, one of the bruising backs who could easily be a tight end.

"We used to call Gale, 'Magic,'" said linebacker Doug Buffone. "The guy would disappear. Walter would take three people with him. Both of those guys, they're probably the two best backs in my mind that ever played."

The short-lived stardom of Sayers was an object lesson. He was a symbol of how easy it is for an NFL player to be cut down in his prime, of how the top-

Doug Plank in action against the Rams in a November 1975 game at Los Angeles Coliseum. The Rams won this encounter 38–10.
NFL/Getty Images

Two popular Chicago Bears: the team mascot, with Walter Payton in 1978.
Bettmann/Corbis

level lifespan of a running back can end suddenly and prematurely. Payton was luckier. He was durable and he had longevity. He was on the Chicago sports scene for 13 seasons and he was a star every step of the way. Payton rushed for a then-record 16,726 yards and was voted to the pro bowl nine times.

He never seemed to age. He never seemed cocky, only self-assured. And he never seemed to take an awkward step so the fans loved him unreservedly. Bears fans appreciated the big-play runs—73 yards in 1977 and 76 yards in 1978—but they loved his steadiness. They recognized his durability, that he played game after game and marveled over his 125 touchdowns. They realized he was not a one-dimensional back, but that he did everything well. That included catching passes and that included blocking, the most unsung task for a superstar imaginable.

It took one to know one and Payton's well-roundedness on the field, in addition to his excellence at running, made Mike Ditka one of his biggest fans. Years after retirement, Ditka recounted how he was an assistant coach with the Cowboys the year Payton was available in the draft. The Cowboy debate centered on whether to choose Payton or defensive lineman Randy White. The Cowboys selected White, hardly a bad pick since he also became a Hall of Famer. "I think things happen because they're supposed to happen," Ditka said. "Walter was supposed to be a Chicago Bear and

he was the greatest one of all."

Payton grew up in Columbia, Mississippi, near the Gulf of Mexico, a place where traditional Southern cooking is deeply ingrained, from salted pork to barbecued pork. Born in 1954, Payton grew up in a segregated state in the heart of the Civil Rights era. He lived only a few blocks from the all-black high school. Payton's father worked two jobs and his mother worked nights. He spent his free time with older brother Eddie and older sister Pam. He said sports was the cornerstone of his life and that he filled his days with all sorts of competitions. Eddie, who had a less-spectacular NFL career, became enamored of golf and later became a very successful college golf coach. Payton played four sports in high school and worked in the yard on the orders of his parents when he was not practicing them, so he never lifted weights or trained in slow times because he never had a slow time.

Later, Payton's Bears teammates used to talk about what a practical joker he was and how he managed to slip under the radar of blame because he had an innocent smile and a first-rate Who, me? look. Payton said he instigated practical jokes in high school, after school desegregation took hold in his community and that firecrackers were always a big part of his repertoire. "Comedy can really bring people together," he said in his autobiography, "so that is what I tried to do."

A TALE OF LOVE
THAT MAKES THE HEART BLEED

The nation was full of hate. It seemed to be ripping apart at its seams, the squiggly lines on maps separating state's borders representing genuine fissures. The Civil Rights movement, a century after the Civil War, was at last beginning to make good on promises to American blacks. At the same time in the 1960s and early 1970s, an unpopular war raged in Southeast Asia and split families and friends, sending hundreds of thousands into the streets to protest against their government.

George Halas was both patriot and old school. The Vietnam War did not outwardly affect the Bears very much. But social relations between whites and blacks had the potential to rend a sports team, destroy its chemistry, and ruin its cohesiveness. Halas, an admirer and friend to Gale Sayers, from the moment the shy black man from the Plains stepped into his Chicago office, suggested that the star running back room with Brian Piccolo, his white back-up who had attended college at Wake Forest in North Carolina.

Sayers came to the Bears nationally touted, a spectacular All-American. Piccolo was like a baby left on the doorstep, nationally forgotten despite leading the NCAA in rushing and scoring his senior season with the Demon Deacons. He was 6 feet tall and weighed 200 pounds, but was deemed too slow for the pros. The Bears gave Piccolo a chance as a free agent and he made the roster in 1966.

By 1967, Sayers and Piccolo were wary roommates on road trips, each learning about friendship and brotherhood, about others with different color skins, breaking through barriers, becoming more

Above left: Bears running back Brian Piccolo in 1970. Piccolo died at age 26 from cancer. *Bettmann/Corbis*

Above right: Star half back Gale Sayers. *Corbis*

partners than teammates. They were the first interracial roommates in professional sports history. They were different personalities, but adapted. As word of their arrangement became known, the men received hate mail at the Bears' offices. The closer they became the more ludicrous they felt were judgments of others. Sometimes they teased interviewers with off-beat answers that were private jokes.

After they figured out life together, Sayers and Piccolo realized that it didn't matter if one was white and one was black. They were just two men sharing a room and sharing a football experience. They didn't dwell on being barrier breakers, though it was brought up often enough. They just did their thing.

And that's where it would have stayed, a footnote in the Civil Rights movement, a symbol to other Bears players and other athletes that whites and blacks with common goals could get along just fine in the team setting. Expect that Piccolo got sick. Very sick. He went from a healthy, physical, professional player to an individual whose strength was sapped by a rare form of cancer. The first indication something was wrong was a persistent, hacking cough that never disappeared.

In late fall of 1969, Piccolo was diagnosed with embryonal cell carcinoma. Surgery removed a tumor, though the illness had spread to his lymph nodes and a lung. He underwent treatment and rehab and seemed to be improving. He needed a second operation in March of 1970 and a third in April that removed his left lung. Sayers was a regular hospital visitor. Piccolo was more adept at cheering his visitors than they were in accepting his disease.

On June 16, 1970, Piccolo died at age 26, survived by his wife Joy and three young daughters. A report from the Sloan-Kettering Cancer Center where he was treated, said that embryonal cell carcinoma had a "zero percent cure rate" at the time.

A few weeks before Piccolo died, Sayers was the honoree at a Pro Football Writers dinner. He had recovered from his first knee surgery to rush for 1,000 yards once again and was being presented with an award as Most Courageous Athlete. Instead, in his speech, Sayers said Piccolo deserved it. "Talk about courage," Sayers said. "My knee injury and courage seem unimportant compared to the courage of Brian Piccolo. I've grown to love Brian Piccolo and I hope you can love him. When you get on your knees to pray tonight, remember Brian Piccolo."

Two days after Piccolo died, a first-person tribute written by Sayers appeared in the *Chicago Daily News*. In part he wrote, "Brian Piccolo was my friend and long before he became ill he was a hero to me. He was a beautiful man. He always hung loose and smiled and said the right thing at the right time."

A book called *I Am Third*, Sayers co-authored about his life was released later that year and a chapter served as the inspiration for the creation of the made-for-television movie *Brian's Song* that caused a sensation as a television landmark. The 1971 film starred Billy Dee Williams as Sayers and James Caan as Piccolo. The movie won awards, boosted Sayers' book into a best-seller, and the sad and true story made millions cry. "He was so young to die, with a future that held so much for him," Halas said when Piccolo passed away. "But Brian made the most of the brief 26 years allotted to him and he will not be forgotten."

Halas paid Piccolo's medical bills and set up a trust fund to pay for his daughters' education—that paramount trait of loyalty. The Bears initiated a Brian Piccolo Award that is given out each year to a rookie and a veteran who best exemplify courage, loyalty, teamwork, dedication and a sense of humor similar to the running back's. The team retired Piccolo's No. 41 jersey and a Brian Piccolo Cancer Research Fund was established. A few years ago, when *Brian's Song* was remade, Piccolo's widow Joy Piccolo O'Connell said it had received $6 million in donations. Bears chairman Ed McCaskey, who was particularly close to the Piccolo family, spearheaded the fundraising until his death in 2003.

When Sayers released a new biography in 2007, he again wrote about his relationship with Piccolo and said that he thinks about him every day.

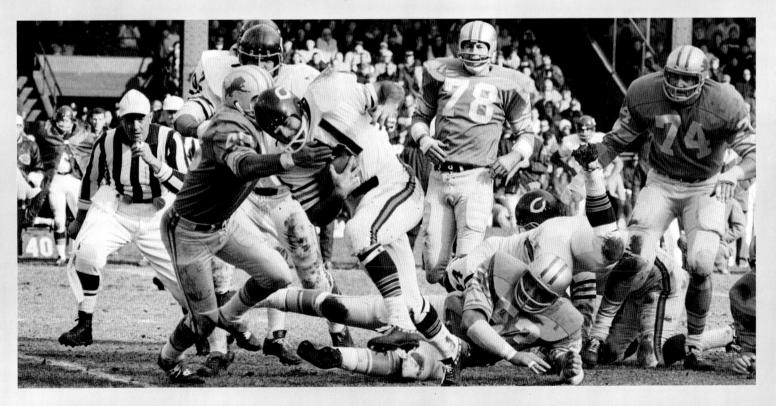

Bears half back Brian Piccolo fights for 9 yards over right tackle before being brought down by the Lions' Tom Vaughn in a 1967 game.
Bettmann/Corbis

1970s BEARS COACHING RECORDS

Jim Dooley	1970, 1971	12–16
Abe Gibron	1972, 1973, 1974	11–30–1
Jack Pardee	1975, 1976, 1977	20–22
Neill Armstrong	1978, 1979	17–15

Chicago defenders Dan Hampton (99), Alan Page (82), Jim Osborne (68), and Mike Hartenstine (73) converge on Green bay quarterback David Whitehurst in a game at Soldier Field on September 2, 1979.
Don Lansu/Getty Images

The pace of integration at the major universities of the South—the Southeastern Conference was tops—was slower than the pace of school integration. No administration wanted to be the first to integrate its sports teams, whether the coaches wanted to tap the pool of black talent in the same city, area, or state, or not. When Payton was ready for college in 1971, the main opportunities were offered by the traditionally black schools of the South, the Gramblings, Tennessee

States, or Jackson States. Payton chose Jackson State and stayed in his home state. He almost went to Kansas, Sayers' alma mater, but followed his brother to Jackson, the state capital.

Later, Payton said he was lucky he wasn't wooed by the SEC powers, that he chose the right school for him. "I needed a school like Jackson State to keep my feet planted," he said. Jackson State wasn't going to be on TV all of the time. Jackson State wasn't going to be playing before crowds of 80,000 every Saturday. At Jackson State, Payton wasn't going to get a big head unless the Tigers made the first bobblehead figure. As it was, Payton gained enough notice to place fourth in the Heisman Trophy voting, so he wasn't a complete unknown.

Payton was selected with the fourth overall pick in the draft. He was nervous about the cold weather and the size of the city, but he ended up loving Chicago and its fans as much as the fans loved him. The once renowned skinflint Bears paid out a three-year, $500,000 contract. By the time it was up, it was clear Payton was worth much more.

During the mid-1970s, when Payton arrived, he was the first building block of the new Bears. The team

had declined and needed total remodeling. Payton was the foundation. After his solid first year, Payton burst into super-stardom. He even did things that amazed his teammates, who realized they were working with someone special. "He's one of the all-time greats," said Bears fullback Matt Suhey, who maintained a close friendship with Payton into retirement. "I have to say he was a tremendously conditioned athlete with a great, competitive spirit."

At the start of the 1979 season, the Bears made an attempt to modernize. For many years, the team's offices in downtown were small and spartanly staffed. As pro football grew, so did the teams' administrative responsibilities and the number of employees. In September the Bears moved into a new $1.6 million headquarters on the campus of Lake Forest College. It was named Halas Hall.

With coach Neill Armstrong in his second year, the Bears were ready to do some damage again on the field. Payton rushed for 1,610 yards and scored 16 touchdowns. The quarterback was Phipps, who completed 52.5 percent of his passes and made fewer mistakes. All season long the Bears were in a dog fight for a playoff berth but on the last weekend of the season, they were faced with a tall order. They had to beat the St. Louis Cardinals by more than 30 points and Dallas had to beat the Washington Redskins. Fans and even friends were skeptical of that combination becoming reality. "Everybody said, 'You guys are nuts to think you're going to go to the playoffs,'" Buffone recalled.

But then the Bears went out and whomped the Cardinals, 42–6. Criterion number one was met. Showered and dressed, the players hung out at Soldier Field listening to the radio or watching TV, tensely rooting for the Cowboys, who trailed, to make a comeback. And then they did, edging the Redskins by one point. The Bears were in. Champagne bottles were opened and bubbly sprayed.

On the same day the team qualified for the playoffs, the front office was struck by tragedy. Founder George Halas' son, George Jr., suffered a heart attack at age 54 and died. He was the heir apparent and had long been involved with the club. His untimely death was a fresh blow to the hierarchy. Ralph Brizzolara, George Sr.'s close friend who had helped rescue the team during the darkest days of the Depression, had died at 76 in 1972. There weren't many of the old guard still around who had forged those original loyalties with George Halas.

The Bears won the right to face the powerful Philadelphia Eagles at Veterans Stadium two days before Christmas. The Eagles were a peaking team, playing their best ball in years. Ron Jaworski, later famed as a TV analyst, was a rock at quarterback. They

1970s CHICAGO BEARS YEAR BY YEAR

Year	Record
1970	6–8
1971	6–8
1972	4–9–1
1973	3–11
1974	4–10
1975	4–10
1976	7–7
1977	9–5
1978	7–9
1979	10–6

had the ingredients of a Super Bowl team while the Bears had barely squeaked into the playoffs with a 10–6 record.

Philadelphia had an almost unstoppable weapon in 6-foot-8 wide receiver Harold Carmichael. The game was hard-fought, with Philly opening the scoring on a 17-yard TD pass from Jaworski to Carmichael. The Bears bounced back with an 82-yard drive climaxed by a two-yard touchdown run from Payton. It was 7–7 after the quarter.

Payton scored again, on a one-yard run, in the second period and kicker Bob Thomas, a future Illinois Supreme Court Justice, booted a 30-yard field goal. The Bears led 17–10 at the half, but never scored again. The Eagles won, 27–17. Carmichael made six catches for 111 yards.

Years later Buffone felt the victory had been in reach and that the Bears had been victimized by an erroneous man-in-motion penalty that probably cost them a touchdown. "That was the game they stiffed us," Buffone remembered.

It was also a season and a game that marked the impending fresh ride to prominence of the Chicago Bears. The 1980s would be their time.

CHAPTER 7
THE 1980s:
YOU CAN GO HOME AGAIN

It gets cold in Chicago and coach Mike Ditka dressed for the weather in this 1982 game.
Ron Vesely/Getty Images

A sense of excitement buzzed around the Bears after the 1979 playoff appearance. They showed every sign of being a team on the way up, of putting the grim results of recent years behind them under coach Neill Armstrong. But the Bears took steps backwards in 1980, finishing 7–9. They lost to Green Bay in the opener, but smashed the Packers, 61–7 late in the season, for the main highlight. Yet some of the usual problems reared up in a discouraging sort of instant replay.

Another new quarterback, Vince Evans, took the majority of snaps under center. He completed 53.2 percent of his passes and completed five more interceptions than touchdown passes. So what was new? Armstrong had bought some goodwill with his playoff season, but when the Bears finished 6–10 in 1981 he was out of chips. Evans had not shown improvement, completing a dismal 44.7 percent of his passes. Despite possessing one of the most feared offensive weapons in the game in Walter Payton, who kept churning out big yardage, the Bears seemed on the verge of slipping back to their recent ugly ways.

Two huge personnel developments were on the horizon that prevented that. Mike Ditka had retired as a player and begun coaching in the Dallas Cowboys' organization under the venerable Tom Landry. While it was not the type of letter that European kings and queens exchanged in diplomatic correspondence to stave off wars or trade off sons and daughters in marriage before the invention of the telephone, Ditka penned a heartfelt note to George Halas. This was a make-up letter. Ditka said he had once been a Bear and

always would be a Bear and that when it came time to hire a new coach he hoped Halas would think of him because no one better understood the meaning of being a Bear and he would bring more passion to the job than anyone else.

Meanwhile, dissension was brewing in Bears land. Halas had brought in Jim Finks as general manager to upgrade football operations. But when George Jr., the heir apparent, died, Halas re-appointed himself team president and began making moves without consulting Finks. He hired his old friend and ex-coach Jim Dooley as an assistant coach and extended the contract of defensive specialist Buddy Ryan. Armstrong was fired and secret negotiations began with Ditka, who was still coaching because Dallas was in the playoffs. In January of 1982, the then 42-year-old Mike Ditka was hired as the Bears new coach. Just like those who had preceded him, he was a product of the Bears system, a former player hand-picked by George Halas. He signed a three-year, six-figure contract. Halas was securing the future.

The concurrent development was that Halas was dying. Age and illness were catching up to the old man who had once paced the sidelines like a caged animal, jaw set in certainty, whose voice once drowned out the decibels of heavy metal rock bands. The Chicago Bears were George Halas' baby. He was the midwife to the birth of the National Football League. He had run the team for more than 60 years, turned it into a Chicago institution. When he passed on he wanted to know his struggling franchise was not only going to be safely held within his family, but successful on the field.

Walter Payton, running against the Green Bay Packers in 1980, is the second most prolific rusher in NFL history.
Focus on Sports/Getty Images

Many did not see it coming, or realize that indeed Ditka returning as head coach was the perfect match. He had been an intimate of the old man, knew the city's moods and likes, was himself a Grabowski, a blue-collar worker, and much of that same fiery, my-way-or-the-highway persona that led Halas to clash with other strong personalities was just as deeply ingrained in Ditka.

Although his authority had been compromised, Jim Finks did not leave immediately. He, Ditka, and personnel director Bill Tobin performed wonders with the draft, picking seven future starters for the Super Bowl team, including No. 1 choice, quarterback Jim McMahon out of Brigham Young University, where he broke numerous passing records. Jerry Vainisi, hired to handle business tasks, signed them all. Soon, Halas decided that it was time to let Finks go and promoted

Vainisi to general manager. As his health began fading, Halas was content that he had ensured a revitalized Bears team by placing the right men in management.

The Bears began the new season slowly, dropping to 3–6 as Ditka, as passionate and loud as ever, made sure the troops understood they were not attending summer camp, but more of a boot camp. Right through early October, Halas was the team's administrative headmaster. Then he became weaker, grew sicker, lapsed into a coma, and on October 31, one of the founders of the NFL died at age 88 of pancreatic cancer. It was Halloween and much of the 1983 team was gathered at a party when the news broke.

A *Chicago Sun-Times* sports columnist wrote that Halas' passing was impossible to believe because "George Halas is too tough to die." Ditka said he had been in regular consultations with Halas until about

Walter Payton flies high to score a touchdown over the New Orleans Saints in 1984.
Bettmann/Corbis

three weeks before he died and the team founder had always ended their discussions with the advice, "Keep your chin up." Tributes poured in. Most praised Halas as a league pioneer who had remarkable foresight, who believed in the sport and the NFL, and always acted that way despite running the Bears as a personal fiefdom. The funeral service at St. Ita's Church in Chicago was attended by about 1,200 mourners, many of them key figures in the NFL paying their respects.

Papa Bear had founded a team, raised it, coached it, saved it, developed it, modernized it, and won more games than any other coach with it. Halas had long imagined his son "Mugs" would run it, but George Jr. pre-deceased him. "Coach George Halas' name is synonymous with the Chicago Bears and the National Football League," said Ronnie Bull, a Bears running back between 1962 and 1970. "I can say that I played for the

WILLIE GAULT
**Wide receiver/
Kick-off returns
1983–1987**

Willie Gault was so fast that if you turned your head you needed to call in a search party. Speed made it particularly difficult for defensive backs to cover the one-time track star when he ran his routes. "I knew that I was the fastest guy on the field," he said. Gault was an Olympic hurdler and world class sprinter who later made a U.S. Winter Olympic team in the bobsled. On a team built on power, Gault's exceptional speed made him the frosting on the cake as the Bears rolled to the Super Bowl title. He scored eight touchdowns as a rookie in 1983 and averaged 26.2 yards per kick-off return in 1985. "I really enjoyed it," Gault said of his kick-off prowess. "I thought I could score every time I got a kick-off."

Many Bears from the title team remained in Chicago, started business careers, or flourished as broadcasters. Gault went Hollywood. He became an actor and has appeared in a multitude of TV shows. Gault has also stayed in shape and later set a world record for the 100 meters for his forties age group.

Although many thought the high-octane team would win several Super Bowls, the Bears had to settle for one. The club's characters have worn well in Chicago and occupy a special place in fans' hearts. "It's a magical moment that will never be lived again," Gault said. "So you look at those moments and you cherish them."

Willie Gault warms up before Super Bowl XX.
Getty Images

Jim McMahon on a rollout in a 1983 game.
Andrew D. Bernstein/Getty Images

The Bears began playing their home football games at Soldier Field in 1971. This is a view of the stadium in 1982 during NFL pre-game entertainment.
Bettmann/Corbis

greatest coach of all time, George Halas."

Succeeding a legend is never an easy task, especially if it is unexpected. Thinking like a legend and carrying on his work is even more daunting. Sid Luckman, the greatest quarterback in club history, said Halas was always "ahead of everybody else by 10 years." Love him or hate him (and there was a fair share of contrarians around the league) Halas made an everlasting mark on the league and for a time single-handedly directed one of sport's great franchises.

Ownership of the Bears passed to Halas' daughter Virginia McCaskey and her husband, Michael, became president.

There were a few bumps along the way before

Willie Gault waits to receive a kick during a game in 1985.
Jonathan Daniel/Getty Images

Above: The 300-plus-pound defensive tackle William Perry was an imposing presence on the gridiron.
B. Bennett/Getty Images

Right: At the height of his fame William "The Refrigerator" Perry appeared on the Bob Hope Christmas Show in 1985.
Jim Smestad/Corbis

Ditka could really jump-start the Bears. Ditka took over in the worst of times. The National Football League Players Association authorized a strike that lasted 57 days. Here Ditka was trying to put his stamp on the team, get his men to pull together, and they ended up on picket lines. It was a fragile situation.

During games Ditka was a human volcano, always on the verge of eruption. He yelled at players. He yelled at officials. He was still frothing when he met the press. There was little doubt Ditka the coach burned to win as much as Ditka the player had and that was what Halas banked on.

Vainisi, who became close friends with Ditka, was put off at first. He told Ditka that by going ballistic so often he might lose his team. "Your technique is you coach by crisis," Vainisi said. "You always have to have some crisis to overcome. It diverts attention from the game itself. The players don't understand it. They think you're crazy." Ditka was an A-plus personality. To him, in the pursuit of perfection, everything WAS a crisis. What

he had to do was separate a major crisis from an irritant. Making sure the Bears bounced back from a strike-interrupted 3–6 season was a real crisis. Finding a truly reliable quarterback was a major crisis.

The Bears improved to 8–8 in 1983, Ditka's first full season, and McMahon was the quarterback designated to run the show. He completed 59.3 percent of his passes, but had to improve his touchdown pass (12) to interception (13) ratio. Payton was till Payton, the cornerstone of the franchise, with 1,421 rushing yards.

Gradually, all of those draft picks began to pay dividends. The young players pushed veterans out of jobs. The talent was upgraded. In 1984, McMahon, whose biggest problem was not being a prankster, but staying healthy, was still the main quarterback. But Steve Fuller, Rusty Lisch, and Bob Avellini also got major chunks of playing time. This was the ongoing Bears nightmare, year after year, decade after decade, that the quarterback seemed to change from month to

Mike Ditka delivers his message on the sidelines during a 1985 playoff game.
Jonathan Daniel/Getty Images

month. Yet the team overcame that. The Bears finished 10–6 and made the playoffs. Defensive coordinator Buddy Ryan's defense was emerging. Payton was unbelievable, rushing for 1,684 yards and catching 45 passes. Linebacker Mike Singletary made 116 tackles and defensive end Richard Dent notched 17½ sacks. The Bears not only qualified for the playoffs for the first time since 1979, they won a first-round game, besting the Washington Redskins, 23–19, the team's first playoff win since 1963. Payton, always a threat with the halfback option, even threw a touchdown pass. "It was another step towards us actually believing in ourselves," said lineman Keith Van Horne.

The unexpected ride came to an end a week later with a 23–0 loss to the San Francisco 49ers. The Bears were bummed, but they felt they had been part of a

growing process and that by winning 10 games, winning in the playoffs, and learning from the defeat they were ready to set up a special year. Something in the atmosphere had changed. Only two years earlier they were lame losers. Now they set their sights on the Super Bowl. "We got some confidence and we started going," center Jay Hilgenberg said.

One thing Ditka did as a public service for Bears fans and no doubt in homage to Halas and his own upbringing as a Bears player was forcefully to rekindle any lagging emotion about the rivalry with the Packers. Packers dominance under Vince Lombardi, combined with the Bears needing to get their own house in order in the 1960s, had deflected some attention away from it. As a former player of the early 1960s, and with Forrest Gregg, a former Packers 1960s' player in charge

Jim McMahon throws against the New York Giants in their playoff game on January 12, 1986.
Ronald C. Modra/Sports/Getty Images

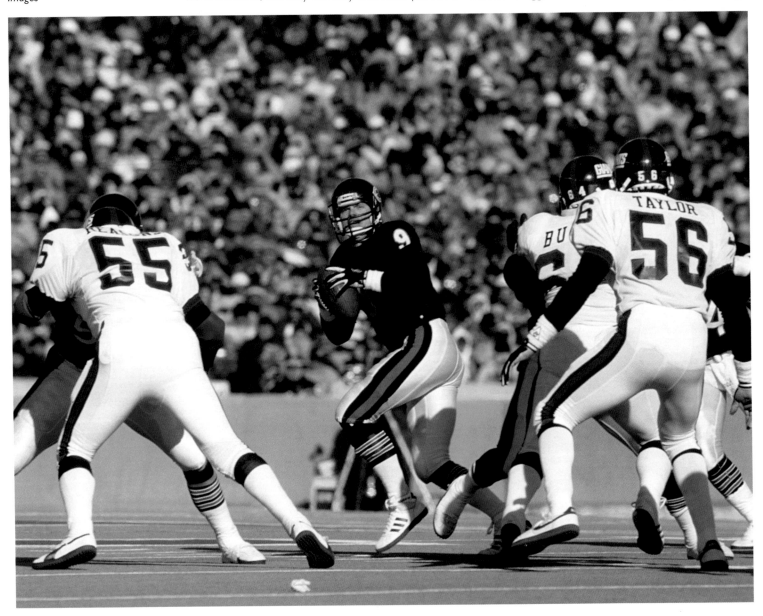

Quarterback Jim McMahon was a character on and off the field. He seemed to enjoy provoking NFL commissioner Pete Rozelle with his head-band graffiti, displayed here during the 1985 playoffs. *Jonathan Daniel/Getty Images*

Guesting on the Johnny Carson show, Bears quarterback Jim McMahon gave the host a pair of red sunglasses that he was modeling. The appearance was just after McMahon was released from the hospital following shoulder surgery in 1986. *Glenn Waggner/Getty Images*

JIM McMAHON
Quarterback
1982–1988

Jim McMahon was a free spirit who tried to hold up the offense's end of the bargain on the Super Bowl team that was over-loaded with quirky defensive guys. Whether he was staggering with a swagger, taunting Pete Rozelle by writing the commissioner's name on a head band after his previous head-band advertising was banned, going the dark glasses route to look cool, stating his disdain for authority, or mooning a helicopter in New Orleans before the Super Bowl, McMahon was a magnet for attention. McMahon said he believed he was destined to be the Bears quarterback at that time and place. "Lots of talent, lots of laughs," he said.

McMahon also had the big-time charisma helpful for leading a team. He was neither the most accurate nor threatening quarterback in the league, but he made the clutch plays and despite his image took care of business on the field and won the admiration of his teammates for playing hurt. McMahon did not have a go-to receiver during the title run. When it wasn't the right thing to hand off to Walter Payton, he could pass to Payton but the Bears had six receivers that year who caught between 24 and 49 passes.

What no one could predict at all was what McMahon would say next. When a reporter asked McMahon who he would like to see the Bears add to the team in the April 1986 draft he said, "I would like to see us draft an owner."

Sack king Richard Dent bearing
down on Giants quarterback Phil
Simms in a 1986 playoff game.
*Ronald C. Modra/Sports/Getty
Images*

of Green Bay, the emphasis was renewed, and not
subtly. The rivalry raged again. "He cranked it up a
notch with Green Bay," Van Horne said of Ditka. "He
just could not stand them and he could not stand
Forrest Gregg, let me tell you." Between 1985 and
1988, the Bears won all eight games against the
Packers.

By 1985 training camp, even rookie kicker Kevin

Butler out of University of Georgia could sense the
growing sense of cockiness that married ability and
confidence. He went home one day and told his fiancée
that they were going to have to postpone the planned
date of their wedding because the Bears were still going
to be playing football in late January. She thought he
was nuts and got angry, but Butler was correct.

What followed was a wild ride of a season that

Bears fans still remember as if it were yesterday. In Chicago, it is wait till next year for the Cubs, but is wait till last time for the Bears in the hopes that they can some day do it all over again with the same pizzazz and domination. The 1985 Bears won their first 12 games, including 23–7 and 16–10 victories over Green Bay. The one that got away was a 38–24 game against Miami, which was protecting the legacy of its own

Dolphins predecessor team that had gone 17–0 to become the only undefeated team to win a Super Bowl. The hype machine was in high gear by week 13 and players were showered with compliments and head-swelling phrases such as "You are the greatest ever!" But Jim McMahon didn't start and the supposed greatest defense of all time gave up five straight touchdowns to the Dolphins to start the game. "We

Defensive coordinator Buddy Ryan exhorts his players during the NFC championship game against the Los Angeles Rams on January 12, 1986.
Ronald C. Modra/Sports/Getty Images

STEVE McMICHAEL

Defensive tackle
1981–1993

Nobody had more fun during the Super Bowl years than the personable, yet ferocious Steve McMichael, aka "Mongo." On a team heavy with big personalities, McMichael was the wildest wild man, who relished his time in the spotlight. The 6-foot-2, 270-pound lineman recorded eight sacks during the Super Bowl run and 44 tackles. The Bears defense was viewed as a swash-buckling 11 and McMichael helped create that image. McMichael described himself and Ivy League safety Gary Fencik appearing at events together as "theatre with the redneck and the conservative republican."

At the end of a playoff game pep talk McMichael picked up a chair and heaved it so hard at the chalkboard it stuck with all four legs. McMichael is regarded as a harsh truth teller with no tolerance for excuses or BS. That was true when he was playing, is true when fans approach to talk to him, and is true when he is on the radio, which he is quite frequently as an honored guest during the football season.

The Bears were so confident going into the January 1986 Super Bowl, McMichael said some began to party before they got to New Orleans. "Actually, I think that we were already drunk when we got off the plane," he said.

The proud defense shut out both playoff opponents, and McMichael's only Super Bowl disappointment was that the 46–10 destruction of the Patriots wasn't a shutout too.

Steve McMichael looms over downed Eric Dickerson in the NFC championship win over the Rams in 1986.
Jonathan Daniel/Getty Images

"Baby, you can *always* get another Mercedes."
—Defensive tackle Steve McMichael to his wife Debi while he chased down refreshments after quarterback Mike Tomczak bumped into his car at Soldier Field sending a case of post-game beer flying.

were more than a little full of ourselves," defensive tackle Steve McMichael admitted.

As had been evident in recent years, the Bears' defense was stronger than its offense, though the offense was no slouch, scoring 456 points. But opponents mustered only 198 points during the regular season, were sacked 64 times and intercepted 30. Ryan fostered unity on the unit by being aggressively egalitarian—treating everyone like dirt, frequently insulting them, sometimes in public—yet mostly by being fiercely protective of his men outside the cocoon. Being outside the inner circle extended to the offense, as well, and sometimes to the head coach. That attitude produced tension between Ryan, garnering extensive attention for his "46" defense named after safety Doug Plank's uniform jersey, and Ditka, who was the boss. Ditka had considerable pride in his resurrection job, and wanted to see team-wide chemistry.

During half-time of the Miami game, one of the few times all season the Bears might have benefited from words of wisdom, Ryan and Ditka were at odds, to the point of nearly breaking into a fist-fight. The men had to be separated. To Ryan it was always "us-versus-them" and the defense circled the wagons yet lapped up the attention lavished on it simultaneously. The defenders loved Ryan, their personal drill sergeant.

One reason the Bears acted so high and mighty going into the Miami game was their prior decimation of the Dallas Cowboys. The day they crushed the Cowboys, 44–0, in Dallas, was the day the Bears knew how good they could be. It was a milestone for several reasons, one being Ditka showing his old bosses that he was not just chopped liver as a head coach.

On the eve of the Dallas showdown game, the *Chicago Tribune* ran a story that examined Ditka's intense desire to win. His family were interviewed and said he had always been like that. Ditka revealed some of his own thinking. "I hate to lose," he said. "You can be gracious in defeat, but boy, I'll tell you what, you can be gracious on the outside, but you better be doing flip-flops inside. If you're not churning and turning, you're going to go out and get your butt whipped next

time out."

The Bears destroyed Dallas with a devastating defensive effort. They crushed the Cowboys with first-string quarterback Jim McMahon sidelined by injury and second-stringer Steve Fuller running the show. Afterwards, Ditka gave game balls to everyone on the team and said he would gold-plate one for Fuller. "Everybody wanted it, more so for Mike," said Payton. "It seemed like the energy and electricity from him just flowed into the other players."

The Bears' first two touchdowns were scored on interceptions and linebacker Otis Wilson hit Dallas quarterback Danny White so hard he knocked him

William Perry and the rest of the Bears defense get set against the Los Angeles Rams in the conference title game in 1986. *Ronald C. Modra/Sports/Getty Images*

The Refrigerettes, female fans of Bears defensive tackle William "The Refrigerator" Perry sign their name to a 36-foot long mural before Super Bowl XX. *Jim Smestad/Corbis*

cold. Ditka called the defense awesome and it had been that way all season long.

There were times Bears football during the 1985 season seemed as serious as a fatal disease. And there were times that it seemed positively cartoonish: When Ditka threw a tantrum, when Buddy Ryan postured, when McMahon cracked wise, and above all when William "The Refrigerator" Perry, a humungous defensive tackle who was the Bears' No. I draft pick out of Clemson, became a cult figure. The nickname linking him to an extra-large domestic appliance came with him.

Perry weighed about 310 pounds in an era when the weights of linemen still hovered in the 280-pound range as often as not. He had a gap-toothed smile, a friendly demeanor, and homespun Southern speech patterns. In contrast to some of his brethren, whose kill-them-all-and-let-God-sort-them-out defensive approach cultivated a convict-type fear, Perry was a cuddly teddy bear.

For much of the season, Perry was a bench-

warmer. Ryan, whose sense of humor had probably been left on a bench overlooking Lake Michigan in the 70s, did not cotton to Perry. Ryan wanted meanness on his defense. So Ditka borrowed Perry for the offense, inserting him at tackle. And then Ditka took it one step further. The Big Man was put in a game at fullback and scored on a 1-yard touchdown plunge that shook Richter scales. Overnight, Perry became a folk hero, pretty much because he was the most unlikely looking ball carrier in history.

Even before the season, Perry had charmed sports writers who were naturally attracted to his nickname. Yes, he was as big as a refrigerator and he burned a lot of electricity, so he had to keep eating. Perry's family in Aiken, South Carolina, veterans of the media onslaught after William had garnered attention in college, seemed to be in on the joke, too. His mother Inez drolly noted of her son's appetite, "He wasn't choosy." And Daryl, one of Perry's seven brothers and 11 siblings said, "We would eat whatever William decided to leave us."

Perry himself uttered one of the classic lines in the

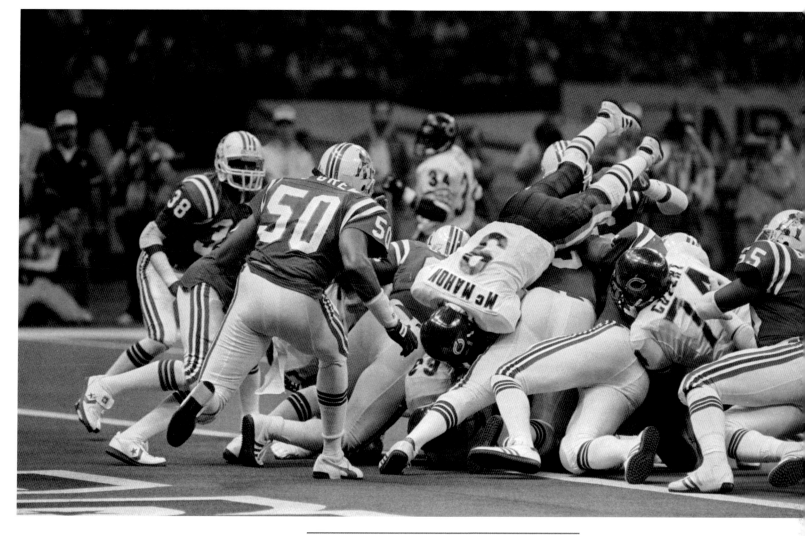

history of American sport by assessing his 300-plus body with the insight of Yogi Berra. "Even when I was little, I was big," Perry said. He stood 6-foot-2 and played in 1985 at around 310 pounds or so, but indisputably grew from there to about 335 pounds. Perry's vital statistics also included size 61 for a sport jacket, 48 inches for his waist and 34 inches for each of his thighs.

Perry's image as more than just a gigantic football guy began to change during the sixth game of the Super Bowl campaign when the Bears defeated the San Francisco 49ers, 26–10. The season before the 49ers had inserted Guy McIntyre, a 275-pound guard into the backfield. The Bears thought it was a ploy by the then-Super Bowl champs to make fun of them in the 23–0 playoff loss. San Francisco coach Bill Walsh called the use of McIntyre his "Angus Formation."

Playing a game of one-upmanship, Ditka put his own raging bull Perry into the backfield and he ran the ball twice on the game's last two plays. The sight of the Hindenburg on legs diving into the run galvanized fans.

"The week before the Super Bowl down there in New Orleans was great fun. It was a work week for us, but [Coach Mike] Ditka let us party and there was no curfew. I think everyone was pretty relaxed."
—Safety Gary Fencik on the lead-up to Super Bowl XX.

The Bears could do no wrong that season and every juicy morsel of off-beat activity they fed to the masses was eaten up. Fullback Matt Suhey joked that The Fridge was after his job. Payton said the 49ers did not "show much courtesy or dignity" when they bested the Bears the year before. "If they can do it, we can do it better," Van Horne said.

Ditka gave reporters a "Who me?" look when accused of payback and said "I'm not that kind of guy," even though everyone knew he was that kind of guy.

Jim McMahon dives for his second touchdown against the New England Patriots in Super Bowl XX.
Ron Kuntz/Corbis

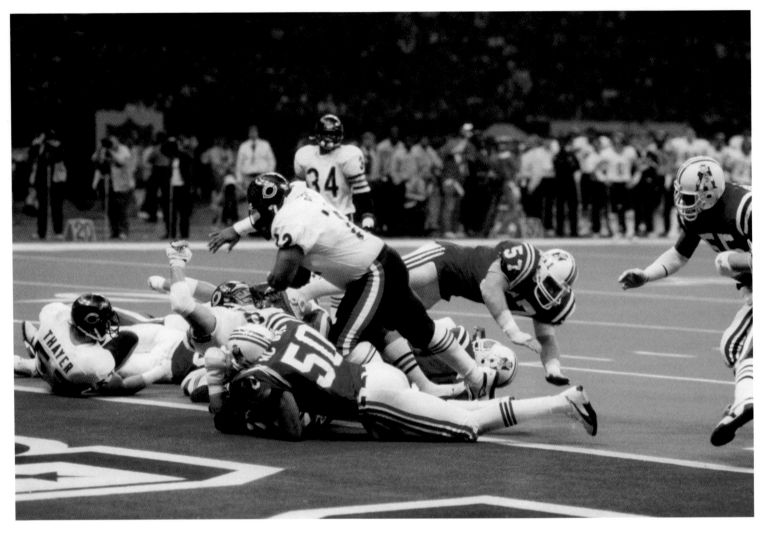

William "The Refrigerator" Perry plays the role of fullback and plows through the New England defense for a touchdown in Super Bowl XX.
Diamond Images/Getty Images

"They ran a big, fat offensive guard in the backfield against us last year," defender Dan Hampton said. "We thought we'd run a big, fat defensive lineman against them."

So there.

It didn't take long before Perry was one of the most sizzling celebrities around. With a rock group called "The Fat Boys," he recorded a rap record called "Chillin' With The Refrigerator." He appeared on a hot selling poster and made so many commercials he was on TV more often than I Love Lucy re-runs. Soon Perry registered his name at the U.S. Patent Office as a trademark and in China he was called "The Electric Ice Box." Perhaps something was lost in the translation.

One reason the Bears' defense was so terrific that season was Hampton, the man they called "Danimal." Another was Richard Dent, who was the primo sackmeister in the league. Mike Singletary was a Hall of Fame linebacker. The defensive secondary did mass damage to wide receivers. But Dan Hampton stood

out on the defensive line. Hampton, a 6-foot-5, 265-pound defensive lineman out of Arkansas, was an old-style Bear, only quicker. The 46 defensive formation required opposing teams to block one-on-one rather than double-team and that just didn't work against Hampton. Hampton's biggest problem in the sport was not in fending off eager blockers, but in keeping his body whole. Not only did he break eight of his fingers at various times, Hampton kept having knee operations, keeping them balanced in number by knee, at least through eight. When he wasn't rehabbing he was a ferocious attacker.

During his playing days, Hampton maintained a 150-acre dairy farm in Cabot, Arkansas, about 22 miles from Little Rock where he grew up, and he always looked powerful enough to wrestle one of those cows to the ground without breaking a sweat. He played much of his career with pain and seemed to have contempt for those who signed up for a man's game, but wouldn't. He was quoted as urging the NFL to change the categories in which it lists players on the

Defensive tackle Steve McMichael helps carry winning coach Mike Ditka off the field at the Super Dome after the Bears won Super Bowl XX in 1986.
Terry Bochatey/Corbis

Reggie Phillips rushes down the right sideline during Super Bowl XX in 1986.
Wally McNamee/Corbis

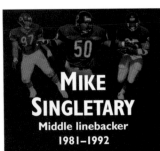

MIKE SINGLETARY
Middle linebacker
1981–1992

Appropriately, the Super Bowl Bears featured a superstar middle linebacker in Mike "Samurai" Singletary. Singletary, soft-spoken and religious off the field, would take your head off on it. Singletary played at 6 feet and 230 pounds and was a defensive weapon that had quarterbacks scanning the horizon at all times. Singletary was an All-American at Baylor and the anchor of the Bears' defense of 1985 that some say was the best ever. During the 15–1 Super Bowl run Singletary was in on 113 tackles.

Singletary has written books, mainly focused on developing character and living a righteous life. His autobiography, *Singletary on Singletary*, deals more with football. "In many ways, football defines me," he wrote. "It requires hard work, preparation, thinking. Lots of things happen at once. The successful player has to overcome fatigue. The field is a place to perform, to excel. It's my arena and I enjoy the privilege and the opportunity to play professionally more than I can say."

Singletary was selected as the NFL's defensive player of the year three times and has been chosen for the Hall of Fame. After playing, Singletary stayed in pro football as an assistant coach with the Baltimore Ravens and San Francisco 49ers, following his dream to become an NFL head coach. When asked if it was difficult to play against his old team, he said, "Mike Singletary will always be a Chicago Bear." One day he hopes to coach the Bears.

injury report prior to weekend games to "Sissy," "Pussing Out," and "Squirreling Out." That might make a few guys think twice about how badly they were injured, he felt. You knew Hampton measured high on the toughness scale when the crusty Ryan referred to him as "My hero."

As part of his machismo image, Hampton wore short sleeves even if it was 10 degrees, and the naked skin of biceps the size of footballs was viewable to intimidate foes. On a team loaded with defensive stars, Hampton was the true leader on the field.

Even as the Bears were crunching Dallas, Payton repeated his weekly mantra: "This team hasn't reached its potential yet."

The loss to Miami could have derailed the freight train, but only minor repairs were needed. The Bears won their last three regular-season games and then they might really have reached their potential. And not as musical performers, either. "The Super Bowl Shuffle" was released near the end of the season, to both critical applause and popular success by touching the funny bones of listeners in Chicago and elsewhere. If you were superstitious it was not difficult to view the song's release as a bad omen, as something that could jinx the rest of the year and kill the team's dream short of reaching its goal. Hampton did not participate in the

making of the song or video out of a sense of cautiousness—the team had not won anything except a National Football Conference Central Division title yet. "I thought it was pretentious," he said.

The Bears did reach their potential, enough even to satisfy Payton, once the playoffs began. The Bears opened before 62,076 fans at Soldier Field, caught up in the magic of the regular season, against the New York Giants. To use the word throttle would be polite. It was a 14-degree day with a 13-mph wind so the conditions favored keep-it-on-the-ground offense and hardy defense, two of the Bears' strengths. The Bears had unlikely scorers, with Shaun Gayle running a punt back for a touchdown and end Dennis McKinnon catching scoring passes of 23 and 20 yards from McMahon. The Giants could barely gain yards, netting 32 rushing and watching quarterback Phil Simms miss 21 of his 35 passing attempts. The Giants were a combined 0-for-14 on third and fourth downs in trying to gain a first down. The final score was 21–0. Rack it.

Step two to the Super Bowl was equally one-sided. The Bears controlled the Los Angeles Rams and shut them out, 24–0. Before the game Buddy Ryan predicted that the Bears defense would be so superior it would force three fumbles from LA star back Eric Dickerson—a rather brash statement. Dickerson did

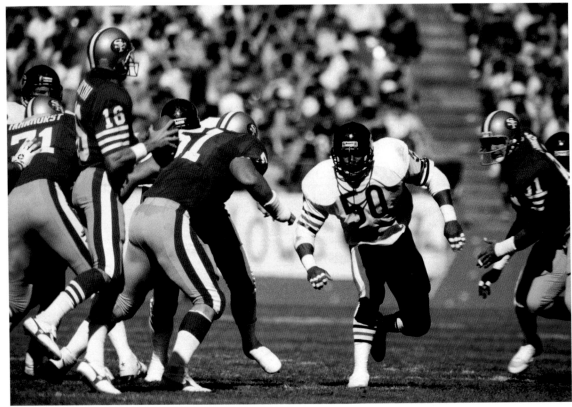

Mike Singletary finds a hole to chase down the quarterback in a 1985 game against San Francisco.
Jonathan Daniel/Getty Images

Dan Hampton became a Hall of Famer for the Bears after his long career.
Ron Vesely/Getty Images

not make that many miscues, but on another cold Chicago day where it snowed during the game the Bears rolled. "Two playoff games, two shutouts," Steve McMichael said. "Bring on New Orleans."

The Bears were a party team going to a party city and although they had the chance to instigate the biggest party in the history of Chicago, they were not going to behave like cloistered nuns in the Big Easy. Ditka did his best to slap on curfews and keep a lid on things, but the Bears were so cocky they would beat the New England Patriots, they had to sample some of the offerings on Bourbon Street.

McMichael, who has seemed to get more outrageous in his radio appearances as time has passed and his playing years receded, has often left listeners laughing. They want to believe the crazy stuff

he says the Bears did. When McMichael co-authored a book with Chicago sports writer Phil Arvia, he claimed he and Hampton always took pops of Crown Royal and 7's in the hotel bar the night before a game.

The first night in New Orleans, McMichael wrote that he did what tourists do—went to Pat O'Brien's and guzzled Hurricanes, the all-encompassing lethal concoction made with a multitude of types of alcohol. "I left a little dissolved Hurricane juice in the alley behind Pat O'Brien's," McMichael wrote. "But it helps when you're a finely tuned athlete. Your body recovers in a few hours and you're able to drink again." A few drinks here, a few drinks there, make some hay in the press conferences on the side—the Bears were outrageous, but avoided doing anything to get arrested. Oddsmakers believed the Bears' image was

real, that they were invincible, and made them 21-point favorites over the Patriots. As it was the line was understated, with the Bears winning 46–10.

In the locker room before the game, Buddy Ryan, who was on his way to becoming the head coach of the Philadelphia Eagles, broke down and told his players he was leaving and that he loved them. They were already fired up, but that was when McMichael threw the chair into the blackboard.

The Bears defense was again dominant, forcing six turnovers and holding the Patriots to minus-19 yards in total offense in the first half. "He is a genius," said Bears defensive back Dave Duerson. "That's all there is to it."

Ditka even pulled out some trick plays. The Fridge attempted a pass, though it landed incomplete. And then, in the third quarter, with the ball at the 1-yard-line, Perry went back in as fullback. He took the hand-off and he scored a touchdown. A touchdown? "I was more concerned with losing yardage," Perry said.

At the time, Perry's play was hailed merely as part

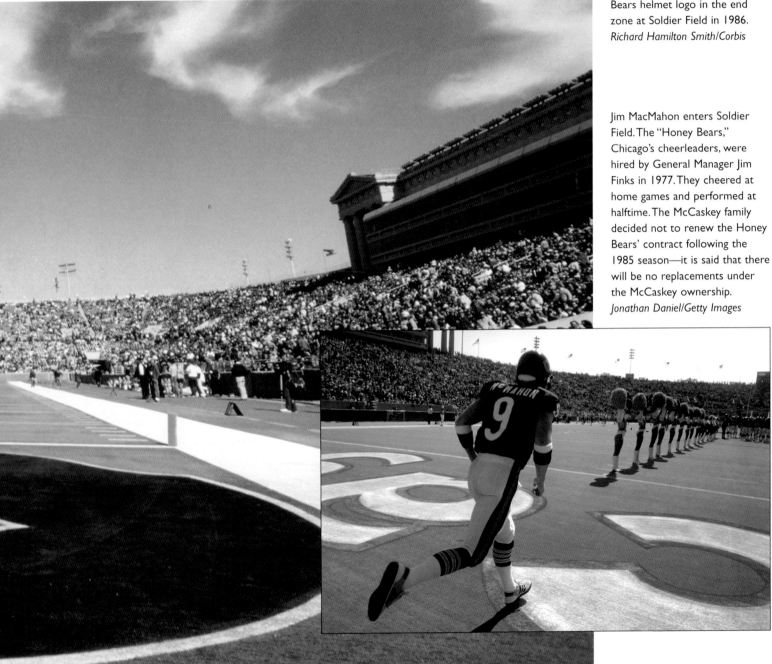

Bears helmet logo in the end zone at Soldier Field in 1986. *Richard Hamilton Smith/Corbis*

Jim MacMahon enters Soldier Field. The "Honey Bears," Chicago's cheerleaders, were hired by General Manager Jim Finks in 1977. They cheered at home games and performed at halftime. The McCaskey family decided not to renew the Honey Bears' contract following the 1985 season—it is said that there will be no replacements under the McCaskey ownership. *Jonathan Daniel/Getty Images*

of the general hilarity, the punch-line to a season of remarkable accomplishment and surreal attention. Only later did it come out that Payton, the NFL's all-time leading ground gainer, was miffed that his number was not called, that he did not get a chance to score a Super Bowl touchdown. Many years later, Ditka admitted he was wrong and that if he had it to do over again he would have rather seen Payton score.

Back in Chicago, about 500,000 people lined a downtown parade route and another 150,000 crammed into Daley Plaza to fete the team on a day when the temperature was 8 degrees with a minus 29 windchill factor. And in some ways, the celebration has never stopped. Bears players from that Super Bowl team remain household names in Chicago. More than two decades after their triumph they still sign autographs at events and make radio and television appearances. The one nagging disappointment that hounds those players and some fans was that the Super Bowl was a one-time thing. The Bears thought

Coach Mike Ditka tries to make himself understood by Bears players at training camp in 1986 at Platteville, WI.
Bettmann/Corbis

they were built for the long haul, ready to win several Super Bowl titles. The immediate departure of Ryan for his new job was the first crack in the foundation.

McMahon was hurt about half of the 1986 season, but Mike Tomczak filled in well. Payton was as great as ever. And the team record nearly matched the season before at 14–2. But the constant attention, or perhaps a bit less hunger, might have taken a toll. The Bears were favored again in the playoffs, but this time lost in the opening round, 27–13 to Washington. Next time around the Bears recorded another excellent 11–4 season but lost in the first round of the playoffs, 21–17 to Washington again. That was Payton's final season and he was not nearly as overpowering, splitting rushing duties with Neal Anderson.

As great was the ride that the Bears took in 1985, there is an emptiness within some players because they felt they should have done more together as a group. "Everybody on the team was too busy with their own selves, who they were, how much air time they got, rather than worrying about the team,"

Hampton said. "They were driven by money and star power, what they could become. I felt that was the team of the decade. If you had told me we weren't going to repeat, I'd have laughed at you." Not only did the Bears not repeat, it took 21 years for the team to return to the Super Bowl.

Ditka was the hand-picked coach of the team patriarch and he had done his duty, leading the Bears back to prominence. Ditka said the group "was the kind of team the Old Man would have loved." Ditka's own image as the rough, tough, gruff guy who brooked no nonsense and hesitated not at all to yell about it, made him as popular as the players with fans. He was selected NFL coach of the year for his work during the 1985 season.

More humorously, it seemed Ditka scared players around the league with his tirades. A poll of 200 NFL players appeared in *Sports Illustrated* during the 1985 season listing him, Don Shula and Tom Landry as the coaches they would least like to play for. Those players were probably "lazy butts who wouldn't want to pay

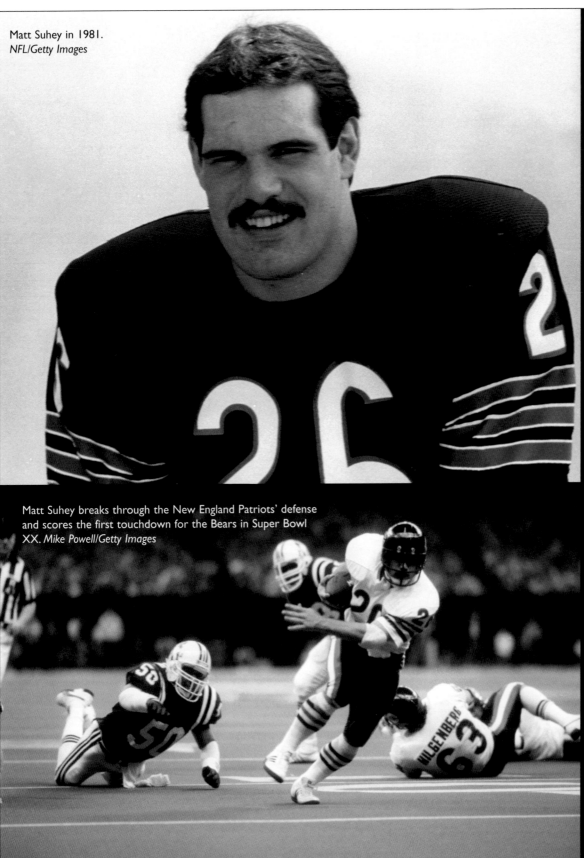

Matt Suhey in 1981.
NFL/Getty Images

Matt Suhey breaks through the New England Patriots' defense and scores the first touchdown for the Bears in Super Bowl XX. *Mike Powell/Getty Images*

MATT SUHEY
Fullback
1980–1989

He was Mr. Reliable. Matt Suhey did not make much noise, but he always delivered. He was Walter Payton's sidekick in the backfield and he was his pal off the field. Suhey was the change-of-pace back, the guy the Bears handed the ball to on the rare occasions when it wasn't Payton's turn. When it was, Suhey was the blocking back who opened the way for Payton's squirts through the line.

A Bears second-round draft pick in 1980, Suhey stood 5-foot-11 and weighed 217 pounds. There weren't many touches to go around with a superstar like Payton in the same backfield, but Suhey rushed for 400-plus yards for the Bears four times. "I hate to complain," Suhey said when his opportunities diminished in 1986. "I can't be selfish at the team's expense. I'd enjoy a chance to carry the ball more, but for whatever reasons I haven't. To win the Super Bowl last year was a sensational feeling, hard to describe."

Suhey carried a team attitude as well as he did the ball, was very fundamentally sound, and did what he was asked to do when he was asked to do it. On a Super Bowl team full of flakes, he fit in, but had a serious side. As a player he already knew he wanted to enter the business world when he parked his cleats and he has become a very successful Chicago businessman since retiring.

1985 SEASON STATISTICS

1985 regular season and playoff record: 18–1

Bears points in regular season: 456

Bears points allowed in regular season: 198

Bears points in playoffs: 91

Bears points allowed in playoffs: 10

Bears regular season first downs: 343

Bears regular season first downs allowed: 236

Passing leader: Jim McMahon, 56.9 percent completed, 2,392 yards, 15 touchdowns

Rushing leader: Walter Payton, 1,551 yards, 4.8 yards per carry

Scoring leader: Kevin Butler, 51 extra points, 31 field goals, 144 points

Pass receiving: Walter Payton, 49 catches, 483 yards

Interceptions: Leslie Frazier, 6

Quarterback sacks: Richard Dent, 17

Fumble recoveries: Mike Singletary and Dan Hampton, 3

Tackles: Gary Fencik, 118

An estimated 500,000 people crowded downtown Chicago for a parade to celebrate the Bears 1986 Super Bowl victory. *John Cary/Corbis*

the price," Ditka said. But it all got a little bit less funny when Ditka suffered a mild heart attack during the 1988 season. Ditka, then 49, had just completed a workout at the Bears' Lake Forest training center when he felt chest pains for at least the second time that week. Assistant coaches had been urging Ditka to get checked out. Now he was hospitalized.

Bears owner Ed McCaskey said he wasn't surprised that Ditka had a heart problem. "He was a prime candidate," McCaskey said. "He eats what he wants, drinks what he wants, smokes what he wants, sleeps when he wants."

Ditka had helped organized a 25th anniversary party for the 1963 team and had to miss it, though he

"We squandered it. There is a saying that caution is a disease that flourishes in opulent environments and that's almost how that team became."
—Defensive end Dan Hampton on how the Bears should have won more Super Bowls in the 1980s.

sent a videotaped welcoming message from the hospital. There was some shock and sadness about Ditka's condition since he was one of the younger

Neal Anderson bursts through the middle for key yards against the Buffalo Bills in October 1988.
Jonathan Daniel/Getty Images

William "Refrigerator" Perry shows why he got the nickname wearing a tight fitting jersey and shorts to a 1988 mini camp.
Ray Foli/Corbis

THE SUPER BOWL SHUFFLE

They made beautiful music together. And that was off the field. As the end of the 1985 NFL regular season loomed, the Bears were the talk of the nation. They won nearly every game and did so in spectacular ways. They featured a voracious, quarterback-eating defense, a swashbuckling quarterback and possibly the best player in the game in Walter Payton.

The coach, Mike Ditka, a Hall of Fame player, was a hard-as-nails mentor who told it like it was and didn't take no guff, though he had a long leash for a mishmash of players who oozed personality if not always charm. The Bears had more characters than a sitcom. On the way to a 15–1 record, they didn't mind telling people how good they were, but pro football fans lapped it up. Chicago was ga-ga over its Bears and the Bears made it fun for all.

You had quarterback Jim McMahon saying outrageous things and winking. There was William "The Refrigerator" Perry, a sudden cult figure for weighing 300 pounds and carrying the ball at the goal line. There was Steve McMichael, whom you definitely didn't want dating your daughter. The Bears were not only good, they had more flavor than the cake contest at the county fair, more big mouths than Congress.

Typically, championship teams won their title, brought the trophy back to their community and showed it off during a parade through downtown. The celebration encompassed the players, the team, the organization, and the town. The Bears went one better. Before the playoffs even began, they recorded a song to let the world know they were better than everyone else. If people withheld judgment on the Bears being arrogant before, they knew it was true now.

"The Super Bowl Shuffle" was recorded as a novelty song for kicks, with a commitment to donate proceeds to charity. It included solo raps by various players accompanied by other players in uniform playing instruments. In all, 24 members of the team participated. What figured to have appeal pretty much confined to Chicago and vicinity became a nationwide sensation. The 45-rpm single record was a hot seller. The whole country laughed. And later the song was nominated for a 1986 Grammy award. It was wild. And after that a parody of the Shuffle was written.

Wide receiver Willie Gault said he never expected it to become such a big deal. "People always remember 'The Super Bowl Shuffle,'" he said. "That's all people talk about."

The lyrics to the "Super Bowl Shuffle" were written by Melvin Owens and Richard E. Meyer. The music was arranged by Bobby Daniels and Lloyd Barry. The song was recorded on Red Label Records and the performers were lumped together as "The Chicago Bears Shufflin' Crew."

The chorus went as follows:

We are the Bears Shufflin Crew
Shufflin' on down, doin' it for you.
We're so bad we know we're good.
Blowin' your mind like we knew we would.
You know we're just struttin' for fun
Struttin' our stuff for everyone.
We're not here to start no trouble.
We're just here to do the Super Bowl Shuffle.

Fans hooted and hollered and rolled in the aisles when individual players, whom they never imagined singing or shuffling, did solos.

Quiet Walter Payton sang in part,

Well, they call me Sweetness,
And I like to dance.
Runnin' the ball is like makin' romance.
We've had the goal since training camp
To give Chicago a Super Bowl champ.
And we're not doin' this
Because we're greedy.
The Bears are doin' it to feed the needy.

There were 10 solo parts that left fans in stitches, brilliantly crafted satire, fitted to the player, yet universal enough in nature with the beat and the rhyme to draw in more casual listeners.

Gault, track star and pass catcher, sang in part, "This is Speedy Willie, and I'm world class. I like runnin', but I love to get the pass."

Middle linebacker Mike Singletary sang in part, "I'm Samurai Mike, I stop 'em cold. Part of the defense, big and bold."

Defensive end Richard Dent referred to himself as "the sack man's comin.'" Quarterback Jim McMahon referred to himself as "the punky QB." Defensive tackle William Perry, alias "The Fridge," said of himself, "I'm the rookie. I may be large, but I'm no dumb cookie."

And linebacker Otis Wilson sang in part, "I'm mama's boy Otis, one of a kind. The ladies all love me, For my body and my mind."

The song was a work of genius, striking just the right tone, a mixture of silliness and reality that was both accurate and funny. Photos of the recording session were superb as well. In one picture, guard Stefan Humphries is playing drums, running back Dennis Gentry is on base guitar, and fullback Calvin Thomas is blowing on a saxophone. Eyes covered, wearing shades and his Bears uniform, Thomas could well have been in a scene from *The Blues Brothers* movie.

Of course, a professional sports team recording a song about how great it was before playing the final game was unprecedented and it put more pressure on the Bears to live up to their notices. It wasn't going to be much of a celebration if the team lost in the playoffs or the Super Bowl. Who would want a souvenir of a season that ended in disappointment even if the money was going to a worthy cause?

Some references indicate the song made $250,000 for charity, though the songwriters were not similarly rewarded. The players did not benefit monetarily, though "The Super Bowl Shuffle's" existence became part of team lore. There had been jokes that the Bears were so popular and famous they had achieved rock star status from their playing exploits. It turned out to be true from their singing exploits. They were rock stars.

The Bears did it on a lark, had a blast making the song, and enhanced the legend of the Super Bowl champs of 1986.

Super Bowl Shuffle video shoot. *NFL/Getty Images*

Kevin Butler kicks a field goal in a loss to the Lions.
Jonathan Daniel/Getty Images

players on the championship club. The players reminisced and swapped stories and when asked if they would do it all again, despite injuries, later in life infirmities, and playing at a time when the pay was less, they all said they would. "I wish I could play today," quarterback Bill Wade said, owning up to once taking 12 painkilling shots in an injured groin before a game.

Former halfback Ronnie Bull helped connect the reunion event to Northwest Community Health

"We stink. We're just not a good football team."
—Coach Mike Ditka, four seasons after the Super Bowl, on the decline of the Bears.

Services as a fund-raiser for the cardiology department. "I thought, 'Gee, Ditka, you didn't have to go this far to emphasize the need,'" Wade said.

A couple of days later Ditka returned to coaching after a two-week leave of absence that had caused him to miss one game. Part of his health pledge involved staying calmer with less yelling and foregoing cigars. Ditka said he got 5,000 pieces of mail and had opened only a small number of them, but one written by a football fan in Massachusetts stuck in his mind. It read, "I don't like you. I don't like the Bears. As a matter of fact, I detest you. But get better. You're good for football."

In 1989, when the team slumped to 6–10, it was not clear if Mike Ditka was quite as good for the Bears as he had been. The first doubts appeared.

The Fridge and Richard Dent in 1989 training camp.
Jonathan Daniel/Getty Images

1980s CHICAGO BEARS YEAR BY YEAR

1980	7–9
1981	6–10
1982	3–6
1983	8–8
1984	10–6
1985	15–1
1986	14–2
1987	11–4
1988	12–4
1989	6–10

W hen the Bears won the Super Bowl after the end of the 1985 season, they looked like a bunch very much in command of their futures. The roster was filled with players in their primes and they seemed likely to win a few more consecutive championships. What no one reckoned with—though signs were plentiful early—was the size of many individuals' egos. Usually, for a team to succeed, the egos of the best players must be submerged so that

everyone pulls together. With the Bears, despite so many colossal egos, the team made it work. They were so talented, so good, and there was more than single helpings of adulation to go around.

The first fissures appeared almost immediately after the victory, when defensive coordinator Buddy Ryan announced his departure for the Philadelphia Eagles. Only a couple of weeks passed before Ryan and coach Mike Ditka were talking about their relationship

Right: Iron Mike Ditka on the sidelines in a 1992 game.
Jonathan Daniel/Getty Images

Below: Buddy Ryan meets with the media after he was named head coach for the Philadelphia Eagles.
Bettmann/Corbis

in the past tense and telling the world they didn't really need one another anyway.

"I'm not happy he's gone, I'm elated," Ditka said. "We'll be better next year."

Ryan was just as snippy. "I should be so lucky to have a Buddy Ryan around," he said. "I'd like to have somebody around to take care of me."

Even if the partnership had been fraught with tension, the men made it work for the common good. The break-up of the team had far-ranging consequences. Ditka was wrong. The Bears were not as good without Ryan as they had been with him. And Ryan never coached a really big winner again.

For the Bears, each season that passed represented a step down from the Super Bowl triumph. In the beginning, in small increments, because Ditka still had the talent and was still a fine coach. And in some ways nationally, the Bears were still riding high because even if they did not repeat as Super Bowl champs, they had stamped their image on the public's mind. They put up records of 11–5 twice to start the 1990s and made the playoffs both times, so the Bears had not gone into hibernation.

In 1991, the Bears reached new heights of national fame when the now signature phrase "Da Bears" was coined in a *Saturday Night Live* comedy skit entitled "Bill Swerski's Superfans." The priceless material, especially if you were from Chicago, was delivered by a high quality group of actors that included at various times Joe Mantegna, Chris Farley, Mike Myers and John Goodman.

The setting was a sports bar with all of the fans drinking beer and eating ribs and Polish sausages (respectable Chicago menu fare) and wearing dark glasses and thick mustaches in homage to their hero, Mike Ditka, "Da Coach." Many discussions tossed in the Chicago Bulls and their star Michael Jordan, too. But it always came around to Da Bears as the greatest sports team in the wide world and to Mike Ditka, as the invulnerable "Da Coach." Once, the characters predicted that Ditka would win the Indianapolis 500 driving the Bears' team bus.

In one of the most sidesplitting of the nine sketches that stretched over two years, the Ditka duplicates competed on a *Jeopardy*-like show where all the right answers revolved around the Bears, Chicago and Ditka. The final *Jeopardy* question was "Da Bears?" or "Da Bulls?" Several years later, the Superfans reappeared on the show on a night when Ditka was the guest host—perfect casting.

The sketches, or off-shoots of them, show up in other satirical comments periodically on *Saturday Night Live* and "Da Bears" or "Da Bulls" is dropped into conversation between Chicago sports fans all of the time. In January 2007, on the eve of the Bears' first return to the Super Bowl since the championship, a *Saturday Night Live* actress gazed at soccer and singing couple David and Victoria "Spice Girls" Beckham and said, "If you guys were a football team, you would be Da Bores."

Besides the disruptive departure of Ryan, there were other signs of cracks in the Bears' homogeneity.

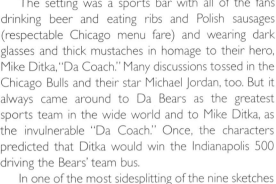
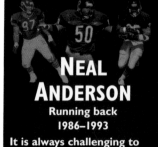

NEAL ANDERSON
Running back
1986–1993

It is always challenging to follow a legend and often thankless. Neal Anderson is the answer to the trivia question: "Who replaced Walter Payton in the Bears' backfield when the Hall of Famer retired?"

Anderson, who grew up in the small town of Graceland, Florida, put together a sterling All-American college career at the University of Florida and was the Bears' No. 1 draft choice in 1986. In the recognition that Payton would not play much longer, the 5-foot-11, 210-pound Anderson was groomed as his successor. The newcomer arrived the season after the Super Bowl championship and his running chances were sparse his rookie season. Anderson carried the ball only 35 times that season, but his average per carry was an impressive 4.2.

In 1987, Payton's last, the backs split the load. Anderson actually out-performed Payton with 586 yards and a 4.5 yards per carry average. When Payton hung up his cleats the Bears felt they were in good hands and Anderson produced 1,106 yards (the first of three 1,000-yard seasons) and 12 touchdowns his first year as the full-time starter.

Injuries stunted some of Anderson's brilliance and he retired young after the 1993 season, but his lifetime statistics indicate a first-rate career. Anderson rushed for 6,166 yards, with a career average of 4.1 yards an attempt and 302 passes caught. Only placed next to the numbers recorded by an all-time great like Walter Payton could Anderson's totals be slighted.

Bears fullback Neal Anderson dives for yardage in a 1992 game against the Atlanta Falcons.
Andy Hayt/Getty Images

Defensive lineman Dan Hampton battles with the Seattle Seahawks in 1990.
Jonathan Daniel/Getty Images

"I thought the world of [Jim] Harbaugh. I thought he was tougher and a better quarterback than people gave him credit for. He was negatively affected by Ditka, and I don't know if Mike was the right coach for him."
—*Former Bears receiver Tom Waddle.*

Ditka and his old favorite Refrigerator Perry were feuding. Ditka told the steadily inflating Perry that enough was enough, that he was fat and must weigh 350 pounds. For all of the good will, attention and fun that stemmed from Ditka's use of The Fridge in the lineup, Perry had to perform. "He is in jeopardy of not being here if he doesn't want to take off the weight," Ditka said.

Perry said he really didn't weigh that much. But he was coy in revealing his true weight, admitting only to weighing between 300 and 350. "I could be 308," Perry said. "But he's the head man and he runs the show. I just sit back and listen." Perry stuck with the Bears through the 1993 season.

The Bears of 1990 were still among the league's elite. They won 11 regular-season games and defeated the New Orleans Saints in the first round of the

Jim Harbaugh fading back to pass against the Packers in 1991.
Jonathan Daniel/Getty Images

JIM HARBAUGH
Quarterback
1987–1993

Jim Harbaugh really did have football in his genes. His father Jack was a college coach, who worked on the staff of Bo Schembechler at the University of Michigan. Eventually son Jim quarterbacked the Wolverines to the Rose Bowl.

Harbaugh was big at 6-foot-3 and 215 pounds and could throw hard. But he and coach Mike Ditka did not seem to have the right chemistry for the Bears' offense. Famously, Ditka once berated Harbaugh harshly on the sidelines. Harbaugh served an apprenticeship on the bench as the Bears shuffled quarterbacks, but when he got the chance to be the main man in 1990 he did well. He completed 57.7 percent of his passes for 10 touchdowns against only 6 interceptions while running the team three-fourths of the time in an 11–5 campaign. He was better in 1991 as the full-time starter with 3,121 yards. And in 1993, Dave Wannstedt's first, Harbaugh completed 61.5 percent of his passes, though his TD–interception ratio was poor. Some of Harbaugh's best years were in Indianapolis. When he led the Colts to several late wins he earned the nickname "Captain Comeback."

Harbaugh said it was an experience to play professionally in Chicago, a city that reveres football, where everything you do on the field matters. "That community just loves, loves football," said Harbaugh, who became a college head coach at the University of San Diego and then Stanford. "They're just so passionate about the game of football."

Quarterback Jim Harbaugh cocks his arm to throw a pass in a 1991 game.
Jonathan Daniel/Getty Images

Right: Mark Carrier catches the ball during a game against the St. Louis Rams in 1995.
Brian Bahr/Allsport/Getty Images

Far right: Steve McMichael, Bears star defensive tackle.
Daniel Stluka/Getty Images

playoffs. But they were crushed, 31–3, by the New York Giants, ending their season.

Neal Anderson rushed for 1,078 yards and Kevin Butler scored 114 points with his foot. Mike Singletary still held the lease to the middle linebacker's job and recorded 151 tackles. They also added an exciting new player in University of Southern California safety Mark Carrier. Carrier had a remarkable rookie year with 10 interceptions, a team record for a season. He was chosen the league's defensive rookie of the year and made the pro bowl. "The interceptions are what you read and hear about, but knowing the game and being able to anticipate are important," Carrier said.

The Bears turned in the same 11–5 record in 1991, but everyone's numbers dropped, except for quarterback Jim Harbaugh, who had his finest season. Anderson's yardage fell to 747, Butler's points fell to 89 and Singletary's tackles fell to 124. And the Bears lost to the Cowboys 17–13, in the first round of the playoffs.

This was a crossroads. Most of the main players from the Super Bowl team were either gone or nearing the end of their careers. The wins piled up during the regular season, but the Bears did not scare opponents. They needed to add some key personnel, a dream quarterback, perhaps, some help in the backfield, and some fresh faces on defense.

None of that happened in 1992. Singletary was still the No. 1 tackler in 1992 with 135, positive evidence of his continuing defensive excellence. But the team seemed to age overnight. Ditka was frantic, his typical tirade leading observers to believe he was ripe for another heart attack, this time on the sidelines during a game. The *Chicago Sun-Times* ran a call-in poll for readers asking, "Will the Bears win another game this season?"

On his radio show—Ditka's main media contact after canceling his regular Monday after-game press conference—he took abuse from callers urging him to quit. He did not discuss the topic gently as if in the setting of courtroom decorum, but fired back at insults. He said he would match his record against any other NFL coach (Ditka would likely win) and occasionally said the callers represented what was wrong with America (he might have been right, but it was an argument he could not win). When the season mercifully ended, with the Bears losing eight of their last nine games to finish 5–11, it was obvious changes were coming.

Shortly after the regular season ended, the biggest change that anyone could have contemplated became reality. The Chicago Bears fired Mike Ditka. Da Coach was a coach without portfolio. After 11 years at the helm, Ditka was out as of January 5, 1993. It was a stunning end to a wildly popular and successful reign. True Bears fans couldn't believe it and questioned the wisdom of the move. To them Ditka should have been like George Halas, coach to as close to forever as possible.

Ditka's record with the Bears was 112–72, a 60.9 winning percentage. He led the team that won the only Super Bowl in team history. And he was five games ahead of Halas for wins in his first 150 games, 100 to 95.

The Bears ended the Ditka era at a press conference at Halas Hall, and even team president Michael McCaskey, who announced the firing, had tears in his eyes. There were definitely Ditka defenders, including Pulitzer Prize winning columnist Mike Royko, known to display temper himself. Ditka participated in the press conference and was also emotional. "I'll try to do this with class," Ditka said. "Scripture tells you that all things shall pass. This, too, shall pass." Royko said Ditka should have been truer to himself, punching McCaskey and walking out without a word. Royko's following prediction from that day was eerie in its accuracy. "This is the beginning of a long, tedious, dull and unsuccessful period for the Bears because McCaskey is no football guy," Royko wrote.

"We did a pretty good job," Ditka said, summing up his tenure on the way out the door.

Mike Singletary, middle linebacker who was the heart and soul of the Bears championship defense, in a 1992 game against Tampa Bay. *Jonathan Daniel/Getty Images*

KEVIN BUTLER
Kicker
1985–1995

Kevin Butler remains the Bears scoring leader more than a decade after he retired as the team's decade-long place kicker. Butler made 387 of the 397 extra points he attempted and he kicked 243 field goals for a total of 1,116 points.

Coming out of the University of Georgia, Butler was a fourth-round draft pick for the soon-to-be Super Bowl champions. He combined two animals that coach Mike Ditka held in disdain on the football field, but couldn't live without—rookies and kickers. The coach yelled at the kicker often, but the kicker's personality allowed him to deflect the abuse or use it for motivation. "I didn't shy away from him getting in my face," Butler said.

At 6-foot and 215 pounds, Butler at least had the size of a football player. One time after Ditka told him he was a lousy kicker Butler yelled back, telling the coach to go get a better kicker if he thought he could find one. Butler showed up at practice to see some bare-footed prospect kicking instead of him. Ditka had no intention of keeping the stranger, but warned Butler not to challenge him again.

After retiring, Butler returned to Georgia and went into business, but said his three children were all born in Illinois and are Bears fans. He is, too, and said Ditka is now a friend. "He is a dear friend and he is a very, very loyal person," Butler said.

Bears kicker Kevin Butler boots a field goal against the Packers in a 1993 game.
Jonathan Daniel/Getty Images

Some might question if the Ditka era ever did pass. Two decades after his dismissal, Ditka was at least as popular a figure in Chicago as he had been when he was producing winning teams. Fans still call him "Coach" or refer to him jokingly as "Da Coach." And that's even after he departed on a "leave of absence" from the city to coach the New Orleans Saints for a few years (a move that did not work out).

If the Bears knew what was in store that day at team headquarters (if they had believed Royko), they might have held on to Ditka tightly, given him a new contract and asked him to start all over and build a new champion. Defensive tackle Steve McMichael, one of the holdovers from the title team, saw it that way. "Ditka was made the scapegoat for a bunch of guys who were not doing their jobs on the field," McMichael said. "If they'd done it right, they'd have fired all the players instead of the coach. It's the players' fault, we bear it on our shoulders."

Whoever was at fault, the Bears were starting all over in 1993.

The only way the reception for the successor coach to Mike Ditka in Chicago would have been warm rather than skeptical was if the coach won big right away. That did not happen. Dave Wannstedt took over for the 1993 season and the Bears finished 7–9.

Wannstedt came with high recommendations. He had been an assistant coach with Pittsburgh (his alma mater), Oklahoma State, Southern Cal and the University of Miami. His long-time friend Jimmy Johnson was winning national championships with the Hurricanes and when Johnson made the leap to the NFL to coach the Dallas Cowboys, he brought Wannstedt with him. Similar success followed and Wannstedt earned considerable recognition as Dallas' defensive coordinator. Pretty soon he was getting attention all around the league as the next breakthrough head coach. Before he landed the Bears' job Wannstedt had been a finalist to take over the Pittsburgh Steelers.

Wannstedt was considered one of the bright young coaches who had paid his dues and who shone when given responsibility. Being a defensive specialist was seen as a plus for a team that had always thrived on that side of the ball. So Wannstedt arrived with great fanfare and… nothing much happened. Butler was still a kicking machine. Anderson ran when he was healthy, but his 3.2 yards per carry was unacceptable long-term. And the defense? Well, the Bears out-scored opponents 234 to 230.

It may not have helped that Mike Singletary went out the door with Ditka. "He was great, fantastic," Singletary said. "I loved him. He was the right guy at the right time in Chicago. It was undoubtedly a great time.

It was a great opportunity for me to to be coached by someone like Coach Ditka and Buddy Ryan at the same time. That was tremendous." Singletary's retirement left his decade of leadership at middle linebacker up for grabs. He had taken great pride in his role and being an anointed successor to Bill George and Dick Butkus. "Coming to Chicago," he said, "I was really, really excited and happy to know that I had to live up to something. Defense meant something and playing defense meant something."

As always, it was unclear where the Bears were going with their quarterback job. The 1990s was an era when prevailing thought still focused on needing a great quarterback to win. Yes, you needed all of the pieces around him, from an offensive line to protect him, to a running back to complement him and a defense to get the ball back, but it was a must to have some dude with a cannon arm back there to win all the marbles. The concept of a "caretaker" quarterback, who was just a cog in the machine, wasn't given much credence and the idea of dinking a team to death with short passes almost as a substitute for the running game, seemed radical.

The Bears just could never find the quarterback they needed. It was ridiculous really that a franchise that dated back to 1920, going on 75 years, had had one bona-fide star quarterback with any longevity. Jim McMahon might have become more, but he was hurt half the time. In an ill-fated personality match, the Bears brought in former Heisman Trophy winner Doug Flutie and his offensive explosiveness which had ruled in the Canadian Football League for a shot. Ditka disparaged him. So the signing of Erik Kramer from the Detroit Lions to lead the team for the 1994 season was a dramatic step. Kramer had an arm. He had experience. He had been a starter. Was he the one? He showed signs of it for six games until he got hurt and missed the rest of the season.

Still, the Bears finished 9–7, and back-up quarterback Steve Walsh had done well taking over. Lewis Tillman, who had attended Walter Payton's old school of Jackson State, rushed for 899 yards and

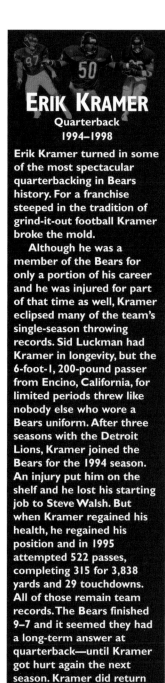

ERIK KRAMER
Quarterback
1994–1998

Erik Kramer turned in some of the most spectacular quarterbacking in Bears history. For a franchise steeped in the tradition of grind-it-out football Kramer broke the mold.

Although he was a member of the Bears for only a portion of his career and he was injured for part of that time as well, Kramer eclipsed many of the team's single-season throwing records. Sid Luckman had Kramer in longevity, but the 6-foot-1, 200-pound passer from Encino, California, for limited periods threw like nobody else who wore a Bears uniform. After three seasons with the Detroit Lions, Kramer joined the Bears for the 1994 season. An injury put him on the shelf and he lost his starting job to Steve Walsh. But when Kramer regained his health, he regained his position and in 1995 attempted 522 passes, completing 315 for 3,838 yards and 29 touchdowns. All of those remain team records. The Bears finished 9–7 and it seemed they had a long-term answer at quarterback—until Kramer got hurt again the next season. Kramer did return to excel in 1997, too.

"We didn't win as many games as I would have hoped, but just living in that city and being part of the Bears family and history is something that I'll always remember and something I was proud to be part of," said Kramer, who became a TV sportscaster in California after retirement. "The Bears are one of the great franchises there is."

CHRIS ZORICH

Defensive tackle
1991–1997

Lineman Chris Zorich was one of the most popular players of the 1990s. Of African-American and Croatian heritage, Zorich succeeded against the odds. He was raised by a single mother, Zora, in poverty on Chicago's South Side and became a star player at nearby Notre Dame, twice winning All-American recognition, as well as the Lombardi Trophy as college football's best lineman.

It took a little while for the 6-foot-1, 278-pound Zorich to make a major impact on the Bears' defense, but 1993 was his breakthrough season, with 121 tackles and 7 sacks. It was the type of season that brought back memories of the 1980s defenders who terrorized quarterbacks so often. Zorich was the latest "Monster of the Midway." Zorich became a pro bowl alternate that season.

In 1994, Zorich recorded 104 tackles with 5½ sacks. Although he was in on 79 tackles a year later, Zorich's career was bedeviled by injuries after that and rarely again did he have the opportunity to show his ability at full strength. He was retired by age 28.

Almost from the first moment he appeared in a Bears uniform, Zorich involved himself in Chicago charitable work, as a rookie establishing the Christopher Zorich Foundation to aid disadvantaged families. He has received national humanitarian awards for his efforts to help those less fortunate. Zorich has worked as a motivational speaker and always credits his mother's devotion and advice for his success in life

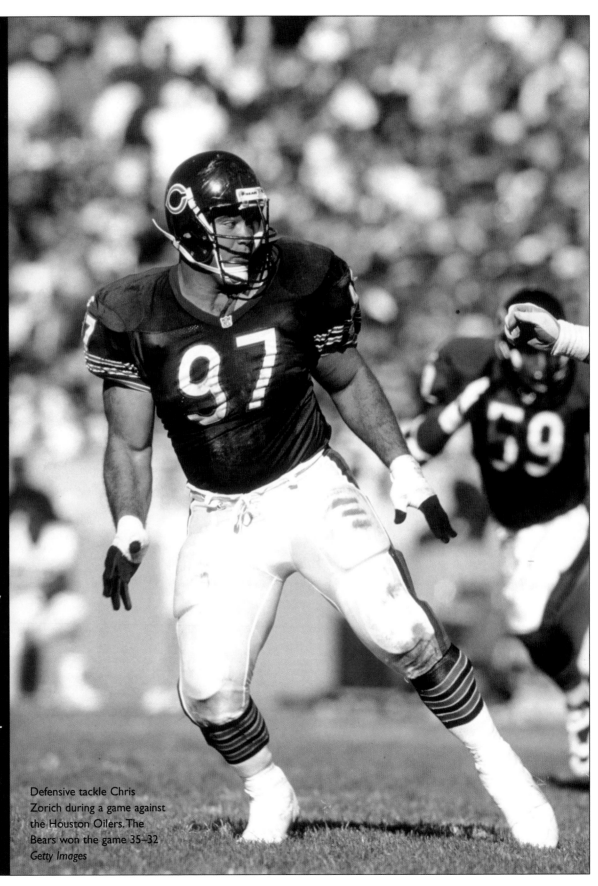

Defensive tackle Chris Zorich during a game against the Houston Oilers. The Bears won the game 35–32
Getty Images

caught 27 passes in the primary running back role. But the defense was not all that special, giving up 307 points while the offense scored 271. The best fan-friendly thing that occurred, however, was qualifying for the playoffs. And then the Bears won a game, taking out Minnesota, 35–18, on the road yet, before losing to the San Francisco 49ers.

The Vikings victory was probably the high point of the Wannstedt era. The team recorded a winning record, uplifting fans' feelings and the playoff win was frosting on the cake. The achievements of the year were worth celebrating. All signs pointed to being No. 1 with a bullet. What Wannstedt and the Bears didn't know was that was all there was. The Bears had peaked again.

The next season Chicago finished 9–7 again, but that record wasn't good enough to get into the playoffs. There were some individual standouts, particularly Kramer, who had the best single season of any quarterback in team history. He threw short, he threw long, and he threw touchdowns, 29 that season, against only 10 interceptions and set the Bears team record of 3,838 yards gained while completing 60.3

percent of his passes. For once, the Bears did not need their defense to score touchdowns on interceptions or fumble recoveries just to be in games. The offense was the workhorse. Everything was in just-so proportion, too, because with their No. 1 draft choice that season the Bears took Colorado's Rashaan Salaam. Salaam had won the Heisman Trophy as the best player in college football after rushing for 2,055 yards.

He was a key addition. Salaam's running prowess—1,074 yards and 10 touchdowns—kept defenses off-balance and allowed Kramer time to throw. Kramer's go-to receiver was Jeff Graham out of Ohio State. As a rookie Graham caught 68 passes from Walsh and Kramer. In his second year, Graham nabbed 82 balls and gained 1,301 yards.

Yet for all of that, the Bears still barely contained opponents on defense. Wannstedt's reputation as a defensive whiz haunted him. A mid-season stretch when the Bears lost four straight games and then extended that to six out of seven before righting themselves took some luster off the winning season. Fans felt the Bears had more talent and that Wannstedt either wasn't using his players properly or

Steve Walsh looks to hand off the ball during the divisional playoff against the San Francisco 49ers at Candlestick Park on January 7, 1995. The 49ers won 44–15. *George Rose/Getty Images*

**"When [coach Dave] Wannstedt was here—I played with him my last year—he just thought it [playing Green Bay] was another game. To me, it was like, 'You don't get it.' That just upset me."
—Bears lineman Keith Van Horne.**

calling the right plays. Something was off. Shouldn't the Bears have been better than 9–7? Shouldn't they have made the playoffs?

Oh well, there was always next year. But there wasn't. In the 1996 season the Bears went backwards in most measurable ways. They were out-scored again, 305 to 283, leading fans to sting Wannstedt by asking where was this defensive wisdom. The leading tackler by far was strong safety Marty Carter, in on 180 tackles. That was far too many for a player who began each play far back from the line of scrimmage. That meant ball carriers were breaking through the line and coming to him; they already had their yardage by the time Carter caught them. Kramer made it through half a season healthy. Salaam made it through half a season healthy. The team never had any consistency. It was win one, lose three, win one, lose two, win one. There was some question of whether or not Wannstedt would make it through the season healthy, or at least with his job.

A sense of frustration eased in like fog from Lake Michigan. The Bears were not improving, they were clawing to stay even. Then in 1997 things got worse. The Bears started 0–7. Salaam was injured and barely a factor, though Raymont Harris filled in nicely with 1,033 yards. But the defense was as much of a sieve as a goalie on a 10-goal night. The team got clobbered most weeks, falling to 4–12, giving up at least 31 points seven times and losing all but one of those. The Bears were out-scored 421 to 263 that season. It was embarrassing.

The Bears finished 4–12 again the next year. The running game was in disarray. Salaam and Harris were both out of the picture. Kramer only made it through half a season healthy and, as galling as anything else, the Packers swept the Bears. That was a disappointing trend in the making. Ever since Green Bay plugged in this strong-armed kid from Southern Mississippi named Brett Favre at quarterback, the Bears were getting shellacked in the rivalry series.

Tackle Keith Van Horne caught only the beginning of the Favre era face-to-face and he said the combination of the Bears not being very good in the last two-thirds of the 1990s and Favre being very good tilted the series Green Bay's way. "Too much Favre," Van Horne said. "We didn't have to deal with Brett much when I was playing. He came in at the end for me." Van Horne had been weaned on the feeling that you hate Green Bay if you play for Chicago. Ditka emphasized that during his tenure. Wannstedt did not play it up as much—neither did assistant coaches—and Van Horne missed that passion. "That was not a good sign," Van Horne said.

Of course by 1998, Wannstedt was worried about winning any game, not just beating the Packers. The Bears started 0–4, then had an 0–6 losing streak in November and December, too. And the Bears were out-scored overall by nearly 100 points again. In the end, Wannstedt was taking flak from all directions. The Bears were mired in mediocrity and did not have the

personnel in place for a quick fix. The first phase of repairs began right after the season. Wannstedt was fired with a 41–57 record.

Strange doings and almost comical misunderstandings ensued. The Bears' first choice for a new coach was a man who wanted the job. It seemed like a good match, with Dave McGiniss having experience as an assistant under Ditka and Wannstedt. The hire got so close to reality that a press conference was called to introduce McGiniss to the media. But then McGiniss balked, saying he had not signed a deal and the Bears had jumped the gun. He recoiled from the Bears and the team was coachless. Quickly, Dick Jauron, former NFL defensive back who had grown up in Massachusetts and attended Yale, became the replacement for the replacement.

Opposite page: Bears coach Dave Wannstedt talks in 1998 training camp with Wasswa Serwanga. *Jonathan Daniel/Getty Images*

Rashaan Salaam in action in 1997. *Jonathan Daniel/Allsport/Getty Images*

THE DEATH OF
WALTER PAYTON

When Walter Payton retired from the Chicago Bears after the 1987 season, he was the National Football League's all-time leading ground gainer. He had accumulated 16,726 yards rushing on an exceptional 4.4 yards per carry and as a byproduct also grabbed an impressive 492 passes. It all added up to 125 touchdowns.

Payton had also run for a single-game rushing record of 275 yards against the Minnesota Vikings in 1977, a mark since broken. It was a day when the Bears needed every one of them because they only won 10–7. Payton scored the Chicago touchdown on a 1-yard burst. He carried the ball 40 times that day and except for one 58-yard dash added up the yards in small chunks.

Payton lugged the ball through some lean times with the Bears and no one was more overjoyed when the team's resurgence lassoed a Super Bowl. In a long and productive career it seemed he had only one regret—not scoring a touchdown in the Bears' 46–10 win. Payton's chance, his carry, went to "The Refrigerator," the 300-pound lineman doubling as a running back and coach Mike Ditka made the call. When he realized later how much Payton lamented his lost chance, Ditka admitted publicly that he had made a mistake.

When he left the game Payton was hailed by many as the greatest running back of all and was on a supersonic path to the Pro Football Hall of Fame. His 13 Bears seasons were marked by class and his nickname of "Sweetness" was as a sign of his pleasing personality. The public loved Payton and so did his teammates. He never bragged about his exploits so they often took to podiums on his behalf, never missing a

Connie Payton (R), widow of the late Chicago Bear great Walter Payton holds her daughter, Brittney (L), as they watch a video tribute to Payton during the public memorial in Chicago's Soldier Field, November 6, 1999.
Reuters/Corbis

chance to tell fans how marvelous the 5-foot-10, 200-pound runner was as a player, man, and as a hard worker. Payton was inducted into the Hall of Fame in 1993. In a moving ceremony, Payton's then 12-year-old son Jarrett, served as his presenter.

It was known that he lived in the Chicago area and that Jarrett was an ever-improving running back just like dad and on his way to the University of Miami to play football. But Payton was not in the spotlight as often as some of his former compatriots with Super Bowl XX rings. Ditka was everywhere, from his restaurant just off the Magnificent Mile, to NFL television pre-game shows. Other teammates were paid commentators and analysts on TV and radio stations, pontificating about and reporting on the activities of the next generation of Bears. Payton not so much. He was not a hermit, but he was not in the gossip columns, seen at night clubs, working in the media, running for mayor or governor or anything quite so high profile.

Payton was a little bit out of mind compared to the days when he was churning out big yards and scoring big touchdowns. So it came to a shock to everyone, from the teammates he hadn't seen lately to the millions of fans who admired him as a player, to hear in 1998 that Payton was battling a debilitating, dangerous, rare liver disease.

It was announced that Payton was going to be placed on a liver transplant list. A sense of hope was imparted that things would still turn out OK. Payton mostly retreated from public view after that. He was sicker than he let on and perhaps sicker than he even knew.

As 1999 wore on, Payton's health deteriorated. Known as the No. 1

practical joker on the Super Bowl champs, Payton stopped seeing many of his teammates who wanted to visit, gradually limiting their stop-overs. Ditka was still in the loop until the final few weeks of Payton's life. Fullback Matt Suhey, Payton's best friend from his playing days, and cohort in many of the half-baked jokes played on teammates, saw him in the last days of his life. So did the linebacker Mike Singletary, a very religious man, who saw Payton the day he died. "He was lying there, no tense look on his face, just peace," Singletary said. "It's difficult to explain. Just peace."

When Payton died on November 1, 1999—the diagnosis was cancer of the liver bile duct—he was 45. Most people who heard of his demise were shocked and disbelieving. An impression had formed that yes, they heard Payton was ill, but the doctors were taking care of it. There was a general feeling that Payton would get well again.

Only those closest to Payton, his wife Connie, brother Eddie, also a former NFL player, and his children, knew the truth, that the odds had tilted against him being able to accept a transplant, or

survive the aggressive cancer. It had been a year-long fight lost by a tough man who had never shirked tough challenges.

Ditka said he had expected Payton to obtain a transplant and go back to "being Walter again." Quarterback Jim McMahon said he had planned to visit Payton the day before he died, but was called to California because his mother-in-law died. "So I never got to say goodbye to him," McMahon said. "I didn't know it was this bad."

It was not until months after Payton died that his autobiography, co-written with sports writer Don Yaeger, reached bookstores. It was called *Never Die Easy*. He did not. In the book, Payton said, "If you ask me how I want to be remembered, it is as a winner." If anyone has ever challenged that assertion, it has been done awfully quietly.

The day Payton died, the Bears lowered the American flag to half staff at Halas Hall, the team's headquarters. "It's a very sad day," team president Ted Phillips said. "If anyone was bigger than life, it was Walter. We're all better off having known him and we're going to miss him greatly."

Current members of the Chicago Bears line up to place a rose at the foot of a large photograph of the late Walter Payton November 6, 1999.
Reuters/Corbis

A makeshift fan memorial at Soldier Field honoring Walter Payton after he died of cancer at age 45 in 1999. *Sue Ogrocki/Getty Images*

BEARS–PACKERS 1992–1999

After Brett Favre arrival

1992	**Bears 30–10 at Green Bay**
	Packers 17–3 at Chicago
1993	**Packers 17–3 at Green Bay**
	Bears 30–17 at Chicago
1994	**Packers 33–6 at Chicago**
	Packers 40–3 at Green Bay
1995	**Packers 27–24 at Chicago**
	Packers 35–28 at Green Bay
1996	**Packers 37–6 at Chicago**
	Packers 28–17 at Green Bay
1997	**Packers 38–24 at Green Bay**
	Packers 24–23 at Chicago
1998	**Packers 26–20 at Green Bay**
	Packers 16–13 at Chicago
1999	**Bears 14–13 at Green Bay**
	Packers 35–19 at Chicago

Above right: Dick Jauron smiles from the sidelines during a Bears mini-training camp at Halas Hall. *Jonathan Daniel /Allsport/Getty Images*

Opposite: Defensive back Tony Parrish tries to break up a scoring pass to the Redskins' Michael Westbrook during a 1999 game. *Jessica Persson/Getty Images*

Jauron was quiet, even stoic from the start, as he took over headed into the 1999 season. Studying tape and scouting, personnel director Mark Hatley decided he had found the future quarterback of the Bears, the man destined to lead the Bears out of the wilderness, UCLA star Cade McNown. Making McNown the No. 1 draft pick was a disaster on several fronts. It turned out to be a waste of a first-round choice. Because Kramer was cut as a result of the pick his talents were lost to the team. McNown did not have the ability to be a pro quarterback and lasted just two seasons on the Bears roster and that was after arriving with a Big Man On Campus attitude that alienated many Bear veterans.

McNown got a chance to play right away and ended up throwing 10 interceptions to 8 touchdowns and giving way to former Florida star Shane Matthews, who completed 60.7 percent of his passes and completed 10 touchdown passes to 6 interceptions. McNown was written off as one of the biggest personnel busts in team history.

The messy quarterback situation—again—saddled Jauron with problems not of his own making. His first Bears team in 1999 finished 6–10.

Jauron's first season coincided with the depressing death of all-time great Walter Payton on November 1, from liver disease complicated by cancer. Payton had been ill for a year, but many expected him to recover, not die at age 45. Although Payton knew his illness was serious and he believed what the doctors at the Mayo Clinic told him, he said he tried to tackle it as he would a football injury. "I'm looking at it as a sprained ankle or a twisted knee," Payton said. "I have to stay positive. Then whatever happens, happens." His demise, funeral, and the out-pouring of sentiment for the classy player who had defined Bears character during his 13-year Hall of Fame career, was a sad backdrop to a season that was a struggle from beginning to end.

Not only was Payton a phenomenal running back,

"To see it happen to Walter is shocking, to not be able to combat this thing like he did everything else in his life."
—Former Bears quarterback Jim McMahon when Hall of Fame halfback Walter Payton died of liver disease.

he impressed his teammates, coaches and whoever else watched with his relentless work ethic, his willingness and ability to block, and his all-around skills catching passes. Payton had retired as the NFL's leading rusher of all time with 16,726 yards, had been inducted into the Hall of Fame, and had caught fans off guard when he publicly revealed his illness in 1998. Payton was given two years to live in February of that year unless he received a liver transplant.

Payton had been diagnosed with sclerosing cholangitis, a rare disease affecting the bile ducts, and was still on the transplant list when cancer struck quickly. Only a few of Payton's old Bears teammates were admitted to the family circle in his final days and hours, notably fullback Matt Suhey, Payton's best friend during his playing days, and linebacker Mike Singletary.

One of the most poignant moments on the day of Payton's death was the sight of his son Jarrett, a member of the University of Miami football team at the time, returning from Florida and meeting with sports writers at Halas Hall to talk about his dad. "The last 12 months have been extremely tough on me and my family," Jarrett Payton said. "We learned a lot about love and life. Our greatest thanks go out to the people of Chicago. You adopted my dad and made him yours. He loved you all."

Team owner Virginia McCaskey, daughter of team founder George Halas, said that when running back Brian Piccolo died of cancer in 1970, the family had decided they would no longer get so close to the players. They pretty much stuck to that, she said, until Payton came along and was so esteemed. They considered him a special man and he became the only retired player, except for Halas himself, to ascend to the team's board of directors.

Many tears were shed for Payton among those who knew him best at a private memorial service and among those who admired him from afar at a public memorial service.

After an emotionally draining experience like that, fans didn't have too many tears left over to cry for the current Bears. They just got angry because the Bears couldn't figure out a way to win again.

1990s CHICAGO BEARS YEAR BY YEAR

1990	11–5
1991	11–5
1992	5–11
1993	7–9
1994	9–7
1995	9–7
1996	7–9
1997	4–12
1998	4–12
1999	6–10

Right: Bears quarterback Jim Miller (left) and receiver David Terrell bump chests in celebration of a win over Tampa Bay in 2001 that gave the team a playoff spot.
Sue Ogrocki/Getty Images

Far right: All-star center Olin Kreutz sets up to block against the St. Louis Rams in a 2003 game.
John Zich/Getty Images

Dick Jauron's first season behind the wheel did not go particularly well and if anything things got worse in 2000. The Bears finished 5–11, were outscored 365 to 216, discovered that Cade McNown was not their quarterback of the future, and were reminded that Shane Matthews was good to have around—as a backup.

There was very little good news. One notable exception being a rookie linebacker named Brian Urlacher bursting on the scene out of New Mexico where he had spent more time as a defensive back. Urlacher was in on 165 tackles and blasted quarterbacks to the tune of 8 sacks. He was an immediate sensation and an all-star as a rookie. Just about the only other good-news development was the sight of running back James Allen dashing for 1,120 yards.

Throughout it all, Jauron was a sideline statue, stoicism being his middle name. Years later fans would be hard-pressed to remember many occasions when Jauron was seen smiling or frowning very deeply. He was one of those football coaches who keep emotions inside, churning his belly, rather than yelling in front of the cameras.

From all outward appearances, 1999 and 2000, the first two years of the Jauron administration, had been disasters. Speculation began on how long Jauron would last as coach. And then came 2001, a completely unexpected turn-around, a totally unanticipated gift, a season that energized Bears fans, provoked them into more pre-game parking lot tailgating than had been witnessed in years. You couldn't walk near Soldier Field

"The new Soldier Field, the face that launched a thousand quips (Monstrosity of the Midway, Eyesore on Lake Shore, Mistake by the Lake) is almost here—a skillful, sometimes brilliant and ultimately jarring failure. With its spaceship-like seating bowl crammed between the stadium's legendary rows of Doric columns, the stadium is Klingon meets Parthenon, an architectural encounter of the worst kind."
—Chicago Tribune *architecture critic Blair Kamin in 2003 as remodeled Soldier Field was about to open.*

for hours before kick-off without inhaling the smell of Polish sausages and other grilled meats. Passers-by were offered beers and were invited to join the cozy parties. The Bears were back!

It was a stunning reversal. Led by Urlacher and a new linebacking partner, Warrick Holdman, the defense limited foes to 203 points while an offense which had scared nobody in pre-season ran up 338 points behind the signal-calling of journeyman quarterback Jim Miller. McNown was last seen hitch-

hiking his way out of town on the Edens Expressway, headed back west someplace. Rookie running back Anthony Thomas came out of the University of Michigan and took over, rushing for 1,183 yards and 7 touchdowns. And wide receiver Marty Booker set pass-catching records, grabbing 100 throws for 1,071 yards and 8 touchdowns. The Bears actually had a multi-dimensional offense.

Maybe this guy Jauron knew what he was talking about, even if he was so close-mouthed he hardly told anyone what he was talking about. The season was a fantasy ride and nothing typified the magical quality of a team on a roll better than two mid-season overtime victories. Defensive back Mike Brown, who intercepted five passes that season, was the central figure in two consecutive beyond-belief comebacks.

On October 28, the Bears went into overtime at Soldier Field against the San Francisco 49ers after trailing by two touchdowns in the fourth quarter. In sudden death play, the team with the ball has a great advantage. There is terrific pressure on the defense. San Francisco had the ball and Brown took it away, intercepting a pass and running it back all of the way for a touchdown and a 37–31 Bears win. "To lose a game like that, this is a shock," said 49ers quarterback Jeff Garcia.

A week later, the Bears were in almost the same circumstances, again at Soldier Field, except the odds were even more overwhelming against them. The

BERNARD BERRIAN

Wide receiver
2004–
Bernard Berrian was a 4th-round draft pick out of Fresno State and heralded by Bears management as a potential go-to wide-out. At 6-foot-1 and 185 pounds, fleetness is of importance to Berrian. He caught nearly 200 passes in college and was a high school star in Modesto, California. Berrian caught 15 passes as a rookie. And he grabbed 13 as a second-year player. Though he was injured part of the time, Berrian averaged a gaudy 18.9 yards per catch that season, displaying speed after the catch. After limited play for those two seasons he caught 51 passes for 6 touchdowns in 2006 and showed opposing defensive backs just how dangerous he could be.

Reaching the Super Bowl in 2007 was a team landmark and Berrian said the experience was great, but merely a warm-up for winning it all. "You know, we have unfinished business to take care of," Berrian said. "We don't want to be a team known for getting to the Super Bowl, or just being there. We want to be known for winning the Super Bowl. My standard is way too high to call just getting to the Super Bowl my career highlight. My standards are way too high."

Berrian was not belittling reaching the Super Bowl game, but being only 26 at the time he spoke, he was hoping for many more chances to win the big game. "That's definitely something to remember," Berrian said of 2007. "But I'm not selling myself short."

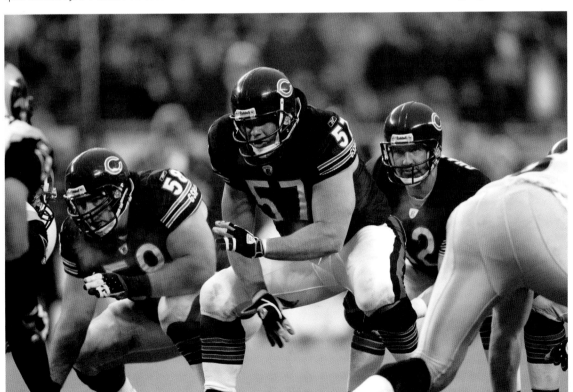

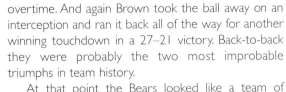

"It's Green Bay. It's all you have to know. It doesn't matter what our records are."
—Bears coach Lovie Smith in 2005 asked how big the game is with his team on an eight-game winning streak and the Packers playing poorly.

Marty Booker makes a key catch in a 2003 game against the Green Bay Packers.
Jonathan Daniel/Getty Images

stadium was clearing out, the fans had given up, when the Bears scored two touchdowns in the last minute to send the game against the Cleveland Browns into overtime. And again Brown took the ball away on an interception and ran it back all of the way for another winning touchdown in a 27–21 victory. Back-to-back they were probably the two most improbable triumphs in team history.

At that point the Bears looked like a team of destiny, a team that would win every game just because they were supposed to. The team's trademark was the defense forcing a turnover and the offense capitalizing.

The season ran long that year because of the September 11, 2001, terrorist attacks. When President John F. Kennedy was assassinated November 22, 1963, a Friday, the NFL went ahead and played its regularly scheduled games that weekend. Commissioner Pete Rozelle was forever criticized for the decision. After the hijacked airplanes crashed into the World Trade Center towers, the Pentagon and a field in Western Pennsylvania, there was no hesitation. All sports activities were suspended. The NFL skipped a week of scheduled games and pushed the season back by a week. As a result, the Bears were still playing a regular season opponent, Jacksonville, on January 6, 2002.

Defense played a huge part again as the Bears crumpled the Jaguars, 33–13, to clinch the National Football Conference Central Division and a first-round bye in the playoffs. The first big play was when James "Big Cat" Williams, 6-foot-7 and 331 pounds, playing on special teams, raised a big paw to swat down an attempted field goal when the score was still 0–0. "I don't even think I got off the ground," Williams said afterwards, laughing about how high he might have jumped.

The defense intercepted three passes and sacked the quarterback four times in the decisive victory. The players, who had suffered through such a rotten season the year before, indulged in a little bit of gloating. "We couldn't be 5–11 again," said defensive end Bryan Robinson. "To prove everybody wrong is the biggest thing."

The Bears season ended with a 33–19 playoff loss to the Philadelphia Eagles two weeks later. It was disappointing that they went down so meekly, but no one had seen the good results of the season coming and it certainly promised better things.

The unexpected extension of the 2001 season, first from the postponed game and then by making the playoffs, led to a construction delay in the revamping of Soldier Field. The plan was to work every possible minute from the end of the Bears season until the start of the 2003 season. The Bears were scheduled to play 2002 home games at Memorial Stadium in Champaign, about 150 miles south, where the University of Illinois football team plays. Within minutes after the final gun

An aerial view of newly
renovated Soldier Field in
October 2003.
John Zich/Getty Images

Above: Brian Urlacher breaks up a pass intended for San Francisco receiver Brandon Lloyd during Chicago's 23–13 win over the 49ers on October 31, 2004.
Jonathan Daniel/Getty Images

Right: 1,000-yard rusher Thomas Jones lugging the football against the Detroit Lions in 2005.
Harry How/Getty Images

Muhsin Muhammad makes an extraordinary diving grab in a 2006 game against the Green Bay Packers.
Tom Hauck/Getty Images

sounded ending the game and the Bears season, heavy equipment operators were maneuvering big rigs onto the field and digging up the earth near the 50-yard-line. Those leaving Soldier Field late could not even depart through the usual exit. Work was underway to provide a new look to the stadium.

There was no catching teams by surprise the next season. The Bears had to prove that they were for real by repeating their effort and results of 2001. Didn't happen. Didn't come close to happening. Brian Urlacher produced a dominating, almost scary season with 214 tackles, and Marty Booker caught 97 passes, but almost no one else produced anything worthwhile. People tried to blame staying at the wrong hotel in Champaign the night before a game or the long drive taking players out of their comfort zone as reasons

why the team couldn't win, but no one seriously bought those excuses. During one stretch the Bears lost eight games in a row. Thomas' running declined. Miller got hurt and Chris Chandler stepped in at quarterback. Miracles were in short supply and sometimes defense was, too. The team had set a high standard the year before and created expectations where there had been none. It was a dismal 4–12 campaign.

If it had not been for the previous feel-good 13–3 season Jauron surely would have been fired. The team's upper management restructured in an unprecedented way, bringing in Jerry Angelo from Tampa Bay as a new general manager, one from outside the family. Angelo and Jauron did not seem to be on the same page and it seemed obvious that

"And now I get to celebrate with my teammates."
—Bears center Olin Kreutz after the team defeated Green Bay, 24–17, to clinch the National Football Conference's North Division in December 2005.

Jauron must take the team to the playoffs in 2003 to retain his job as his contract ran out.

He did not make it. The Bears finished 7–9. As usual, Urlacher excelled and Thomas churned out another solid rushing season with 1,024 yards. There was also considerable attention focused on the new-look Soldier Field. While never has been heard a discouraging word about the sight lines or it being difficult to watch a game, the outside of the stadium was condemned in many quarters for being a blight on the lakefront. Construction had indeed preserved the outer columns and for two-thirds of its height, the old concrete structure. The inside had been gutted and redone to provide a better viewing experience. Again, nobody complained about that. But using modern materials and a futuristic look built on top of the old framework was an affront to the eyes. The jarring picture never improved with age and soon there were threats to have the stadium removed from the National Historic Landmark list.

Remodeling didn't help Jauron, either. He was fired and Angelo hired a new coach. Lovie Smith, a veteran assistant coach with a reputation for shaping excellent defenses, was brought in to save the day. Smith became the first black head coach in Bears history. At his introductory press conference, Smith seemed in tune with Bears tradition. Most new coaches would have talked about instilling a winning habit, of taking the team to the playoffs and the Super Bowl. It's not as if Smith wasn't conscious of those goals, but he also said something very important that fans never forgot. Goal number one, he said, was to beat the Green Bay Packers. Already Smith was making friends.

He would need them in 2004 when the Bears showed little improvement with a 5–11 record. However, Angelo had acquired some key new players through the draft and trades. Rookie linebacker Lance Briggs led the team with 168 tackles. Rookie defensive back Nathan Vasher worked his way into the starting lineup, intercepted five passes and ran one back 71 yards for a touchdown. Angelo picked up running back Thomas Jones in a trade with the Arizona Cardinals and Jones ran for 948 yards. And after the free agent signing of Kordell Stewart did not work out at quarterback, the Bears reeled in throwers as if they were fish biting on a hot day. Angelo had drafted Florida's Rex Grossman in the first round in 2003, with the idea of grooming him to become the franchise's quarterback of the future. He started the last three games of the season and all systems were go for 2004.

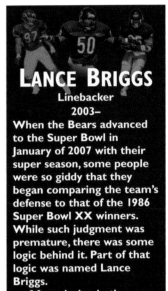

LANCE BRIGGS
Linebacker
2003–
When the Bears advanced to the Super Bowl in January of 2007 with their super season, some people were so giddy that they began comparing the team's defense to that of the 1986 Super Bowl XX winners. While such judgment was premature, there was some logic behind it. Part of that logic was named Lance Briggs.

After playing in the shadow of middle linebacker Brian Urlacher since he arrived as a third-round draft pick for the 2003 season, Briggs had come into his own and become closer to Urlacher's equal, a fact that terrified opponents. Briggs was selected to play in the pro bowl in Hawaii after the 2005 and 2006 seasons and in 2004, 2005, and 2006 he averaged more than 10 tackles per game. His seasonal high was 176 in 2006. After the 2006 season Briggs became embroiled in a contract dispute with the team, but when the Bears slapped the "franchise" player tag on him he received $7.2 million for the 2007 season and opened the door to becoming a Bear for the rest of his career.

Briggs grew up in Sacramento and became a three-time All-Pac-10 all-star linebacker at Arizona after shifting from fullback. At 6-foot-1 and 240 pounds, Briggs not only packed a huge wallop with his tackles, he had fast wheels and excellent lateral movement. Much like Urlacher, Briggs' talents allowed him to roam sideline-to-sideline to make plays and those skills helped put a stamp on the Bears' defense.

Lance Briggs rearranges Green Bay tight end Bubba Franks' head on a hit in a 2005 game. *John Gress/Getty Images*

RUBEN BROWN
Guard
2004–2007

Ruben Brown was already well on his way along the road that might carry him to the Hall of Fame before he became a Chicago Bear. Cut loose by the Buffalo Bills, Brown signed as a free agent in 2004 and solidified a rebuilding offensive line. He then used his 6-foot-3, 300-pound bulk to help carry the Bears to the Super Bowl.

Being an offensive lineman is the most unheralded role on a football team. And being a guard at war in the line of scrimmage trench means being the most unheralded of all. Centers and tackles, especially the tackle protecting the quarterback's back, get more attention. Brown played collegiately at Pittsburgh and was a No. I draft pick by the Bills in 1995. He is a grinder who opens holes and is one of those anonymous players given gold watches by appreciative runners and quarterbacks who achieve the flashier statistical goals. Yet there are experts who watch line play and Brown has been chosen for the pro bowl nine times.

Brown said playing for the Bears is special because it's apparent how much love Chicago gives the team. "I had heard that even when the Bulls were winning championships that everyone was in love with the Bears," Brown said. "It's definitely nice to be the town favorite. I smile when I see little kids wearing Bears jerseys. The parents are doing a great job of educating the youth in Bears history."

Safety Chris Harris holds his hand up to his ear as if to encourage more applause from the Soldier Field crowd after he batted away a Carolina Panthers pass in 2005. *John Gress/Getty Images*

Quarterback Kyle Orton hands off to running back Cedric Benson in a 2005 game. *John Gress/Getty Images*

In 2004, Grossman started the first three games then tore up a knee. Fans were horrified and other teams feasted as the Bears achingly progressed through the year, switching quarterbacks in and out of the lineup, playing lifetime backups as starters. Chad Hutchinson, Craig Krenzel and Jonathan Quinn each took a turn, none produced, and were last seen waving goodbye at O'Hare International Airport. It takes a trivia expert to recall the names of Bears QBs that season.

The keys to the car were at last turned over to Grossman for the start of the 2005 season. Smith and Angelo had re-stocked the shelves, built a team they liked. Now they needed someone to run it. Grossman broke his ankle and missed 13 games. The only one left to run the lemonade stand was Kyle Orton, a rookie from Purdue. Orton was in no way prepared to supervise a playoff-caliber NFL offense, but he and the Bears made it work better than anyone expected. Urlacher and Briggs were everywhere on defense, Vasher intercepted 8 passes, and Jones ran for 1,335 yards. Acquisition Muhsin Muhammad from Carolina caught 64 passes. Orton made rookie mistakes, but the Bears made up for them. They finished the season 11–5 and reached the playoffs, only to lose 29–21 to the Carolina Panthers. Grossman returned and played in the playoff loss, capping a tumultuous season for

him. "It's been a crazy year," Grossman said. "Nothing that I would have expected happened. I'm going to do everything I can physically and mentally to come back and be the best quarterback in the league."

One thing that seemed to revive on Smith's watch right away was a focus on the Packers. The Bears won, 21–10, the first time the teams met under Smith in 2004. The next year the Bears swept and that felt very good. Former coach Mike Ditka was even asked to reminisce about going against the Packers when he was in charge. He and Packer coach Forrest Gregg, who had been rivals on the field as players, too, seemed to despise one another. Ditka said the rivalry was at its worst when Gregg coached. Recalling the occasion Packer defensive lineman Charles Martin wore a towel with the names and numbers of Bears players on his hit list, Ditka said things got out of hand. "It became mayhem because it was stupid, trying to hurt people," Ditka said of the 1980s showdowns. "All I know is it did not happen when Bart Starr was the Packers' coach, or Lindy Infante, or Mike Holmgren."

Running back Adrian Peterson blows past the 49ers defense and adds to his career-best 120 yards rushing against San Francisco on November 13, 2005.
Jonathan Daniel/Getty Images

ADRIAN PETERSON
Running back
2002–

Adrian Peterson was a longshot to make the pros. He was a star in college, but it was at Division I-AA Georgia Southern, the second tier of NCAA football. He was strong, but not exceptionally large at 5-foot-10 and 210 pounds. But he showed heart and year after year he has thrown himself into the tasks Bears coaches have asked of him. Sometimes that was being part of the kamikaze crew running full-speed downfield to make the tackle on special teams. Sometimes it was being a blocking back. Other times it was being asked to play in the backfield just on third downs. Peterson did it all well, never complaining that he deserved more chances to carry the ball, but always hoping he would get that chance. In his first six seasons, Peterson's best production came in 2005 when he gained 391 yards. Yet his career average was a first-rate 4.7 yards per carry.

It felt right to Peterson when the Bears, as one of the original NFL teams, reached the Super Bowl again. "It's almost like this is the rightful place for a championship team," Peterson said. "It had been a while since we had gotten back to the pinnacle." Peterson is also impressed by how much Chicagoans appreciate their Bears. "This is a great town to be a football player," he said. "Chicago ranks at the top. They say Chicago is a Bears town and when you win it's even more of a Bears town."

Quarterback Rex Grossman at
the controls in a 2006 game
against the Buffalo Bills.
Anne Ryan/Getty Images

Bears owner Virginia Halas McCaskey, daughter of Bears founder George Halas, cheers the Bears triumph over New Orleans in the NFC playoffs in 2007.
Hans Deryk/Getty Images

Tank Johnson talks to the media at Super Bowl XLI.
Maury Tannen/Getty Images

In the 2000s, fans were certainly caught up in the rivalry. A packerssuck.com site was created on the Internet and jokes galore making fun of the team and the city appeared. One item read, "Did you hear about the tragic death of two ice-fishing Packer fans? They got run over by the Zamboni!" Also, "Why don't Packer fans ever sky dive? What good is a parachute if you can't count to 10?" And, "How do you know when a Packer fan is angry at you? He grits his tooth at you."

For years since future Hall of Fame quarterback Brett Favre appeared on the scene, the Packers had held the upper hand in the rivalry. But as Favre reached the shadow of the end of his career, the Packers fell back in the pack and went through a rebuilding phase. In 2005, the team stumbled to its first losing season since Favre came aboard. "I'm sure people in Chicago are tickled to death with the Packers," Favre said.

In 2006, the Bears opened the season with a 26–0 victory over the Packers in Green Bay and there were extenuating circumstances when Chicago lost in the season finale. For once, the Green Bay game took a back seat to the playoffs. It was definitely produce or else time for Grossman in 2006. The fans were out of patience. The coaches were trying to give his strong arm a chance to make big plays. Could he lead a team? No one really knew. Just in case he could not, Angelo would not risk repeating history by sticking an inexperienced wanderer into the most important role on the field. He signed veteran Brian Griese as a back-up. For once the Bears had an insurance policy that was more than wishful thinking.

Grossman, a 6-foot-1 and 217-pound star in high school in Bloomington, Indiana, and at Florida, stayed in one piece throughout the 2006 season. He passed for 3,193 yards and 23 touchdowns, but he was also guilty of 20 interceptions. He was a good leader at times and maddeningly inconsistent at other times. The media played "Good Rex" and "Bad Rex" games and fans booed mistakes. Grossman was perpetually under a microscope, scrutinized so closely that if the number of cells in his body changed it would have been reported on the front page of the city's sports sections.

Additions through the draft made Angelo look smart. Charles "Peanut" Tillman became a quick contributor in the defensive backfield. Robbie Gould, who scored 143 points, took over the place kicking. Thomas Jones was unhappy that the team brought in Texas rookie Cedric Benson to push him, but he refused to be beaten out and rushed for 1,210 yards. Above all, the defense was voracious and premature comparisons were made to the 1985 defense. Lovie Smith, who proved to be as tough to read as Dick Jauron, was more restrained than others. "If you don't let them score you

have a heck of a chance to win," Smith said.

The Bears started 7–0, but the sixth win was one players remembered later. The Bears met the Arizona Cardinals on a *Monday Night Football* game in the desert. Chicago was heavily favored because of its early-season play and the Bears were being touted as the team of the year. Then they went out and played their worst game, embarrassing themselves with ineptitude on national television.

The Cardinals led 20–0 at the half and the Bears

Veteran tackle Fred Miller.
Thomas E. Witte/Getty Images

BRIAN URLACHER

Linebacker
2000–

From the moment Brian Urlacher joined the Bears for the 2000 season after being drafted out of New Mexico, the 6-foot-4, 258-pound guided missile injected himself into the sweepstakes of best Chicago Bear Middle Linebacker of All-Time. He fit right in with the tradition of the franchise, immediately claiming ownership of the position. Urlacher's speed, determination and ability to cover massive amounts of territory roughly the size of his home state of New Mexico, were noticed immediately, not only by Bears fans. He was named the NFL's defensive rookie of the year and in 2005 was selected as the league's defensive player of the year.

Each season Urlacher led the Bears in tackles, including 2002 when he was in on an astounding 214 plays, and he was chosen for the pro bowl every year. The player's speed for a big man set him apart. He was capable of running down running backs and receivers (as well as picking off the occasional interception and recovering fumbles) and when he exploded off the line he often met quarterbacks with vicious hugs when they would have preferred a handshake. He totaled 32½ sacks through his first six seasons.

Urlacher has become a symbol of the team to the public. Urlacher's No. 54 jersey is one of the most popular for sale among NFL fans across the country and on game day in Chicago hundreds of rooters can be seen wearing the replicas at Soldier Field.

Brian Urlacher holds up the NFC Championship trophy named for Bears founder George Halas after Chicago's victory over New Orleans in 2007 as coach Lovie Smith looks on.
Maury Tannen/Getty Images

had shown no offensive punch whatsoever. They got a break when Mike Brown recovered a fumble and ran it 3 yards for a touchdown, but it was still 23–10 after three quarters. The clock was ticking down in the fourth quarter, fans at University of Phoenix Stadium were filing out, and televisions were being clicked off all over the United States.

The defense created another big play when Tillman recovered another Cardinals' fumble and ran it back 40 yards for another touchdown. The score was Arizona 23, Chicago 17. Even that didn't make Arizona fans very edgy. There simply was not enough time left for the Bears to mount a drive. The Cardinals ran the clock down and punted. They hadn't counted on Devin Hester. He gathered the ball, surveyed the defenders, made a move and was gone. Almost impossibly, he ran the punt back 83 yards for a touchdown, Robbie Gould kicked the extra point and the Bears won.

The players celebrated wildly in the locker room.

The Bears clinched their weak division with weeks left in the season. They finished 13–3 in the regular season, out-lasted Seattle, 27–24 in overtime, and

Tight end Desmond Clark leaps over fallen St. Louis linebacker Dexter Coakley after catching a pass in a 2006 game.
John Gress/Getty Images

DEVIN HESTER
THE TOUCHDOWN MACHINE

He was drafted out of the University of Miami on potential, his dreadlocks a trademark blowing in the breeze as he blew past collegiate tacklers. But no one, not the Bears' hierarchy, teammates or fans, realized up front that Devin Hester would virtually overnight become the most electrifying player in the National Football League.

The odds against running back any single punt or kick-off for a touchdown are huge. Some players who specialize in returns run back one for a touchdown in their entire career. That's the history of the role, even amongst the best return men. The job is to get field position for the offense, run the kick back as far as you can before the 11 guys on coverage catch up to you. Except in the case of Hester, who is fast enough, but 10 times more elusive than any other kick returner they see. He is Superman in cleats, a bolt of lightning in a football jersey, a zig-zag on a page.

What the Bears and opponents swiftly discovered was that Hester, all 5-foot-11 and 186 pounds of him, could get out of tighter spots than Houdini. Gale Sayers, the previous best-ever kick returner in Bears history, used to say all he needed was 18 inches of daylight and he was gone. If so, Hester makes good on the boast with a ruler's length of space, 12 inches. Hester leaves observers groping for superlatives. He leaves teammates jumping up and down on the sidelines in glee. Reporters search for fresh descriptions to apply to his breakaway runs. It all added up to six touchdown runbacks as a rookie in 2006 and selection to the pro bowl.

His first season, Hester led the NFL in punt returns made, punt return yardage and in scoring three touchdowns on punts with a long gain

Devin Hester has become an all-pro kick return star
for the Bears.
Scott Boehm/Getty Images

of 84 yards. He scored twice more on kick-offs, with a long of 96 yards. Not included in the stats, apparently defying categorization, Hester also ran a missed field goal back 108 yards for a touchdown against the New York Giants. Hester then introduced himself to millions of new fans by jump-starting the Super Bowl against the Indianapolis Colts in January of 2007 in Miami by running the opening kick-off 92 yards for another touchdown.

Of course Hester is fast, but a lot of guys are fast. He just has an instinct for the opening and a stupendous ability to adjust on the fly, cut back when he needs to and slash at an angle away from the oncoming tide. He was not particularly surprised to run back the kick-off in the Super Bowl that the Bears lost 29–17. "This is what I had been envisioning all week and actually for two weeks," he said. "We had a chance to come out with the kick-off return on the first play of the game. But the bad part is that we didn't come out with the victory." Still, Hester was feted by fans and announcers and in the off-season he was even a guest of the Chicago Cubs to throw out a ceremonial first pitch at a game at Wrigley Field and then lead the singing of "Take Me Out to the Ballgame" during the seventh-inning stretch.

By the middle of his second season, Hester was such a feared weapon that teams game-planned around kicking to him. Some were so worried that he would run back a critical punt or kick-off for a score that they kicked the ball out of bounds, giving the Bears good field position instead of chancing a Hester runback.

Sometimes that worked to the opponent's favor and sometimes it gave the Bears an edge. In the 11th game of the 2007 season, the Denver

Broncos chose to kick to Hester and he ran back two kicks, first a punt for 75 yards, then an 88-yard kick-off return, for touchdowns in the same quarter. By the end of that game, after only 1⅔ seasons, Hester had authored touchdown runbacks 12 times. He was the chief reason the Bears prevailed over the Broncos in overtime that day. The next morning's *Chicago Tribune* ran a huge headline reading, "Devin Almighty."

Most humorously, at the end of the punt return, Hester ran straight through the end zone and down a tunnel under the stands, disappearing for a few moments. "I had to slow myself down," he said. "I couldn't stop." Chicago fans were used to seeing Hester perform magic, but no one had ever seen him disappear. No one gets tired of these type of plays. Because of the unpredictability of kick returns, no one knows when it's coming either, when the coverage will part like the Red Sea. It is a gift that cannot really be taught. The talent must be in place and only some experience in reading the field and the unfolding play is what can be improved on. There have been many great players, however, who have tried, been given the opportunity, but never approached what Hester has accomplished in a very short time.

Tom Waddle, who was a Bears receiver between 1989 and 1994, and later a sports radio host, had no qualms rating the performance against the Denver Broncos as one achieved by a special player. "He is the most exciting player in the game," Waddle said on his radio show.

Whether it was humility, the nature of his unpredictable job, or flat out true, not even Hester seemed prepared for his immediate explosive impact. Not even at the start of the 2007 season when he started repeating the plays of 2006. Early in his second Bears season, Hester ran a punt back 73 yards for his fourth punt-return touchdown, a team record. He was asked if he ever amazes himself and Hester said yes. "Every day," he said. That only indicates Devin Hester is human. Because all the other mortals watching think he is pretty amazing too.

In Super Bowl XLI, Devin Hester started things off with a bang by running the opening kickoff back 92 yards for a touchdown. *Jed Jacobsohn/Getty Images*

surprisingly thumped New Orleans, 39–14, in the second round of the playoffs to advance to the Super Bowl in Miami against the Indianapolis Colts. In the pre-game hype, Lovie Smith came perilously close to making a prediction. A man who worked overtime to avoid saying anything confrontational, controversial, or perhaps even meaningful, said, "We are a good football team and we know how to finish the job. Teams like this deserve to have a championship."

The night before the Super Bowl, Bears linebacker

Hunter Hillenmeyer's mother Sally obtained a picture of downtown Chicago with its skyscrapers lit up forming words to encourage the team. "Go Bears" was written out by coordinated window lighting. Sally Hillenmeyer had the image blown up into a huge poster and gave it to her son as a gift. "That was a big moment for me," said Hillenmeyer talking about his favorite Super Bowl-related souvenir. "There were blue and orange lights and there were like 20 different buildings with Bears stuff on it."

The Super Bowl began in the most auspicious way possible for the Bears. Rookie sensation Devin Hester, the most dazzling kick returner to enter the NFL in years, took the opening boot from the Colts and ran it back 92 yards for a touchdown. Hester, a 5-foot-11, 186-pound whippet, had exploded on the league during the regular season, returning six kicks of different types for touchdowns. He was the king of special teams, a bonus offensive weapon that other teams did not have. Unfortunately for the Bears, the team peaked right there. The Colts, behind legendary quarterback Peyton Manning, were the superior team that day and won 29–17. "We knew deep down that we were capable of returning one," Hester said. "But when it all boils down that return didn't mean a thing. The only thing that really matters is who came out with the victory."

Thomas Jones, who had done so much to stabilize the Bears' running game with three straight solid seasons, was from Miami and he so wanted to win a Super Bowl in front of family and friends in the city that he knew so well. He took his time getting dressed afterwards, trading a work suit with grass stains on it for slightly more formal attire. "Right now I am just trying to stay positive about the season," he said. "Otherwise you can drive yourself crazy."

Although it had been nearly 15 years since he coached the Bears, Mike Ditka remained one of the most popular sports figures in Chicago. He opened a popular steak house that thrived downtown. He endorsed cigars and wine. His opinion was sought by television and radio sports shows. Briefly, he was tempted to run for the U.S. Senate representing Illinois after the Republicans invited him.

But in 2007 Ditka took on a cause that straddled politics and sport. He vigorously campaigned to convince the National Football League and the NFL Players Association to increase their pension payments and disability checks to needy former players who did not make big bucks when they played. Ditka became a visible spokesman for the Gridiron Greats Assistance Fund lobbying for help for disabled ex-players who were short on funds, and testifying before Congress about the need. The battle

Kicker Robbie Gould shouts with happiness after kicking the winning field goal in overtime as the Bears bested the Seattle Seahawks 27–24 in a 2007 playoff game.
Maury Tannen/Getty Images

"Bears fans, they're true and blue. They've been through some lean years. Until they carry the Lombardi Trophy off, we'll still be their favorite kids."
—*Kevin Butler, Bears Super Bowl XX kicker, reminiscing in 2005.*

between organizations became quite bitter, but Ditka never wavered in his determination to speak out for individuals who needed help and were in some cases living in dire circumstances. "All we're here for is for the system to get fixed," Ditka testified to the House Judiciary Subcommittee on Commercial and Administrative Law in June. "The system does not work." In a later discussion with a Congressman, Ditka said, "The responsibility has to go back to the league and the owners. Come on. It's a bunch of red tape and bureaucracy."

In July, the players' union and the NFL agreed to start a fund with $7 million to provide much needed assistance. A few months later Ditka announced he was auctioning off a Super Bowl ring he had won with the Dallas Cowboys with the proceeds going to the assistance fund. And then in October, the NFL announced the allocation of $10 million to a medical fund to help disabled retired players. "Ten million," Ditka said. "Terrific. Great gesture. I hope it changes

Thomas Jones bursts into the clear for a key touchdown in the Bears 2007 playoff victory over Seattle.
Scott Boehm/Getty Images

Safety Chris Harris leaps in front of Colts receiver Marvin Harrison to intercept a Peyton Manning pass in the first quarter of Super Bowl XLI.
Jed Jacobsohn/Getty Images

about 75 miles south of Chicago. "Recent history has been bad for Super Bowl teams getting back," Hillenmeyer said. "But I look around and it feels like we're hungrier this year than we were last year. I think definitely everything is in gear."

That was the mood, but that was not the reality. The Bears seemed out of sync from the start of the 2007 season. Something seemed off every game. One day it was the quarterbacking. One day it was the running game. One day it was the defense. After a few weeks, Rex Grossman was benched, replaced by Brian Griese. Cedric Benson had stepped in as the new running back following the trade of Thomas Jones at his own request. Injuries disrupted the defense and opposing teams began piling up unprecedented yardage and 30-point games.

It was unfathomable. The Bears that were only months removed from the Super Bowl did not look like a team that could make the playoffs—they were a team that might not even compile a winning record. There was a lot of soul searching at Halas Hall. At the halfway point the Bears were 3–5, very un-Bear-like. "If you look at our games, we're about taking the ball away and we haven't been able to get any turnovers," Smith said. "They have been able to run the ball at us and we have not been able to run the ball at them."

Bears players were perplexed. There seemed to be no specific explanation for why things weren't clicking. "You go back to the basics of what you set your team up to be in training camp," said offensive lineman Patrick Mannelly, who joined the team in 1998. Then you go back to what your identity should be. Run the ball. Cause turnovers. We're not doing it." In some ways, Mannelly said he felt as sorry for the fans as anything. "It's truly amazing that they live and die and their work weeks depend on whether we win or lose," he said. "If we won on Sunday they're going to have a great week till the next Sunday. That's the true fan and it's pretty unbelievable. You hear about people watching the game with their grandfathers and stuff like that. It's truly a great football town."

Bears players seemed to be shocked glancing at the standings and seeing themselves with a 3–5 record, almost as if the newspaper was behind held upside down. "We've got to play football on a consistent basis," said defensive end Alex Brown. "We've got to make plays. We've got to cause the fumbles. We're not doing that. We're not doing it, for whatever reason. It's frustrating."

The one player who waged a personal crusade in making big plays was runback star Devin Hester. Any team that booted a punt in his direction or a kick-off in his direction was in danger of being burned. When he had the ball cradled against his chest, Hester

some lives."

In the hot days of training camp before the 2007 season began, the Bears said they were not satisfied with just reaching a Super Bowl. Their rise under Lovie Smith had been swift, but they wanted more. They wanted to get back to the big game and win it. And they brought that attitude to pre-season training camp at Olivet Nazarene University in Bourbonnais, Illinois, created more excitement than fireworks on Fourth of July. By mid-November, Hester had run back four kicks for touchdowns and teams were avoiding him. When the Denver Broncos tried to play normally, kicking deep, Hester scored two more touchdowns.

On a team with a sputtering offense, even after Grossman returned to the lineup when Griese suffered a shoulder injury, with a defense that was not living up to its reputation, Hester was the most important player. Ways were being formulated to use him as a wide receiver or maybe even a running back, just to put the ball into his hands more often and give him a chance to increase his touchdown production.

It grew into a national debate. Should coaches kick to Hester? The Oakland Raiders did it and got away with it. There were no openings for Hester to

2000s
CHICAGO BEARS
YEAR BY YEAR

2000	5–11
2001	13–3
2002	4–12
2003	7–9
2004	5–11
2005	11–5
2006	13–3
2007	7–9

squirt through to daylight. The Bears were listless and being out-performed, dragged up and down the field by the Broncos when they met in late November. Kick away, was the Denver strategy, and Hester went to the house—twice—on a long punt return and a long kick-off return. Broncos kicker Todd Sauerbrun, who had spent four seasons kicking for the Bears, was victimized in every way possible. On a play that was shown on highlights a thousand times, Hester ran back one kick where Sauerbrun was the last line of defense and was shown sprawling on the Soldier Field turf with Hester leaping over him on the run like a high hurdler. Sauerbrun said he had provided tickets to about 40 friends and relatives in his old hometown where he still owns a house, only to end up having the worst game of his career. "I think I'm going to sell my house now," Sauerbrun said, though he was laughing. "But all props to Devin. The guy belongs in the pro bowl."

It was not clear if the Bears would revive themselves and need some patching and fix-it pickups in the off-season, or if they would have to delve into a wholesale rebuilding phase. They had been in both positions before over the long years of the franchise. What was clear was that they had the most spectacular player in the league in Hester. If anyone could offer lessons on how to run to daylight Devin Hester could.

Bears mascot Staley Da Bear in 2007.
David Stluka/Getty Images

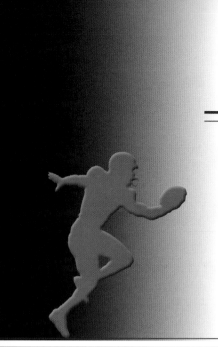

BIBLIOGRAPHY

Books

Claerbaut, David, *Bears Essential*, Chicago, Triumph Books, 2006

Davis, Jeff, *Papa Bear: The Life and Legacy of George Halas*, New York, McGraw-Hill, 2005

Dent, Jim, *Monster of the Midway*, New York, Thomas Dunne Books, 2003

Freedman, Lew, *Chicago Bears Game of My Life*, Champaign, Illinois, Sports Publishing LLC, 2006

Halas, George (with Gwen Morgan and Arthur Veysey), *Halas: An Autobiography*, Chicago, Bonus Books, 1986

McMahon, Jim (with Bob Verdi), *McMahon!*, New York, Warner Books, 1986

McMichael, Steve (with Phil Arvia), *Steve McMichael's Tales from the Chicago Bears Sideline*, Champaign, Illinois, Sports Publishing LLC, 2004

Mullin, John, *Tales from the Chicago Bears Sidelines*, Champaign, Illinois, Sports Publishing LLC, 2003

Payton, Walter (with Don Yaeger), *Never Die Easy*, New York, Villard, 2000

Peterson, Robert W., *Pigskin: The Early Years of Pro Football*, New York, Oxford University Press, 1997

Sayers, Gale (with Al Silverman), *I Am Third*, New York, Penguin Books, 1970

Sayers, Gale (with Fred Mitchell), *Sayers: My Life and Times*, Chicago, Triumph Books, 2007

Singletary, Mike (with Jerry Jenkins), *Singletary on Singletary*, Nashville, Tennessee, Thomas Nelson Publishers, 1991

Whittingham, Richard, *What Bears They Were*, Chicago, Triumph Books, 1991

Youmans, Gary and Youmans, Maury, *'63: The Story of the 1963 World Champion Chicago Bears*, Syracuse, N.Y., Campbell Road Press, 2004

Personal Interviews

Doug Atkins, Bernard Berrian, Alex Brown, Ruben Brown, Doug Buffone, Kevin Butler, Rick Casares, Gary Fencik, Willie Gault, Jim Harbaugh, Hunter Hillenmeyer, Harlon Hill, Stan Jones, Erik Kramer, Patrick Mannelly, Adrian Peterson, Rich Petitbon, Matt Suhey, Charles Tillman, Keith Van Horne,

Press Conferences

Mike Brown, Dick Jauron, Jim Miller, Lovie Smith, Anthony Thomas

Web Sites

www.bearshistory.com
www.chicagobears.com
www.packerssuck.com
www.wikipedia.com

Publications

Chicago Bears 2007 Media Guide
Chicago Daily News
Chicago Sun-Times
Chicago Tribune
Football Digest
Game Day NFL Programs
Sport Magazine
Sports Illustrated

Archives

Pro Football Hall of Fame Library, Canton, Ohio
Chicago Tribune Library

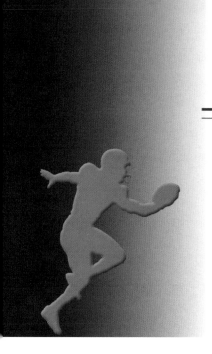

APPENDIX
CHICAGO BEARS RECORD BOOK

*	denotes an NFL record
**	tied for an NFL record

PLAYER RECORDS
SERVICE

Player

Pro Bowls (years are when Pro Bowl was played)

10	Mike Singletary, 1984–93
9	Walter Payton, 1976; 76–81; 84–87
8	Dick Butkus, 1966–73
	Doug Atkins, 1958–64; 66
	Bill George, 1955–62

Seasons

14	Doug Buffone, 1966–79
	Bill George, 1952–65
13	Keith Van Horne, 1981–93
	Steve McMichael, 1981–93
	Walter Payton, 1975–87
	Jim Osborne, 1972–84
	Clyde "Bulldog" Turner, 1940–52
	George Trafton, 1920–32
12	Last: James Williams, 1991–2002

Games

191	Steve McMichael, 1981–93
190	Walter Payton, 1975–87
186	Doug Buffone, 1966–79

Starts

184	Walter Payton, 1975–87
172	Mike Singletary, 1981–92
169	Keith Van Horne, 1981–93

Consecutive games

191	Steve McMichael, 1981–93
186	Walter Payton, 1975–87
179	Mike Hartenstine, 1975–86

Coach

Seasons

*40	George Halas, 1920–29, 1933–42, 1946–55, 1958–67
11	Mike Ditka, 1982–92
6	Dave Wannstedt, 1993–98
5	Dick Jauron, 1999–2003
4	Neill Armstrong, 1978–81
	Jim Dooley, 1968–71
	"Hunk" Anderson / Luke Johnsos co-coaches, 1942–45

Consecutive Seasons

11	Mike Ditka, 1982–92
10	George Halas, 1958–67
	George Halas, 1946–55
	George Halas, 1933–42

	George Halas, 1920–29
6	Dave Wannstedt, 1993–98
5	Dick Jauron, 1999–2003

OFFENSE
SCORING

Points

Lifetime

1,116	Kevin Butler, 1985–95 (387 XP, 243 FG)
750	Walter Payton, 1975–87 (125 TD)
629	Bob Thomas, 1975–84 (245 XP, 128 FG)

Season

144	Kevin Butler, 1985 (51 XP, 31 FG)
143	Robbie Gould, 2006 (47 XP, 32 FG)
132	Gale Sayers, 1965 (22 TD)

Game

36	Gale Sayers, vs. SF, 12/12/65 (6 TD)
24	Last: Bobby Douglass, at GB, 11/4/73

Consecutive games

83	George Blanda, 10/28/51–11/9/58
66	Kevin Butler, 9/9/90–9/12/94
55	Bob Thomas, 12/2/79 –12/16/84

Touchdowns

Rushes–receptions–returns

Lifetime

125	Walter Payton, 1975–87 (110–15–0)
71	Neal Anderson, 1986–93 (51–20–0)
59	Rick Casares, 1955–64 (49–10–0)

Season

22	Gale Sayers, 1965 (14–6–2)
16	Walter Payton, 1977, 1979 (14–22–0)
15	Neal Anderson, 1989 (11–4–0)

Game

**6	Gale Sayers, vs. SF, 12/12/65 (4–1–1)
4	Last: Bobby Douglas, at GB, 11/4/73 (4–0–0)

Consecutive games

8	Rick Casares, 11/1/59–9/25/60
7	Last: Curtis Conway, 9/24–11/12/95

Extra Points Made

Lifetime

387	Kevin Butler, 1985–95
247	George Blanda, 1949–58
245	Bob Thomas, 1975–84

Season

52	Roger Leclerc, 1965
51	Kevin Butler, 1985
47	Robbie Gould, 2006

Game

8	Bob Snyder, at NYG, 11/14/43
7	Last: Bob Thomas, vs. GB, 12/7/80

Extra Points Attempted

Lifetime

397	Kevin Butler, 1985–95
268	Bob Thomas, 1975–84
250	George Blanda, 1949–58

Season

52	Roger Leclerc, 1965
	Ray "Scooter" McLean, 1947
51	Kevin Butler, 1985
47	Robbie Gould, 2006
	George Blanda, 1956

Game

9	Bob Thomas, vs. GB, 12/7/80
8	Roger Leclerc, at Bal, 11/25/62
	George Blanda, vs. Bal, 10/21/56
	Bob Snyder, at NYG, 11/14/43

Consecutive Extra Points

Lifetime

156	George Blanda, 10/28/51–10/21/56
143	Mac Percival, 11/19/67–11/4/73
133	Paul Edinger, 9/3/00–01/2/05

Season

52	Roger Leclerc, 1965
51	Kevin Butler, 1985
47	Robbie Gould, 2006

Game

8	Bob Snyder, at NYG, 11/14/43
7	Last: Bob Jencks, at LA Rams, 10/13/63

Field Goals Made

Lifetime

243	Kevin Butler, 1985–95
128	Bob Thomas, 1975–84
110	Paul Edinger, 2000–04

Season

32	Robbie Gould, 2006
31	Kevin Butler, 1985
28	Kevin Butler, 1986

Game

5	Mac Percival, at Phi, 10/20/68
	Roger Leclerc, vs. Det, 12/3/61
4	Last: Robbie Gould, at Det, 12/24/06

Long

55	Kevin Butler, at TB, 12/12/93
	Kevin Butler, vs. Min, 10/25/93
	Bob Thomas, at LA Rams, 11/23/75

54	Last: Paul Edinger, at Den, 11/23/03
53	Last: Paul Edinger, vs. Min, 12/5/04

50+ Yards (lifetime)

16	Kevin Butler, 1985–95
13	Paul Edinger, 2000–2004
4	Bob Thomas, 1975–84

50+ Yards (season)

5	Paul Edinger, 2002
	Kevin Butler, 1993
4	Kevin Butler, 1990
3	Paul Edinger, 2004
	Paul Edinger, 2003

Field Goal Attempts

Lifetime

333	Kevin Butler, 1985–95
205	Bob Thomas, 1975–84
201	George Blanda, 1949–58

Season

41	Kevin Butler, 1986
38	Kevin Butler, 1985
37	Kevin Butler, 1990

Game

7	Roger Leclerc, vs. GB, 11/17/63
6	Last: Kevin Butler, at GB, 11/8/87
5	Last: Robbie Gould, vs. GB, 12/4/05

Consecutive Field Goals

Lifetime

26	Robbie Gould, 12/25/05–1/19/06
24	Kevin Butler, 10/16/88–12/3/89
21	Jeff Jaeger, 11/3/96–1/16/97

Game (no misses)

5	Mac Percival, at Phi, 10/20/68
	Roger Leclerc, vs. Det, 12/3/61
4	Last: Robbie Gould, at Det, 12/24/06

Games

22	Robbie Gould, 10/23/05–11/26/06
13	Kevin Butler, 9/9–12/9/90
	Kevin Butler, 11/10/85–10/12/86
12	George Blanda, 11/11/56–11/3/57

Field Goal Percentage

Lifetime (25+ attempts)

84.1	Robbie Gould, 2005–06 (53 of 63)
75.9	Jeff Jaeger, 1996–99 (63 of 83)
75.3	Paul Edinger, 2000–04 (110 of 146)

Season (10+ attempts)

88.9	Robbie Gould, 2006 (32 of 36)
83.9	Paul Edinger, 2001 (26 of 31)
82.6	Jeff Jaeger, 1996 (19 of 23)
81.6	Kevin Butler, 1985 (31 of 38)

Missed Field Goal Returns

Touchdowns

*1	Nathan Vasher, vs. SF, 11/13/05
**	Devin Hester, at NYG, 11/12/06

Two Point Conversions

(Since 1994)

Lifetime

1	13 times, Last: Craig Krenzel, 2004

Season
(same as lifetime)

Game
(same as lifetime)

Safeties

Lifetime

3	Steve McMichael, 1981–93

NET YARDS

(rushes + receptions + returns)

Attempts

Lifetime

4,368	Walter Payton, 1975–87
1,619	Neal Anderson, 1986–93
1,579	Rick Casares, 1955–64

Walter Payton diving for yards in a November 1981 game against Tampa Bay. As the statistics on these pages show, Payton truly excelled at everything he did in football. *Ronald C. Modra Sports/Getty Images*

Season
427 Walter Payton, 1984
402 Walter Payton, 1979
383 Walter Payton, 1978
Game
41 Walter Payton, vs. Min, 11/20/77; at Buf, 10/7/79
40 James Allen, vs. NE, 12/10/00
     Walter Payton, at Dal, 11/26/81
39 Walter Payton, vs. SD, 10/25/81

Total Yards
Lifetime
21,803 Walter Payton, 1975–87
9,435 Gale Sayders, 1965–71
8,929 Neal Anderson, 1986–93
Season
2,440 Gale Sayers, 1966
2,272 Gale Sayers, 1965
2,216 Walter Payton, 1977
Game
339 Gale Sayers, vs. Min, 12/18/66
336 Gale Sayers, vs. SF, 12/12/65
300 Walter Payton, at NO, 12/21/75

RUSHING

Lifetime Attempts
3,838 Walter Payton, 1975–87
1,515 Neal Anderson, 1986–93
1,386 Rick Casares, 1955–64
Season Attempts
381 Walter Payton, 1984
369 Walter Payton, 1979
339 Walter Payton, 1977; 1981
Game Yards
275 Walter Payton, vs. Min, 11/20/77
205 Walter Payton, at GB, 10/30/77
     Gale Sayers, at GB, 11/3/68
197 Gale Sayers, vs. Min, 12/18/66
Long
86 Bill Osmanski, (TD) 10/15/39
85 Pete Stinchcomb, (TD) 11/20/21
82 Beattie Feathers, (TD) 10/10/34

1,000-Yard Seasons
Lifetime
10 Walter Payton, 1976–81, 1983–86
3 Neal Anderson, 1988–90
2 Thomas Jones, 2005–2006
    Anthony Thomas, 2001, 2003
    Gale Sayers, 1966, 1969
Consecutive seasons
6 Walter Payton, 1976–81
4 Walter Payton, 1983–1986
3 Neal Anderson, 1988–90

200-Yard Games
Lifetime
2 Walter Payton, 1975–87 (both 1977)
1 Gale Sayers, 1965–71 (1968)

100-Yard Games
Lifetime
77 Walter Payton, 1975–87
20 Gale Sayers, 1965–71
14 Neal Anderson, 1986–93
Season
10 Walter Payton, 1977, 1985
9 Walter Payton, 1979, 1984
8 Walter Payton, 1980
Consecutive Games
10 Walter Payton, 10/13–12/8/85
6 Walter Payton, 09/9–10/14/84
5 Walter Payton, 11/13–12/11/77

Average Gain
Lifetime (250+ attempts)
6.6 Bobby Douglass, 1969–75
5.8 Beattie Feathers, 1934–37
5.0 Gale Sayers, 1965–71

Season (100+ attemots)
*8.4 Beattie Feathers, 1934
6.9 Bobby Douglass, 1972
6.2 Gale Sayers, 1968
Game (10+ attempts)
11.8 Joe Maniaci, at Pit, 10/2/39
11.6 Gale Sayers, vs. Min, 12/18/66
11.2 Rick Casares, vs. Det, 12/16/56

Touchdowns
Lifetime
110 Walter Payton, 1975–87
51 Neal Anderson, 1986–93
49 Rick Casares, 1955–64
Season
14 Walter Payton, 1977; 1979
     Gale Sayers, 1965
13 Walter Payton, 1976
12 Neal Anderson, 1988
     Rick Casares, 1956
Game
4 Bobby Douglass, at GB, 11/4/73
    Gale Sayers, vs. SF, 12/12/65
    Rick Casares, vs. Pit, 12/6/59; at SF 10/28/56
3 Last: Rashaan Salaam, vs. TB 12/17/95
Consecutive games
7 Walter Payton, 10/3–11/14/76
    Gale Sayers, 10/26–12/6/69
6 Gale Sayers, 11/14–12/19/65
    Rick Casares, 11/1–12/6/69
    Johnny Lujack, 10/1–11/12/50
    Beattie Feathers, 9/30–10/28/34
5 Last: Neal Anderson, 10/7–11/11/90

PASSING

QB Rating
Lifetime (400+ attempts)
80.7 Erik Kramer, 1994–98
80.4 Jim McMahon, 1982–88
76.7 Jim Miller, 1998–2002
Season (100+ attempts)
107.8 Sid Luckman, 1943
97.8 Jim McMahon, 1984
95.5 Sid Luckman, 1941
93.5 Erik Kramer, 1995

Attempts
Lifetime
1,759 Jim Harbaugh, 1987–93
1,744 Sid Luckman, 1939–50
1,557 Erik Kramer, 1994–98
Season
522 Erik Kramer, 1995
480 Rex Grossman, 2006
478 Jim Harbaugh, 1991
Game
60 Erik Kramer, vs. NYJ, 11/16/97
57 Bill Wade, at Was, 10/25/64
52 Johnny Lujack, at NYG, 10/23/49

Completions
Lifetime
1,023 Jim Harbaugh, 1987–93
913 Erik Kramer, 1994–98
904 Sid Luckman, 1939–50
Season
315 Erik Kramer, 1995
275 Eik Kramer, 1997
     Jim Harbaugh, 1991
262 Rex Grossman, 2006
Game
34 Jim Miller, vs. Min, 11/14/99
33 Bill Wade, at Was, 10/25/64
32 Erik Kramer, vs. NYJ, 11/16/97
     Erik Kramer, at Mia, 10/27/97
Consecutive
15 Shane Mathews, vs. NE, 12/10/00
14 Steve Walsh, at Min, 12/1/94
13 Jim Harbaugh, at GB, 10/23/92
     Rudy Bukich, 11/22–11/26/64

Long
98 Bill Wade, at Det, 10/8/61 (TD to Farrington)
93 Jack Concannon, vs. StL Cards, 11/19/67 (TD to Gordon)
91 Ed Brown, vs. SF, 10/16/60 (TD to Dewveall)

Completion Percentage
Lifetime (300+ completions)
61.1 Shane Matthews, 1996, 99–01 (366 of 599)
58.6 Erik Kramer, 1994–98 (913 of 1557)
58.5 Jim Miller, 1998–2002 (565 of 965)
Season (75+ completions)
65.1 Shane Matthews, 2001 (84 of 129)
64.0 Chris Chandler, 2002 (103 of 161)
63.2 Jim Miller, 1999 (110 of 174)
Game (10+ completions)
86.7 Bob Williams, vs. Dal, 10/12/52 (13 of 15)
83.3 Bill Wade, vs. Bal, 11/8/64 (10 of 12)
     Ed Brown, at Det, 11/20/55 (15 of 18)
     Gene Ronzani, vs. Det, 10/22/44 (10 of 12)

Yards
Lifetime
14,686 Sid Luckman, 1939–50
11,567 Jim Harbaugh, 1987–93
11,203 Jim McMahon, 1982–88
Season
3,838 Erik Kramer, 1995
3,193 Rex Grossman, 2006
3,172 Bill Wade, 1962
Game
468 Johnny Lujack, 12/11/49
466 Bill Wade, 11/18/62
433 Sid Luckman, 11/14/43

300-Yard Games
Lifetime
9 Bill Wade, 1961–66
7 Erik Kramer, 1994–98
4 George Blanda, 1949–58
3 Jim Miller, 1998–2002
    Vince Evans, 1977–83
    Johnny Lujack, 1948–51
    Sid Luckman, 1939–50
Season
4 Bill Wade, 1962
3 Erik Kramer, 1995
    Bill Wade, 1961
Consecutive games
2 Jim Miller, 11/14–11/21/99
    Bill Wade, 10/14–10/21/62; 11/18–11/25/62
    George Blanda, 10/17–10/24/54
    Sid Luckman, 1012–10/19/47

Touchdown Passes
Lifetime
137 Sid Luckman, 1939–50
68 Bill Wade, 1961–66
67 Jim McMahon, 1982–88
Season
29 Erik Kramer, 1995
28 Sid Luckman, 1943
24 Sid Luckman, 1947
Game
**7 Sid Luckman, at NYG, 11/14/43
6 Johnny Lujack, vs. Chi Cards, 12/11/49
5 Ray Buivid, vs, Chi Cards, 12/5/37
Consecutive games
19 Sid Luckman, 11/22/42–11/26/44
14 Sid Luckman, 10/12/47–10/17/48

Passes Intercepted
Lifetime
132 Sid Luckman, 1939–50
88 Ed Brown, 1954–61
70 George Blanda, 1949–58
Season
31 Sid Luckman, 1947
24 Bill Wade, 1962
     George Blanda, 1953
22 Johnny Lujack, 1949

Game
7 Edmund "Zeke" Bratkowski, at Bal, 10/2/60
5 Last: Kyle Orton, vs, Cin, 9/25/05

Passes Not Intercepted
Consecutive
174 Erik Kramer, 11/19–12/24/95
173 Jim Harbaugh, 10/28–12/9/90
162 Erik Kramer, 9/11–10/22/95
Game
50 Erik Kramer, at Mia, 10/27/97
47 Jim Miller, vs. GB, 11/11/01
46 Bill Wade, vs. LA Rams, 10/11/64

Lowest Interception Percentage
Lifetime (400+ attempts)
2.69 Jim Miller, 1998–2002 (26 int, 965 att)
2.89 Erik Kramer, 1994–8 (45 int, 1,557 att)
3.01 Shane Matthews, 1996, 99–01 (18 int, 599 att)
3.18 Jim Harbaugh, 1987–93 (56 int, 1,759 att)
Season (100+ attempts)
1.40 Jim McMahon, 1984 (2 int, 143 att)
1.90 Chad Hutchinson, 2004 (3 int, 161 att)
1.91 Erik Kramer, 1995 (10 int, 522 att)

Average Gain Per Attempt
Lifetime (400+ passes)
8.42 Sid Luckman, 1939–50
8.23 Bernie Masterson, 1934–40
7.79 Johnny Lujack, 1948–51
Season (100+ attempts)
10.86 Sid Luckman, 1943
9.92 Sid Luckman, 1941
9.92 Ed Brown, 1956
Game (10+ attempts)
17.1 Charlie O'Rourke, at Det, 11/22/42
16.9 Sid Luckman, at Cle Rams, 10/5/41
16.7 Gene Ronzani, vs. Det, 10/22/44

Punter Brad Maynard kicks against New Orleans in the 2007 playoffs. His 2004 season record of 4,638 yards shows the importance of a good punter in the modern game.
John Zich/Getty Images

RECEIVING
Receptions
Lifetime
492 Walter Payton, 1975–87
356 Johnny Morris, 1958–67
329 Curtis Conway, 1993–99
Season
100 Marty Booker, 2001
97 Marty Booker, 2002
93 Johnny Morris, 1964
Game
14 Jim Keane, at NYG, 10/23/49
13 Bobby Engram, at StL, 12/26/99
   Mike Ditka, at Was, 10/25/64
12 Marty Booker, vs. GB, 10/7/02
Consecutive games
58 Marty Booker, 9/24/00–12/28/03
57 Bobby Engram, 10/6/96–9/17/00
49 Mike Ditka, 12/3/61–10/10/65
45 Walter Payton, 12/16/84–12/27/87

Yards
Lifetime
5,059 Johnny Morris, 1958–67
4,616 Harlon Hill, 1954–61
4,538 Walter Payton, 1975–87
Season
1,400 Marcus Robinson, 1999
1,301 Jeff Graham, 1995
1,200 Johnny Morris, 1964
Game
214 Harlon Hill, at SF, 10/31/54
201 Johnny Morris, at Dal, 11/18/62
198 Marty Booker, vs. Min, 9/8/02
   Harlon Hill, vs. Bal, 10/21/56
Long
98 John Farrington (TD), 10/8/61
93 Dick Gordon (TD), 11/19/67
91 Willard Dewveall (TD), 10/16/60

1,000-Yard Seasons
Lifetime
2 Marty Booker, 2001–02
   Curtis, Conway, 1995–96
   Harlon Hill, 1954, 1956

100-Yard Games
Lifetime
19 Harlon Hill, 1954–61
15 Johnny Morris, 1958–67
14 Mike Ditka, 1961–66
12 Curtis Conway, 1993–99
Season
7 Jeff Graham, 1995
   Harlon Hill, 1954
   Ken Kavanaugh, 1947
6 Johnny Morris, 1964
   Harlon Hill, 1956
5 Marcus Robinson, 1999
   Mike Ditka, 1961
Consecutive games
3 Jeff Graham, 11/5–11/19/95
   Harlon Hill, 11/11–11/25/56
2 Last: Marcus Robinson, 11/14–11/21/99

Average Gain
Lifetime (100+ attempts)
22.4 Ken Kavanaugh, 1940–41, 45–50
21.7 Ray "Scooter" McLean, 1940–47
20.4 Harlon Hill, 1954–61
Season (30+ attempts)
25.6 Ken Kavanaugh, 1946
25.0 Harlon Hill, 1954
24.0 Harlon Hill, 1956
Game (4+ attempts)
44.8 Dick Gordon, vs. StL Cards, 11/19/67
37.5 Gene Schroeder, vs. Chi Cards, 12/16/51
37.0 Billy Stone, vs. Det, 11/23/52

Touchdowns
Lifetime
50 Ken Kavanaugh, 1940–41, 45–50
40 Harlon Hill, 1954–61
35 Dick Gordon, 1965–71
Season
13 Dick Gordon, 1970
   Ken Kavanaugh, 1947
12 Curtis Conway, 1995
   Mike Ditka, 1961
   Harlon Hill, 1954
11 Harlon Hill, 1956
Game
4 Mike Ditka, at Rams, 10/13/63
   Harlon Hill, at SF, 10/31/54
3 Last: Marty Booker, at TB, 11/18/01
Consecutive games
7 Curtis Conway, 9/24–11/12/95
   Ken Kavanaugh, 11/2–12/14/47
5 Dennis McKinnon, 9/8–10/5/85
   Mike Ditka, 10/22–11/19/61

DEFENSE
INTERCEPTIONS
Player
Lifetime
38 Gary Fencik, 1976–87
37 Richie Petitbon, 1959–68
32 Donnell Woolford, 1989–96
Season
10 Mark Carrier, 1990
9 Roosevelt Taylor, 1963
8 Nathan Vasher, 2005
   Vestee Jackson, 1988
   Richie Petitbon, 1963
   Johnny Lujack, 1948
   Clyde "Bulldog" Turner, 1942
Game
3 Mark Carrier, at Was, 12/9/90
   Ross Brupbacher, vs. Den, 12/12/76
   Curtis Gentry, vs. StL. Cards, 11/19/67
   Richie Petitbon, at GB, 9/24/67
   Johnny Lujack, at GB, 9/26/48
   Bob Margarita, vs. Det, 11/11/45
2 Last: Charles Tillman, at NE, 11/26/06
Consecutive games
4 Last: Dave Duerson, 9/14–10/5/86

Yards Returned
Lifetime
643 Richie Petitbon, 1959–68
485 Bennie McRae, 1962–70
483 Gary Fencik, 1976–87
Season
212 Richie Petitbon, 1962
182 J.C. Caroline, 1956
177 Nathan Vasher, 2004
Game
101 Richie Petitbon, vs. LA Rams, 12/9/62 (TD)
96 Roosevelt Taylor, at Phi, 10/20/68 (TD)
   Clyde "Bulldog" Turner, at Was, 10/26/47 (TD)
95 Charles Tillman, vs. GB, 12/4/05
Long
Same as game

Touchdowns
Lifetime
4 Mike Brown, 2000–06
   Bennie McRae, 1962–70
3 Roosevelt Taylor, 1961–69
   Richie Petitbon, 1959–68
Season
2 Last: Mike Brown, 2001
Game
1 Last: Ricky Manning, vs. Min, 12/3/06

PUNTING

Attempts
Lifetime
884 Bob Parsons, 1972–83
833 Bobby Joe Green, 1962–73
534 Brad Maynard, 2001–06
Season
**114 Bob Parsons, 1981
108 Brad Maynard, 2004
99 Bob Parsons, 1976
Game
14 Keith Molesworth, 12/10/33
12 Todd Sauerbrun, 10/5/97
11 Last: Brad Maynard, 11/14/04

Yards
Lifetime
35,056 Bobby Joe Green, 1962–73
34,180 Bob Parsons, 1972–83
22,625 Brad Maynard, 2001–06
Season
4,638 Brad Maynard, 2004
4,531 Bob Parsons, 1981
4,059 Todd Sauerbrun, 1997
Game
524 Todd Sauerbrun, vs. NO, 10/5/97
517 Keith Molesworth, vs. GB, 12/10/33
509 Brad Maynard, at Ten, 11/14/04
Long
94 Joe Lintzenich, vs. NYG, 11/15/31
87 Dave Finzer, vs. NO, 10/7/84
81 Bob Parsons, vs. NE, 12/5/82

Gross Average
Lifetime (75+ punts)
44.5 George Gulyanics, 1947–52
42.4 Brad Maynard, 2001–06
42.2 Todd Sauerbrun, 1995–98
Season (30+ attempts)
46.5 Bobby Joe Green, 1963
44.8 Todd Sauerbrun, 1996
44.5 Bobby Joe Green, 1964
Game (4+ attempts)
57.3 Fred Morrison, vs. LA Rams, 11/16/52
54.6 Maury Buford, vs. GB, 10/21/85
54.0 Maury Buford, at TB, 10/6/85

Inside 20
Lifetime
167 Brad Maynard, 2001–06
158 Bob Parsons, 1972–83
94 Maury Buford, 1985–86; 89–91
Season
36 Brad Maynard, 2001
34 Brad Maynard, 2004
31 Bob Parsons, 1981
Game
6 Brad Maynard, at GB, 12/9/01
5 Brad Maynard, vs. TB, 12/17/06
   Bob Parsons, at Hou, 11/6/77
4 Last: Brad Maynard, vs. Min, 12/3/06

Had Blocked
Lifetime
5 Ed Brown, 1954–61
   Bob Parsons, 1972–83
   Maury Buford, 1985–86; 89–91
4 Fred "Curley" Morrison, 1950–53
Season
2 Brad Maynard, 2003
Game
2 Jon Kilgore, at LA Rams, 12/8/68
   Ray Stachowicz, at Min, 12/11/83
1 Last: Brad Maynard, at Min, 1/1/06

PUNT RETURNS

Returns Made
Lifetime
127 Dennis McKinnon, 1983–85; 87–89
123 Jeff Fisher, 1981–84
112 George McAfee, 1940–41; 45–50
Season
58 Jeff Fisher, 1984
57 Lew Barnes, 1986
47 Devin Hester, 2006
Game
8 Jeff Fisher, at Det, 12/16/84
7 R.W. McQuarters, vs. Was, 10/17/04
   Dennis McKinnon, at GB, 12/4/83
   Steve Schubert, at TB, 12/4/77
   Ron Smith, at Cle, 10/15/72
   George McAfee, vs. GB, 10/15/50
6 Last: Devin Hester, vs. TB, 12/17/06

Yards
Lifetime
1,431 George McAfee, 1940–41; 45–50
1,171 Dennis McKinnon, 1983–85; 87–89
1,137 Jeff Fisher, 1981–84
Season
600 Devin Hester, 2006
509 Jeff Fisher, 1981
492 Jeff Fisher, 1984
Game
152 Devin Hester, at Arz, 10/16/06
134 Gale Sayers, vs. SF, 12/12/65
   Dennis McKinnon, vs. NYG, 9/14/87
108 George McAfee, vs. LA Rams, 10/10/48

Average
Lifetime (50+ returns)
*12.8 George McAfee, 1940–41; 45–50
11.3 J.R. Boone, 1948–51
10.6 R.W. McQuarters, 2000–04
Season (15+ returns)
14.9 Gale Sayers, 1965
14.5 George McAfee, 1947
13.9 George McAfee, 948
Game (3+ attempts)
36.0 George McAfee, vs. LA Rams, 10/10/48
34.0 Ray McLean, vs. Chi Cards, 10/11/42
29.7 Dennis McKinnon, at TB, 10/25/87

Touchdowns
Lifetime
3 Devin Hester, 2006
   Dennis McKinnon, 1983–85; 87–89
   Steve Schubert, 1975–79
   Ray McLean, 1940–47
2 R.W. McQuarters, 2000–04
   Gale Sayers, 1965–71
   George McAfee, 1940–41; 45–50
Season
3 Devin Hester, 2006
2 Dennis McKinnon, 1987
Game
1 Last: Devin Hester, vs. Min, 12/3/06

Fair Catches
Lifetime
66 Glyn Milburn, 1998–2001
47 Steve Schubert, 1975–79
40 Jeff Fisher, 1981–84
Season
26 Glyn Milburn, 2000
21 Steve Schubert, 1978
20 Terry Obee, 1993
   Jeff Fisher, 1981
Game
6 Bobby Engram, vs. Min, 9/15/96
5 Last: Glyn Milburn, vs. GB, 12/3/00
4 Last: Terry Obee, vs. Min, 12/25/93

KICK-OFF RETURNS

Attempts Made
Lifetime
192 Glyn Milburn, 1998–2001
   Dennis Gentry, 1982–92
119 Jerry Azumah, 1999–2005
Season
63 Glyn Milburn, 2000
62 Glyn Milburn, 1998
61 Glyn Milburn, 1999
Game
9 Ahmad Merritt, at SF, 9/7/03
8 Brian Baschnagel, at Hou, 11/6/77
7 Last: Glyn Milburn, at TB, 9/10/00

Yards
Lifetime
4,596 Glyn Milburn, 1998–2001
4,353 Dennis Gentry, 1982–92
2,885 Jerry Azumah, 1999–2005
Season
1,550 Glyn Milburn, 1998
1,468 Glyn Milburn, 2000
1,426 Glyn Milburn, 1999
Game
225 Devin Hester, at StL, 12/11/06
221 Nate Lewis, at Min, 12/1/94
208 Ron Smith, vs. SF, 11/19/72
Long
103 Gale Sayers, at Pit, 9/17/67 (TD)
100 Don Bingham, vs. LA Rams, 11/18/56 (TD)
99 Willie Galimore, at Bal, 10/4/58 (TD)
   Willie Gault, vs. Was, 9/29/85 (TD)

Average
Lifetime (50+ returns)
*30.6 Gale Sayers, 1965–71
26.6 Ron Smith, 1965; 70–72
25.6 Willie Galimore, 1957–63
Season (1+ per game)
37.7 Gale Sayers, 1967
32.7 Cecil Turner, 1970
31.7 Walter Payton, 1975
Game (3+ attempts)
56.3 Devin Hester, at StL, 12/11/06
52.0 Cecil Turner, at NYG, 9/19/70
48.7 Dick Gordon, at LA Rams, 9/16/66

Touchdowns
Lifetime
*6 Gale Sayers, 1965–71
4 Cecil Turner, 1968–73
3 Dennis Gentry, 1982–92
Season
4 Cecil Turner, 1970
3 Gale Sayers, 1967
2 Last: Devin Hester, 2006
Game
**2 Devin Hester, at StL, 12/11/06
1 Last: Jerry Azumah, at GB, 12/7/03

COMBINED KICK RETURNS

Returns Made
Season
98 Glyn Milburn, 2000, p–35, k–63
91 Glyn Milburn, 1999, p–30, k–61
87 Glyn Milburn, 1998, p–25, k–62

Yards
Lifetime
5,566 Glyn Milburn, 1998–2001, p–970, k–4,596
4,477 Dennis Gentry, 1982–92, p–124, k–4,353
3,172 Gale Sayers, 1965–71, p–391, k–2,781
Season
1,841 Glyn Milburn, 1999, p–291, k–1,550
1,772 Glyn Milburn, 1998, p–346, k–1,426
1,768 Glyn Milburn, 2000, p–300, k–1,468
Game
246 Devin Hester, at StL, 12/11/06, p–21, k–225

221   Nate Lewis, at Min, 12/1/94, k–221
216   Glyn Milburn, vs. SF, 9/20/98, p–106, k–110

Touchdowns
Lifetime
8   Gale Sayers, 1965–71, p–2, k–6
5   Devin Hester, 2006, p–3, k–2
4   Cecil Turner, 1968–73, p–0, k–4
Season
*5   Devin Hester, 2006, p–3, k–2
4   Cecil Turner, 1970, k–4
     Gale Sayers, 1967, p–1, k–3
3   Glyn Milburn, 1998, p–1, k–2
Game
**2   Devin Hester, at StL, 12/11/06

FUMBLES
Fumbles Made
Lifetime
85   Walter Payton, 1975–87
38   Jim Harbaugh, 1987–93
35   Rick Casares, 1955–64
Season
15   Jim Harbaugh, 1993
14   Gary Huff, 1974
13   Carl Garrett, 1973
Game
4   Last; Rusty Lisch, vs. GB, 12/9/84
3   Last: Anthony Thomas, at Det, 10/20/02

Own Recovered
Lifetime
18   Walton Payton, 1975–87
13   Gale Sayers, 1965–71
10   Jim Harbaugh, 1987–93
     Ed Brown, 1954–61
Season
7   Gary Huff, 1974
6   Jack Concannon, 1970
5   Bobby Douglass, 1972
Game
3   Gary Huff, vs. Det, 9/15/74

Opponents' Recovered
Lifetime
25   Dick Butkus, 1965–73
22   Joe Fortunato, 1955–6
17   Mike Hartenstine, 1975–86
Season
6   Dick Butkus, 1965
5   Ed O'Bradovich, 1962
4   Last: Mike Green, 2004
Game
3   John Thierry, vs. Hou, 10/22/95
     Virgil Livers, at Min, 10/5/75
2   Last: Bryan Knight, vs. NO, 9/22/02

Yards Returned Own Fumbles
Lifetime
36   John Adams, 1959–62
24   Ike Hill, 1973–74
22   Ron Bull, 1962–70
Season
36   John Adams, 1961
24   Ike Hill, 1973
21   Ron Bull, 1962
Game
Same as season
Long
Same as season

Yards Returned Opponents' Fumbles
Lifetime
218   Mike Brown, 2000–06
158   Brian Urlacher, 2000–06
128   Charlie Sumner, 1955; 58–60
Season
101   Brian Urlacher, 2001
     Charlie Sumner, 1958
98   George Halas, 1923

Game
98   George Halas, (TD) vs. Oorang, 11/4/23
95   Mike Brown, (TD) at GB, 9/19/04
     Charles Tillman, vs. GB, 12/4/05
90   Brian Urlacher, (TD) at Atl, 11/7/01
Long
Same as game

Touchdowns Own Fumbles
Lifetime
2   Ken Kavanaugh, 1940–41; 45–50
     Mike Ditka, 1961–66
Season
1   Last: Johnny Musso, 1976
Game
1   Last: Johnny Musso, vs. Min 10/31/76

Touchdowns Opponents' Fumbles
Lifetime
3   Mike Brown, 2000–06
2   Fred Evans, 1948
     Ed Sprinkle, 1944–55
Season
2   Fred Evans, 1948
Game
2   Fred Evans, vs. Was, 11/28/48
1   Last: Charles Tillman, at Arz, 10/16/06

TAKEAWAYS
Player
(Interceptions and Opponents' Fumbles Recovered)
Lifetime
50   Gary Fencik, 1976–87 (38 int, 12 fum)
47   Dick Butkus, 1965–73 (22 int, 25 fum)
44   Richie Petitbon, 1959–68 (37 int, 7 fum)
Season
12   Mark Carrier, 1990 (10 int, 2 fum)
     Roosevelt Taylor, 1963 (9 int, 3 fum)
11   Dick Butkus, 1965 (5 int, 6 fum)
Game
4   Bill George, vs. Det, 12/3/61 (2 int, 2 fum)
3   Last: John Thierry, vs. Hou, 10/22/95 (3 fum)

SACKS
Player (since 1970)
Lifetime
124.5   Richard Dent, 1983–93; 95
92.5   Steve McMichael, 1981–93
82.0   Dan Hampton, 1979–90
Season
17.5   Richard Dent, 1984 (16 games)
17.0   Richard Dent, 1985 (16 games)
15.0   Jim Osborne, 1976 (14 games)
Game
4.5   Richard Dent, vs. Raid, 11/4/84; at Raid, 12/27/87
4.0   Jim Osborne, vs. Min, 9/23/73
     Alex Brown, at NYG, 11/7/04
Consecutive games (at least .5 sack)
8   Roosevelt Colvin, 12/23/01–10/07/02
7   Alonzo Spellman, 12/1/94–9/17/95
6   Steve McMichael, 10/29–12/3/89

TEAM RECORDS
WON–LOST
Wins
Highest winning percentage, season
**1.000   1942   11–0
           1934   13–0
.938   1985   15–1
.923   1926   12–1–3
Lowest winning season
.071   1969   1–13
.214   1973   3–11
.250   Last: 2002,   4–12
Wins, at home
9   1926   (11 games at Wrigley)
8   1985   (8 games at Soldier Field)

      1922   (9 games at Wrigley)
      1921   (9 games at Wrigley)
7   2005   (8 games at Soldier Field)
      2001   (8 games at Soldier Field)
      1990   (8 games at Soldier Field)
      1988   (8 games at Soldier Field)
      1986   (8 games at Soldier Field)
      1933   (7 games at Wrigley)
Wins on the road, season
7   2006   (8 road games)
      1986   (8 road games)
      1985   (8 road games)
      1934   (7 road games)
      1920   (9 road games)

Consecutive Games
Won
*17   11/26/33–12/2/34
16   11/9/41–12/6/42
Without losing
24   11/9/41–11/14/43 (23–0–1)
Wins at home
19   11/20/32–10/20/35
Wins on the road
10   9/28/41–12/6/42
Lost
8   Last: 9/22/02–11/18/02
Without winning
11   11/3/29–10/5/30 (0–9–2)
Losses at home
8   11/25/69–11/8/79
Losses on the road
16   11/12/73–11/30/75

SCORING
Points
Most, season
456   1985   (16 games)
427   2006   (16 games)
409   1965   (14 games)
Fewest, season
133   1933   (13 games)
141   1982   (9 games)
145   1931   (13 games)
216   2000   (16 games)
Most, game
61   vs. GB, 12/7/80 (win, 61–7)
     vs. SF, 12/12/65 (win, 61–20)
58   vs. Bal, 10/21/56 (win, 58–27)
57   at Bal, 11/25/62 (win, 57–0)
Most, first half (by quarters)
41   vs. SF, 10/29/06 (24, 17)
     vs. Was, 11/28/48 (20, 21)
31   vs. Det, 9/18/05 (10, 21)
     vs. Was, 9/29/85 (0, 31)
Most, second half (by quarters)
49   at Phi, 11/30/41 (21, 28)
33   vs. GB, 12/17/80 (13, 20)
Most, first quarter
24   vs. SF, 10/29/06
21   vs. Cin, 9/28/86
     vs. Cle, 9/7/86
     vs. Was, 11/9/80
     vs. Chi Cards, 10/11/42
Most, second quarter
31   vs. Was, 9/29/95
28   vs. TB, 9/26/93
     vs. GB, 12/7/80
Most, third quarter
27   vs. Chi Cards, 9/5/37
24   at Min, 9/19/85
Most, fourth quarter
28   vs. Min, 9/17/89
     vs. Phi, 11/30/41
22   at Phi, 9/12/94
21   Last: vs. Arz 11/30/03
Margin of victory
57   at Bal, 11/25/62 (57–0)
54   vs. GB, 12/7/80 (61–7)
49   at NYG, 11/14/43 (56–7)

vs. Det, 10/19/41 (49–0)

Margin of defeat
52   at Bal, 9/27/64 (52–0)
49   at GB, 9/30/62 (49–0)
47   at Hou, 11/6/77 (47–0)

Touchdowns

Most, season
56	1941	(11 games)
54	1965	(14 games)
51	1985	(16 games)
	1948	(12 games)
	1947	(12 games)

Fewest, season
16	1982	(9 games)
	1933	(13 games)
22	2000	(16 games)
	1993	(16 games)

Most, game
9   vs. GB, 12/7/80
    vs. SF, 12/12/65
8   at Was, 10/26/47
    at NY Giants, 11/14/43

Extra Points Made

Most, season
52	1965	(14 games)
51	1985	(16 games)
	1948	(12 games)
47	2006	(16 games)

Fewest, season
15	1933	(13 games)
	1932	(14 games)
16	1982	(9 games)
20	1997	(16 games)

Most, game
8   at Was, 10/26/47 (8 of 8)
    at NYG 11/14/43 (8 of 8)
7   vs. GB, 12/7/80 7 of 9)
    vs. SF, 12/12/65 (7 of 9)
    at Rams, 10/13/63 (7 of 7)
6   Last: at StL, 12/11/06 (6 of 6)

Most, season (no misses)
51	1985	(16 games)
47	2006	(16 games)
45	1995	(16 games)

Extra Points Missed

Season
11	1941		(11 games)
	1939		(11 games)
4	1976	27 of 31	(14 games)
	1975	18 of 22	(14 games)
3	1983	35 of 38	(16 games)
	1979	34 of 37	(16 games)
	1978	26 of 29	(16 games)
	1977	27 of 30	(14 games)

Most, game
3   Last: vs. Cle, 11/9/41
2   Last: vs. GB, 12/7/80

Field Goals Made

Most, season
32	2006	(16 games)
31	1985	(16 games)
28	1986	(16 games)

Fewest, season
**0	1947	(12 games)
	1944	(10 games)
8	1969	(14 games)
9	1982	(9 games)
1974	(14 games)

Most, game
5   at Phi, 10/20/68
    vs. Det, 12/3/61
4   Last: at Det, 12/24/06

Field Goals Attempted

Most, season
| 41 | 1986 | (16 games) |
| 38 | 1985 | (16 games) |

| 37 | 1990 | (16 games) |

Fewest, season
0	1944	(10 games)
13	1974	(14 games)
18	1980	(16 games)

Most, game
7   vs. GB, 11/17/63
6   Last: at GB, 11/8/87

Field Goals Missed

Most, season
18	1971	15 of 33 made	(14 games)
15	1999	17 of 32 made	(16 games)
	1965	11 of 26 made	(14 games)
14	1970	20 of 34 made	(14 games)

Fewest, season
4	2006	32 of 36 made	(16 games)
	1989	15 of 19 made	(16 games)
	1988	15 of 19 made	(16 games)
	1974	9 of 13 made	(16 games)
5	2001	26 of 31 made	(16 games)

1998	21 of 26 made	(16 games)
1997	21 of 26 made	(16 games)
1980	13 of 18 made	(16 games)
1978	17 of 22 made	(16 games)

Most, game
4   Last: vs. Phi, 9/14/86 (2 of 6)
3   Last: at Min, 10/10/99 (1 of 4)

Two-Point Conversions

Most, season
5	1997	(16 games)
2	2003	(16 games)
	1994	(16 games)

Most, game
1   Last: at NYG, 11/7/04

Safeties

Most, season
3	2004	(16 games)
	1985	(16 games)
2	Last: 1986	(16 games)

Devin Hester is in the clear as the Bears' best returner with a remarkable record already—including an unbelievable kickoff return touchdown in Super Bowl XLI in 2007. *Gary I. Rothstein/Getty Images*

Most, game
2   vs. Pit, 11/9/69
1   Last: vs. Min, 12/ 3/06

POSSESSION

Time of Possession (since 1978)
Highest average, season
35:08   1984   (16 games)
34:33   1985   (16 games)
33:38   1994   (16 games)
Lowest average, season
27:42   2002   (16 games)
28:20   2004   (16 games)
28:30   2000   (16 games)
Highest, game
48:50   vs. SD, 1025/81 (OT)
45:32   vs. Mia, 9/4/88
44:53   at Mia, 10/27/97 (OT)
Lowest, game
18:01   at Dal, 12/27/92
18:57   at Min, 10/27/02
19:20   at LA Rams, 1/2/94

FIRST DOWNS

Total
Most, season
343   1985   (16 games)
340   1995   (16 games)
319   1987   (15 games)
Fewest, season
114   1937   (11 games)
115   1933   (13 games)
153   1982   (9 games)
226   1993   (16 games)
Most, game
33   vs. GB, 12/7/80
30   at NY Yanks, 12/9/51
29   vs. SF, 10/28/01
       vs. Cle, 11/4/01
Fewest, game
2   vs. GB, 12/10/33
4   vs. Det, 11/22/81
5   vs. NE, 10/14/79

Rushing
Most, season
176   1985   (16 games)
166   1986   (16 games)
164   1984
Fewest, season
55   1970   (14 games)
56   1982   (9 games)
79   2002   (16 games)
Most, game
19   at GB, 10/30/77
       vs. GB, 11/6/55
18   vs. Det, 11/10/85
17   Last: vs. Mia, 9/4/88
Fewest, game
0   at Jax, 12/12/04
       at GB, 12/11/94
       at Bal, 10/5/57
       vs. Chi Cards, 10/14/45
1   at Dal, 11/25/04
       at TB, 11/18/01
       at Det, 11/25/99
       at Oak, 9/26/99
       at NE, 9/21/97
       at KC, 11/17/96

Passing
Most, season
203   1999   (16 games)
201   1995   (16 games)
188   1997   (16 games)
Fewest, season
41   1940   (11 games)
48   1942   (11 games)
54   1972   (14 games)

83   1982   (9 games)
98   1979   (16 games)
Most, game
21   vs. NYJ, 11/16/97
       at Dal, 11/18/62
20   vs. Cle, 11/4/01
       at StL, 12/26/99
18   vs. TB, 12/17/06
       vs. Was, 11/2/97
Fewest, game
0   at GB, 9/28/41
       vs. GB, 11/7/37
1   vs. Min, 12/3/06
2   Last: vs. GB, 12/4/05

By Penalty
Most, season
*42   1987   (15 games)
36   2006   (16 games)
32   1988   (16 games)
       1963   (14 games)
Fewest, season
5   1939   (11 games)
7   2000   (16 games)
12   1977   (14 games
       1972   (14 games)
Most, game
9   at Cle, 11/25/51
7   at TB, 9/8/91
6   vs. Mia, 11/5/06
       at GB, 10/25/92
       vs. Det, 11/22/87

Net Yards
(Rushing and passing)

Yards
Most, season
5,837   1985   (16 games)
5,830   1983   (16 games)
5,673   1995   (16 games)
Fewest, season
2,493   1982   (9 games)
2,641   1937   (11 games)
3,129   1973   (4 games)
3,717   1993   (16 games)
Most, game
682   at NYG, 11/14/43
596   vs. Chi Cards, 12/11/49
594   vs. GB, 12/7/80
Fewest, game
24   vs. Det, 11/22/81
66   at Den, 12/5/71
75   at Det, 10/28/62

RUSHING

Attempts
Most, season
674   1984   (16 games)
634   1978   (16 games)
627   1979   (16 games)
Fewest, season
275   1982   (9 games)
353   1970   (14 games)
        1954   (12 games)
383   2002   (16 games)
Most, game
*72   vs. Brooklyn, 10/20/35
63   vs. Min, 10/20/77
62   vs. Buf, 10/7/79
Fewest, game
11   at Phi, 9/12/94
12   at Min, 10/27/02
        at Det, 11/25/99
13   vs. Phi, 10/3/04
        vs. GB, 11/22/92

Yards
Most, season
2,974   1984   (16 games)

2,847   1934   (13 games)
2,761   1985   (16 games)
Fewest, season
988   9182   (9 games)
1,344   2002   (16 games)
1,387   1999   (16 games)
Most, game
408   vs. Brooklyn, 01/20/35
406   vs. GB, 11/6/55
375   at GB, 10/30/77
Fewest, game
1   at LA Rams, 10/26/52
27   at GB, 12/11/94

Average
Highest, season
5.19   1934   (13 games)
4.75   1968   (14 games)
4.52   1985   (16 games)
Lowest, season
3.08   1953   (12 games)
3.09   1970   (14 games)
3.26   1994   (16 games)
Highest, game
13.75   at Cin, 9/30/34
6.94   at GB, 10/30/77 (54 or 375)
6.34   at Cin, 9/28/86 (35 for 222)
Lowest, game
0.03   at LA Rams, 10/26/52 (33 for 1)
1.72   vs. GB, 11/11/01 (25 for 43)
1.86   at Dal, 12/27/92 (15 for 28)

Touchdowns
Most, season
30   1941   (11 games)
27   1985   (16 games)
25   1988   (16 games)
Fewest, season
3   1970   (14 games)
        1933   (13 games)
4   1999   (16 games)
5   1982   (9 games)
Most, game
6   vs. Det, 10/19/41
5   vs. Mia, 9/4/88
4   Last: at TB, 10/8/89

Fumbles
Most, season
**56   1938   (11 games)
40   1973   (14 games)
        1972   (14 games)
37   1988   (16 games)
Fewest, season
16   1982   (9 games)
        1963   (14 games)
21   2001   (16 games)
        1994   (16 games)
        1979   (16 games)
Most, game
8   at NYG, 12/18/77
        at ChiCards, 9/11/38
7   vs. GB, 10/21/85
        at Bal, 12/5/65

Fumbles Lost
Most, season
26   1973   (14 games)
Fewest, season
8   2001   (16 games)
        1982   (9 games)
        1978   (16 games)
9   2003   (16 games)
        1996   (16 games)
10   Last: 1994   (16 games)
Most, game
5   vs. Det, 10/4/98
        vs. Dal, 9/16/73
4   Last: at Car, 12/22/02

Own Recovered

Most, season

*37	1938	(11 games)
20	1981	(16 games)
19	1977	(14 games)
	1942	(11 games)
	2005	(16 games)

Fewest, season

5	1963	(14 games)
	1955	(12 games)
6	1989	(16 games)
8	1998	(16 games)
	1979	(16 games)

Most, game

7	at NYG, 12/18/77
	at Chi Cards, 9/11/38
6	at GB, 11/15/81
5	at Min, 10/5/75

PASSING

Attempts

Most, season

684	1999	(16 games)
595	1997	(16 games)
551	1996	(16 games)

Fewest, season

147	1937	(11 games)
205	1972	(14 games)
262	1982	(9 games)
352	1978	(16 games)

Most, game

65	vs. NYJ, 11/16/97
63	at Was, 10/31/99
59	at NYG, 10/23/49

Fewest, game

4	vs. Det, 10/15/67
7	vs. TB, 1126/78
8	vs. Det, 10/19/08
	vs. Buf, 10/7/79

Completions

Most, season

404	1999	(16 games)
336	1997	(16 games)
318	1996	(16 games)

Fewest, season

56	1937	(11 games)
78	1972	(14 games)
186	1978	(16 games)

Most, game

36	at Was, 10/31/99
34	vs. Min, 11/14/99
	at NYG, 10/23/49
33	vs. NYJ, 11/16/97
	at Was, 10/25/64

Fewest, game

1	Last: at Phi, 12/10/72

Completion Percentage

Highest, season

61.4	1994	308 of 502	(16 games)
60.2	1995	315 of 523	(16 games)
59.7	2001	315 of 528	(16 games)

Lowest, season

29.7	1934	57 of 192	(13 games)
38.0	1972	78 of 205	(14 games)
44.2	1976	123 of 278	(14 games)
44.9	1973	136 of 303	(14 games)
45.4	1981	222 of 469	(16 games)

Highest, game (10+ attempts)

83.3	vs. GB, 12/7/80 (20 of 24)
81.5	vs. NYJ, 12/15/02 (22 of 27)
	vs. NE, 12/10/00 (22 of 27)
78.1	vs. SF, 10/29/06 (25 of 32)

Lowest, game (10+ attempts)

11.7	vs. Den, 12/12/76 (2 of 17)
16.7	vs. GB, 12/31/06 (2 of 12)
21.7	vs. KC, 12/29/90 (5 of 23)

Net Yards (Gross yards minus sack yards)

Most, season

4,136	1999	(16 games)
3,743	1995	(16 games)
3,281	2006	(16 games)

Fewest, season

955	1934	(13 games)
1,108	1972	(14 games)
1,505	1982	(9 games)
1,933	1978	(16 games)

Most, game

488	at NYG, 11/14/43
468	vs. Chi Cards, 12/11/49

Fewest, game

−20	vs. Det, 11/22/81
−16	at Hou, 11/6/77

Times Sacked

Most, season

66	2004	(16 games)
55	1969	(14 games)
52	1983	(16 games)

Fewest, season

15	1995	(16 games)
17	2001	(16 games)
20	1963	(14 games)

Most, game

9	vs. GB, 1/2/05
	vs. Min, 10/25/93
	at Den, 12/5/71
	at Min, 11/2/69

Yards Lost

Most, season

449	2004	(16 games)
439	1969	(14 games)
395	1973	(14 games)
392	1971	(14 games)
359	1974	(14 games)
358	1983	(16 games)

Fewest, season

95	1995	(16 games)
109	1947	(12 games)
120	2001	(16 games)

Most, game

78	at Min, 11/2/69
70	at Den, 12/5/71

Touchdown Passes

Most, season

29	1995	(16 games)
	1947	(12 games)
28	1943	(11 games)
26	1949	(12 games)

Fewest, season

5	1990	(12 games)
6	1973	(14 games)
7	1993	(16 games)
	1978	(16 games)

Most, game

**7	at NYG, 11/14/43
4	Last: vs. Det, 9/17/06

Had Intercepted

Most, season

35	1954	(12 games)
	1947	(12 games)
28	1978	(16 games)

Fewest, season

10	1995	(16 games)
11	1982	(9 games)
	1941	(11 games)

Most, game

8	at Det, 9/22/68
7	at Cle, 12/22/60
	at Bal, 10/2/60
	vs. LA Rams, 10/9/49

Returned for TD, season

*6	1992	(16 games)

Interception Percentage

Highest, season

14.95	1942		(11 games)	
7.95	1978	28 int, 352, att		(16 games)

Lowest, season

1.91	1995	10 int, 523 att.		(16 games)
2.63	1998	13 int, 494 att		(16 games)
2.79	1990	12 int, 430 att		(16 games)

PUNTING

Punts

Most, season

114	1981	(16 games)
110	2004	(16 games)
100	1976	(14 games)

Fewest, season

32	1941	(11 games)
38	1947	(12 games)
58	1995	(16 games)
	1965	(14 games)

Most, game

17	vs. GB, 10/22/33
14	vs. GB, 12/10/33
12	vs. NO, 10/5/97

Fewest, game

0	vs. Det, 10/1/72
	at NYG, 11/28/65
	vs. GB, 11/6/55

Gross Average

Highest, season

46.5	1963	(14 games)
45.5	1964	(14 games)
44.8	1996	(16 games)

Lowest, season

35.7	1945	(10 games)
36.2	1983	(16 games)
36.9	1976	(14 games)

Highest, game (4+ punts)

57.3	vs. LA Rams, 11/16/52
54.6	vs. GB, 10/21/85
54.0	at TB, 10/6/85
53.6	at Det, 11/27/97

Lowest, game (4+ attempts)

22.1	at Min, 10/10/76
25.0	at Card-Pitt, 12/3/44
26.4	vs. GB, 10/21/74

PUNT RETURNS

Returns Made

Most, season

64	1984	(16 games)
60	1950	(12 games)
57	1986	(16 games)

Fewest, season

19	1968	(14 games)
22	1967	(14 games)
23	1992	(16 games)

Most, game

11	vs. Chi Cards, 10/8/50
8	vs. NE, 9/16/85
	at Det, 1/16/84

Yards

Most, season

781	1948	(14 games)
607	2006	(16 games)
561	1984	(16 games)

Fewest, season

81	1968	(14 games)
97	1966	(14 games)
142	1982	(9 games)
176	1992	(16 games)

Most, game

152	at Arz, 10/16/06
151	vs. Chi Cards, 10/12/41
134	vs. NYG, 9/14/87
	vs. SF, 12/12/65

Fewest, game
-6   vs. Min, 12/19/65
-5   vs. Dal, 11/24/68
       vs. GB, 10/16/06

Average
Highest, season
20.2   1941   (11 games)
12.1   2006   (16 games)
11.8   2003   (16 games)
Lowest, season
3.4   1957   (12 games)
3.9   1966   (14 games)
6.7   1989   (16 games)

Touchdowns
Most season
3   2006   (16 games)
2   1987   (15 games)
      1941   (11 games)
Most, game
1   Last: vs. Min, 12/3/06

Fair Catches
Most, season
28   1967   (14 games)
Fewest, season
3   1975   (14 games)
Most, game
6   vs. Min, 9/15/96
      vs. Min, 12/10/67
      at StL. Cards, 10/31/66

KICK-OFF RETURNS

Returns Made
Most, season
83   2002   (16 games)
79   1997   (16 games)
      2004   (16 games)
      1975   (14 games)
Fewest, season
20   1942   (11 games)
26   1963   (14 games)
34   1982   (9 games)
43   1985   (16 games)
Most, game
10   at Chi Cards, 11/27/55
9   at SF, 9/7/03
      at GB, 12/11/94
      at SF, 12/23/91
8   Last: vs. Ind, 11/21/04
Fewest, game
0   Last: at TB, 11/6/94

Yards
Most, season
1,762 2002   (16 games)
1,738 2003   (16 games)
1,696 1997   (16 games)
Fewest, season
424   1963   (14 games)
632   1982   (9 games)
879   1990   (16 games)
Most, game
304   vs. GB, 11/9/52
251   at Pit, 9/17/67
226   at Atl, 10/14/73

Fewest, game
0   Last: at TB, 11/6/94

Average
Highest, season
*29.4 1972   (14 games)
27.9   1966   (14 games)
25.3   1985   (16 games)
Lowest, season
16.3   1990   (16 games)
       1963   (14 games)
16.4   1983   (16 games)

Touchdowns
Most, season
**4   1970   (14 games)
3   1967   (14 games)
2   Last: 2006   (16 games)
Most, game
**2   at StL, 12/11/06
      vs. GB, 11/9/52
      at GB, 9/22/40

SACKS

Team (since 1972)
Most, season
72   1984   (16 games)
70   1987   (15 games)
64   1985   (16 games)
Fewest, season
18   2003   (16 games)
23   1972   (14 games)
24   1974   (14 games)

Steelers Jon Kolb (55) and Terry Bradshaw (12) join in a tackle on Dick Butkus (51) after Butkus itercepted a Bradshaw pass in a September 1971 game. The play was called back for a penalty but Butkus intercepted Bradshaw's pass on the next play as well. *Bettmann/Corbis*

28   1998   (16 games)
        1994   (16 games)
Most, game
12   at Det, 12/16/84
11   at Phi, 10/4/87
        vs. Min, 10/28/84
9   Last: at LA Raiders, 12/27/87

Opponents' Yards Lost
Most, season
583   1984   (16 games)
503   1986   (16 games)
484   1987   (15 games)
Fewest, season
105   2003   (16 games)
154   1953   (12 games)
163   1972   (14 games)
173   2004   (16 games)
        1974   (14 games)
Most, game
114   vs. Min, 12/17/61
107   vs. Det, 11/20/60
101   vs. Min, 10/28/84

PENALTIES

Penalties Conceded
Most, season
124   2004   (16 games)
122   1948   (12 games)
121   1981   (16 games)
Fewest, season
57   1955   (12 games)
58   1982   (9 games)
63   2001   (16 games)
Most, game
**22   at Phi, 11/26/44
17   at Oak, 9/26/99
16   at TB, 10/21/84
        at Den, 10/16/78
        at Bal, 12/5/65
Fewest, game
**0   vs. Phi, 12/24/95
        at StL, 9/24/95
        at Det, 11/28/91
        vs. Min, 10/23/72
        at Cle, 10/9/38
1   Last: at Pit, 12/11/05

Yards Penalized
Most, season
1,194   1968   (14 games)
1,005   1981   (16 games)
984   1976   (14 games)
Fewest, season
422   1982   (9 games)
498   1955   (12 games)
503   1994   (16 games)
Most, game
170   at Phi, 11/26/44
147   at Den, 10/16/78
        vs. Was, 10/3/67
144   vs. LA Rams, 10/10/77
Fewest, game
**0   vs. Phi, 12/24/95
        at StL, 9/24/95
        at Det, 11/28/91
        vs. Min, 10/2/72
        at Cle, 10/9/38
5   Last: at Pit, 12/11/05

OPPONENTS' SCORING

Points Allowed
Most, season
421   1997   (16 games)
379   2002   (16 games)
        1975   (14 games)
        1964   (14 games)
377   1989   (16 games)

Fewest, season
21   1920   (13 games)
35   1923   (12 games)
44   1922   (12 games)
Since 1932
44   1932   (14 games)
187   1986   (16 games)
198   1985   (16 games)
202   2005   (16 games)
Most, game
55   at Det, 11/27/97
53   at ChiCards, 11/27/55
52   at SF, 12/23/91
        at SF, 9/19/65
        at Bal, 9/27/64
Most, first half (by quarter)
34   at Bal, 10/4/58 (27, 7)
33   at SF, 9/7/03 (10, 23)
31   at Was, 10/31/99 (14, 17)
        at TB, 12/22/96 (7, 24)
        at Mia, 12/2/85 (10, 21)
Most, second half (by quarter)
38   at Det, 11/27/97 (17, 21)
35   at GB, 9/30/62 (21, 14)
32   vs. Min, 9/18/94 (18, 14)
Most, first quarter
27   at Bal, 10/4/58
20   at TB, 10/25/87
Most, second quarter
31   at Mia, 12/2/85
24   at TB, 12/22/96
        at SF, 9/19/65
23   at SF, 9/7/03
Most, third quarter
24   at Dal, 12/27/92
21   Last: at SEA, 9/23/84
Most, fourth quarter
28   at SF, 2/23/91
        vs. GB, 11/6/55
        at LA Rams, 10/26/52
21   Last: vs. TB, 12/17/06

Touchdowns Allowed
Most, season
50   1997   (16 games)
48   1975   (14 games)
47   1964   (14 games)
43   2000   (16 games)
        1992   (16 games)
        1989   (16 games)
Fewest, season
**6   1932   (14 games)
**8   1963   (14 games)
20   2005   (16 games)
        1986   (16 games)
        1982   (9 games)
Most, game
7   Last: at Det, 11/27/97
6   Last : at Was, 10/31/99

Extra Points Allowed
Most, season
47   1975   47 of 48   (14 games)
46   1964   46 of 47   (14 games)
45   1997   45 of 45   (16 games)
Fewest, season
4   1932   (14 games)
18   1982   18 of 20   (9 games)
        1963   18 of 18   (14 games)
19   2005   9 of 20   (16 games)
        2001   19 of 20   (16 games)
        1986   19 of 20   (16 games)
Most, game
7   at Det, 11/27/97
        at SF, 12/23/91
        at SF, 9/19/65
        at Bal, 9/27/64
        at GB, 9/30/62
6   Last: at Was, 10/31/99

Opponents' Extra Points Missed
Most, season
6   1955   (12 games)
4   1978   28 of 32   (16 games)
        1974   29 of 33   (14 games)
        1970   27 of 31   (14 games)
3   Last: 1990 28 of 31   (16 games)
Most, game
3   vs. Cle, 11/24/40
2   Last: at TB, 10/22/79

Field Goals Allowed
Most, season
37   2002   (16 games)
31   2003   (16 games)
30   1994   (16 games)
Fewest, season
**0   1942   (11 games)
        1932   (14 games)
10   1967   (14 games)
12   1982   (9 games)
12   1979   (16 games)
Most, game
5   vs. Oak, 10/05/03
        at SF, 9/7/03
        vs. TB, 12/29/02
        at Min, 10/10/99
        vs. KC, 1/29/90
        vs. Min, 9/23/73
        vs. Was, 11/14/71

Field Goal Attempts Allowed
Most, season
44   2002   (16 games)
41   1994   (16 games)
        1971   (14 games)
39   1973   (14 games)
38   2003   (16 games)
Fewest, season
2   1942   (11 games)
17   1985   (16 games)
        1982   (9 games)
        1963   (14 games)
Most, game
7   vs. Dal, 11/24/68
6   Last: vs. Phi, 10/3/04
5   Last: at Arz, 1016/06

Opponents' Field Goals Missed
Most, season
18   1968   13 of 31   (14 games)
15   1971   24 of 39   (14 games)
14   1967   10 of 24   (14 games)
13   1987   18 of 31   (16 games)
        1980   14 of 27   (16 games)
Fewest, season
3   1078   16 of 19   (16 games)
Most, game
5   vs. Dal, 11/24/68   2 of 7
4   vs. Atl, 9/26/76 1 of 5
        at NO, 10/7/73 0 for 4
3   Last: vs. GB, 10/7/02   2 of 5

Opponents' Safeties Against
Most, season
2   Last: 1988   (16 games)
Most, game
1   Last: at Jax, 12/12/04

OPPONENTS' FIRST DOWNS

Total Allowed
Most, season
332   1989   (16 games)
328   2002   (16 games)
316   1995   (16 games)
Fewest, season
98   1942   (11 games)
166   1982   (9 games)
219   1984   (16 games)

Most, game
35	at Was, 11/26/89	
31	vs. Ind, 11/21/04	
	at Cle, 11/3/80	

Fewest, game
3	at Det, 11/23/41	
	at Cle, 10/9/38	
5	at GB, 10/17/91	
6	Last: vs. SEA, 9/9/90	

Rushing Allowed

Most, season
138	1973	(14 games)
128	1978	(16 games)
124	1977	(14 games)

Fewest, season
*35	1942	(11 games)
53	1982	(9 games)
67	1986	(16 games)

Most, game
19	vs. Den, 12/12/76	
	at Min, 10/17/65	
17	vs. LA Rams, 12/2/73	
15	vs. Ind, 11/21/04	
	vs. Min, 9/15/94	

Fewest, game
**0	vs. Det, 11/20/94	
	vs. Buf, 10/2/88	
	at TB, 10/6/85	
	at Det, 10/28/45	
	at Chi Cards, 12/6/42	
	at Cle, 10/10/37	

Passing Allowed

Most, season
212	1995	(16 games)
196	1999	(16 games)
191	2001	(16 games)
	1989	(16 games)

Fewest, season
*33	1943	(10 games)
90	1973	(14 games)
96	1963	(14 games)
122	1984	(16 games)

Most, game
23	at SF, 12/17/00	
22	at Min, 9/19/85	
21	at TB, 11/18/01	
	at Was, 11/26/9	
	at LA Rams, 12/26/82	

Fewest, game
**0	Last: vs. Atl, 11/24/85	

By Penalty

Most, season
36	1968	(14 games)
33	2002	(16 games)
30	1988	(16 games)
29	2003	(16 games)

Fewest, season
10	1953	(12 games)
11	1982	(9 games)
	1977	(14 games)
12	1994	(16 games)

Most, game
7	at Phi, 11/26/44	
5	vs. Was, 9/15/68	
4	Last: at GB, 12/25/05	

OPPONENTS' NET YARDS

Rushing and Passing

Most, season
5,729	1989	(16 games)
5,704	1999	(16 games)
5,606	2002	(16 games)

Fewest, season
1,703	1942	(11 games)
2,846	1982	(9 games)
3,176	1963	(14 games)
3,869	1984	(16 games)

Most, game
583	at LA Rams, 12/26/82	
557	at LA Rams, 10/24/54	
550	at Cle, 11/25/61	

Fewest, game
33	vs. Phi, 10/25/42	
54	at Pit, 10/2/39	
86	vs. Pit, 11/9/69	
88	vs. LA Rams, 11/10/63	
92	vs. TB, 11/26/78	

OPPONENTS' RUSHING

Attempts Allowed

Most, season
564	1978	(16 games)
563	1973	(14 games)
547	1973	(14 games)

Fewest, season
260	1982	(9 games)
294	1942	(11 games)
358	1964	(14 games)
359	1985	(16 games)

Most, game
59	vs. Den, 12/12/76	
55	at Dal, 10/24/76	
54	at NE, 10/30/88	

Fewest, game
10	vs. Atl, 9/27/92	
	vs. Buf, 10/2/88	
	vs. Mia, 9/4/88	
11	vs. GB, 11/27/88	
12	vs. Det, 11/22/88	

Yards Allowed

Most, season
2,509	1973	(14 games)
2,174	1978	(16 games)
2,157	1977	(14 games)

Fewest, season
*519	1942	(11 games)
897	1982	(9 games)
1,313	2001	(16 games)

Most, game
393	at Det, 11/26/36	
356	vs. Den, 12/12/76	
304	at Min, 10/17/65	

Fewest, game
-36	vs. Phi, 11/19/39	
-17	at Chi Cards, 12/6/42	
0	vs. Buf, 10/2/88	
11	at Min, 10/28/96	

Average Allowed

Highest, season
5.28	1955	(12 games)
4.45	1994	(16 games)
4.44	1973	(14 games)

Lowest, season
1.77	1942	(11 games)
3.17	1970	(14 games)
3.32	1974	(14 games)
3.41	1988	(16 games)

Highest, game
9.52	at Den, 11/23/03 (21 for 200 yards)	
9.11	at NYJ 9/25/94 (18 for 164 yards)	
8.30	at Min, 10/10/99 (20 for 166 yards)	
8.03	at Cle, 11/25/51 (N/A)	

Lowest, game
-0.89	at Chi Cards, 12/6/42 (N/A)	
0.00	vs. Buf, 10/2/88 (10 for 0 yards)	
0.80	at Min, 10/28/96 (14 for 11 yards)	
0.85	at Det, 11/9/03 (20 for 17 yards)	

Touchdowns Allowed

Most, season
25	1975	(14 game)
21	1989	(16 games)
20	1964	(14 games)

Fewest, season
3	1942	(11 games)

	1932	(14 games)
4	1986	(16 games)
	1982	(9 games)
5	1988	(16 games)
	1987	(15 games

Most, game
6	at Chi Cards, 11/28/29	
5	vs. GB, 11/4/62	
	at GB, 9/30/62	
4	Last: at Det, 11/27/67	

OPPONENTS' PASSING

Attempts Allowed

Most, season
602	2001	(16 games)
595	1995	(16 games)
583	1999	(16 games)

Fewest, season
187	1933	(13 games)
294	1982	(9 games)
296	1969	(14 games)
435	1984	(16 games)

Most, game
62	vs. Phi, 10/2/89	
58	vs. GB, 12/4/05	
57	at TB, 11/18/01	
	at Det, 10/9/88	

Fewest, game
3	at Det, 11/28/35	
	vs. NYG, 11/17/35	
9	vs. Atl, 9/17/72	
10	vs. GB, 11/12/72	

Completions Allowed

Most, season
374	1995	(16 games)
355	2001	(16 games)
354	1999	(16 games)

Fewest, season
59	1935	(12 games)
150	1969	(14 games)
164	1982	(9 games)
197	1984	(16 games)

Most, game
41	at TB, 11/18/01	
36	vs. NE, 11/20/02	
	at SF, 12/17/00	
	vs. GB, 12/5/93	
34	at StL, 12/11/06	
	vs. Pit, 11/5/95	

Fewest, game
**0	at GB, 9/25/49	
	at Bos, 11/5/33	
	vs. Chi Cards, 10/15/33	
1	vs. SF, 11/13/05	
3	vs. Atl, 11/24/85	
	vs. GB, 12/16/73	
	at GB, 11/4/73	

Opponents' Completion Percentage

Highest, season
64.0	1998	(16 games)
62.9	1995	(16 games)
62.6	2000	(16 games)

Lowest, season
30.4	1935	(12 games)
42.6	1967	(14 games)
4.4	1981	(16 games)

Highest, game (10+ attempts)
86.7	at Bal, 9/27/64	
85.0	at Atl, 10/14/73	
81.8	at SF, 12/17/00	

Lowest, game (10+ attempts)
0.0	at GB, 9/25/49	
7.7	vs. SF, 11/13/05	
17.4	vs. Atl, 11/24/85	
	at Det 11/5/67	

Net Yards Allowed

Most, season

4,240	1995	(16 games)
4,041	2002	(16 games)
3,832	1989	(16 games)

Fewest, season

691	1933	(13 games)
1,674	1973	(14 games)
1,765	1963	(14 games)
2,492	1984	(16 games)

Most, game

506	at LA Rams, 12/26/82
411	at Min, 9/19/85
395	at TB, 11/18/01

Fewest, game

−22	vs. Atl, 11/24/85
−12	at GB, 11/4/73
−7	vs. TB, 11/26/78

TD Passes Allowed

Most, season

27	1998	(16 games)
	1995	(16 games)
	1964	(14 games)
	1961	(14 games)
25	2000	(16 games)
	1997	(16 games)
	1968	(14 games)

Fewest, season

2	1934	(13 games)
3	1936	(12 games)
	1932	(14 games)
7	1977	(14 games)
10	2005	(16 games)
	1968	(14 games)

Most, game

5	at GB, 11/12/95
	at Min, 11/28/82
	at Pit, 9/28/80
	vs. SF, 11/19/72
4	Last: vs. Ind, 11/21/04

TURNOVERS

Takeaways

Most, season

58	1947	(12 games)
54	1985	(16 games)
51	1963	(14 games)

Fewest, season

20	2003	15 int, 5 fum	(16 games)
	2000	11 int, 9 fum	(16 games)
	1982	13 int, 7 fum	(9 games)
22	1994	12 int, 10 fum	(16 games)

Most, game

**12	at Det, 11/22/42	7 int, 5 fum
9	vs. StL Cards, 11/19/67	7 int, 2 fum
8	vs. TB, /2/84	6 int, 2 fum
	at GB, 9/24/67	5 int, 3 fum
	vs. Phi, 10/27/63	4 int, 4 fum
	at LA Rams, 10/13/63	6 int, 2 fum

Opponents' Fumbles Lost

Most, season

26	1952	(12 games)
24	1965	(14 games)
	1962	(14 games)
23	1976	(14 games)
	1971	(14 games)
22	1981	(16 games)
	1966	(14 games)

Fewest, season

5	2003	(16 games)
6	1946	(10 games)
	1943	(10 games)
7	1982	(9 games)

Most, game

5	at Oak, 9/26/99
	at KC, 11/8/81
	at Den, 9/30/73
4	Last: at Det, 12/22/85

Touchdowns from Fumbles

Most, season

5	1942	(11 games)
2	Last: 2006	(16 games)

Most, game

2	at Arz, 10/16/06
	vs. Was, 11/28/48
1	Last: at GB, 9/19/04

INTERCEPTIONS BY OPPONENTS

Number Made

Most, season

37	1935	(12 games)
36	1963	(14 games
34	1985	(16 games)

Fewest, season

9	2002	(16 games)
10	1964	(14 games)
	1960	(12 games)
11	2000	(16 games)

Most, game

7	vs. StL Cards, 11/1967
	at Chi Cards, 12/5/54
	at Det, 11/22/42
	at GB, 9/22/40
6	vs. TB, 9/2/84
	at LA Rams, 10/13/63

Yards Returned

Most, season

585	1941	(11 games)
546	2004	(16 games)
537	1963	(14 games)
524	2005	(16 games)

Fewest, season

60	1997	(16 games)
69	1987	(15 games)
99	1982	(9 games)

Most, game

149	vs. LA Rams, 10/11/64
140	vs. GB, 12/4/05

Touchdowns

Most, season

5	2004	(16 games)
4	Last: 2005	(16 games)
3	Last: 2001	(16 games)

Most, game

2	Last: vs. GB, 12/5/93

PUNTING BY OPPONENTS

Number Made

Most, season

100	2006	(16 games)
	1986	(16 games)
	1984	(16 games)
99	1983	(16 games)
98	1981	(16 games)

Fewest, season

42	1945	(10 games)
49	1982	(9 games)
62	1995	(16 games)
	1972	(14 games)
	1964	(14 games)

Most, game

16	vs. Chi Cards, 11/30/33
15	vs. NYG, 11/17/35
11	vs. TB, 12/17/07
	vs. NE, 9/16/85
	at Cle, 10/15/72

Fewest, game

**0	vs. GB, 12/17/89
	at Mia, 9/23/79
	at GB, 9/24/67
	at Det, 12/2/56

Gross Average Allowed

Highest, season

46.6	1964	(14 games)
43.5	1997	(16 games)
43.3	1963	(14 games)

Lowest, season

35.4	1978	(16 games)
36.3	1976	(14 games)
37.1	1995	(16 games)

Highest, game (4+ punts)

61.8	vs. Det, 11/24/46
55.3	at Dal, 9/28/97
54.5	at SF, 11/19/61

Lowest, game (4+ punts)

23.6	vs. Atl, 11/19/78
25.5	at Pit, 11/30/58
26.0	vs. Den, 12/12/76

OPPONENTS' PUNT RETURNS

Returns Allowed

Most, season

66	1981	(16 games)
58	1974	(14 games)
57	2004	(16 games)

Fewest, season

20	1941	(11 games)
22	1993	(16 games)
	1965	(14 games)
24	1986	(14 games)
	1972	(14 games)

Most, game

9	at Chi Cards, 11/29/59
8	vs. Was, 10/11/81
	at Atl, 10/13/74
7	Last: TB, 21/17/06

Yards Allowed

Most, season

727	1997	(16 games)
633	1974	(14 games)
594	1981	(16 games)

Fewest, season

106	1969	(14 games)
110	1972	(14 games)
115	1993	(16 games)

Most, game

147	vs. GB, 11/8/59
117	at Atl, 10/13/74
116	at TB, 12/21/97

Average Return Allowed

Highest, season

17.0	1941	(11 games)
14.0	1997	(16 games)
13.0	1987	(15 games)

Lowest, season

3.8	1969	(14 games)
4.1	1967	(14 games)
5.2	1993	(16 games)

Touchdowns Allowed

Most, season

2	1997	(16 games)
	1996	(16 games)
	1954	(12 games)
	1952	(12 games)
	1947	(12 games)
	1941	(11 games)
	1933	(13 games)

Most, game

1	Last: vs. GB, 12/25/05

Fair Catches Forced

Most, season

38	1993	(16 games)
33	2000	(16 games)
26	1973	(14 games)
	1972	(14 games)

Fewest, season

5	1090	(16 games)

6   1990   (16 games)
7   1987   (15 games)
       1989   (9 games)
       1980   (16 games)
Most, game
7   vs. Det, 11/21/76
6   at GB, 12/16/73

OPPONENTS' KICK-OFF RETURNS

Number made
Most, season
83   2006   (16 games)
78   1985   (16 games)
73   1990   (16 games)
Fewest, season
30   1982   (9 games)
32   1971   (14 games)
44   1981   (16 games)
Most, game
10   at Det, 9/24/89
9   vs. TB, 9/25/93
       vs. GB, 12/7/80
       vs. Bal, 10/21/56
       at Boston, 11/21/48
8   Last: at TB, 10/21/84
Fewest, game
**0   Last: vs. NO, 9/19/82

Yards Allowed
Most, season
1,827   1985   (16 games)
1,730   2006   (16 games)
1,583   1965   (14 games)
Fewest, season
435   1940   (11 games)

537   1982   (9 games)
700   1974   (14 games)
       1945   (10 games)
918   1993   (16 games)
Most, game
275   at Det, 9/24/89
254   at LA Rams, 10/13/63
234   vs. GB, 12/7/80
Fewest, game
*0   Last: vs. Min, 9/18/94

Average Allowed
Highest, season
27.8   1960   (12 games)
25.6   1971   (14 games)
24.7   1973   (14 games)
Lowest, season
16.0   1946   (11 games)
16.6   1999   (16 games)
17.3   1993   (16 games)

Touchdowns Allowed
Most, season
1   Last: 2003
Most, game
1   Last: vs. Det, 10/26/03

OPPONENTS' PENALTIES

Number Conceded
Most, season
132   2006   (16 games)
129   1980   (16 games)
120   2004   (16 games)
       1987   (15 games)

Fewest, season
34   1942   (11 games)
43   1941   (11 games)
52   1982   (9 games)
66   1969   (14 games)
78   2000   (16 games)
Most, game
21   at Cle, 11/25/51
16   at GB, 11/8/87
15   at TB, 10/21/84
       at Det, 9/2/68
Fewest, game
**0   Last: vs. Den, 12/18/93
1   Last: vs. TB, 11/19/00

Yards Penalized
Most, season
1,109   1980   (16 games)
1,103   1987   (15 games)
1,084   2006   (16 games)
Fewest, season
110   1937   (11 games)
451   1982   (9 games)
611   1965   (14 games)
645   1994   (16 games)
Most, game
209   at Cle, 11/25/51
149   vs. NO, 10/8/00
147   at Det, 9/22/68
Fewest, game
**0   Last: vs. Den, 1/18/93
5   Last: vs. LA Rams, 12/18/94

Brian Griese (left) and Kyle Orton, two of the Bears' 2007 quarterbacks. *Jonathan Daniel/Getty Images*

INDEX